From Passion
to Objectivity

International and Cross-Disciplinary
Perspectives on Service-Learning Research

a volume in
Advances in Service-Learrning Research

Series Editor:
Shelley H. Billig
RMC Research Corporation, Denver

Advances in Service-Learning Reserach

Shelley H. Billig, Series Editor

Advancing Knowledge in Service-Learning:
Research to Transform the Field (2006)
edited by Shelley H. Billig, Georgia Davidson,
Nicole C. Springer, and Karen McKnight Casey

Improving Service-Learning Practice:
Research on Models to Enhance Impacts (2005)
edited by Susan Root, Jane Callahan, and Shelley H. Billig

New Perspectives in Service Learning: Research to Advance the Field (2004)
edited by Andrew Furco and Shelley H. Billig

Deconstructing Service-Learning: Research Exploring Context,
Participation, and Impacts (2003)
edited by Janet Eyler and Shelley H. Billig

Service Learning Through a Multidisciplinary Lens (2002)
edited by Shelley H. Billig and Andrew Furco

Service Learning: The Essence of the Pedagogy (2002)
edited by Andrew Furco and Shelley H. Billig

From Passion to Objectivity

International and Cross-Disciplinary Perspectives on Service-Learning Research

edited by

Sherril B. Gelmon
Portland State University, Portland

and

Shelley H. Billig
RMC Research Corporation, Denver

Information Age Publishing, Inc.
Charlotte, North Carolina • www.infoagepub.com

Library of Congress Cataloging-in-Publication Data

From passion to objectivity : international and cross-disciplinary perspectives on
service-learning research / edited by Sherril B. Gelmon and Shelley H. Billig.
   p. cm. — (Advances in service-learning research)
   Includes bibliographical references and index.
   ISBN 978-1-59311-845-7 (pbk.) — ISBN 978-1-59311-846-4 (hardcover)
   1. Service learning—Congresses. I. Gelmon, Sherril B., 1955- II. Billig, Shelley.
   LC220.5.F76 2007
   361.3'7—dc22

                                                                    2007033623

ISBN 13: 978-1-59311-845-7 (pbk.)
ISBN 13: 978-1-59311-846-4 (hardcover)
ISBN 10: 1-59311-845-7 (pbk.)
ISBN 10: 1-59311-846-5 (hardcover)

Printed in the United States of America

CONTENTS

INTRODUCTION

Sherril B. Gelmon and Shelley H. Billig

This volume is the seventh in the *Advances in Service-Learning Research* series, and presents a collection of papers selected from those presented at the Sixth International Service-learning Research, hosted by Portland State University in Portland, Oregon in October 2006. The theme of the conference, which is also the title of this volume, was "From Passion to Objectivity: International and Cross-Disciplinary Perspectives on Service-Learning Research." This theme was selected to showcase several important topics in contemporary service-learning and community engagement research. Of key importance is the way in which the chapters selected for this volume reflect the evolution and maturation of research in the field of service-learning—moving from descriptive narratives of the passion for addressing social problems and inequities that was evident in much of the early research (and is still reflected today) to increasingly sophisticated research that draws on multiple methodologies, presents solid evidence, and offers the basis for replication and further exploration through future research.

Section I is titled "International and Cross-Cultural Perspectives." The first chapter is a summary of one of the keynote plenaries at the 2006 conference, highlighting models of engagement around the world, with participants from Australia, Canada, South Africa, the United Kingdom, and

From Passion to Objectivity: International and Cross-Disciplinary Perspectives on Service Learning Research, pp. vii–xi

the United States. The study of community engagement offers many different perspectives, which often are derived from local context and culture. The authors discuss motivations for community engaged research; college/university responsibilities to address the public good; institutional, governmental and other internal and external drivers of community engagement; government, nongovernmental organizations, and philanthropic funding and support of research; community development as a driver of research; and barriers to university-community engagement.

Chapter 2 provides an analysis of data using five intercultural theories to interpret student learning outcomes in nine international/intercultural service-learning programs. Merrill and Pusch describe the process and outcomes of a qualitative study of alumni of International Partnership for Service-Learning semester-long programs in Ecuador, Mexico, Jamaica, South Dakota, (with the Lakota and Dakota Native American peoples), India, France, the Philippines, and England between 1986 and 2001. This study was conducted to determine the impact of participation within the International Partnership for Service-Learning and Leadership programs on the students' intercultural competence and the impact on their subsequent life choices, such as careers and further education. The chapter demonstrates that intercultural theory is essential to understanding service-learning in a culturally different environment, and shows the usefulness of the theories both in exploring the student experience and for establishing international programs and related student services.

Sallee and Harris, in Chapter 3, explore the experiences of 41 Taiwanese and South Korean international graduate students enrolled in a Teaching English as a Foreign/Second Language program who were engaged in service-learning in urban schools in the United States. The authors explore two primary questions: (1) How can service-learning help international students learn more about the United States and the American educational system; and (2) How does being from another culture affect their experiences and perspectives? They found that participants gained insight into American culture and the differences between Asian and American approaches to education in ways that traditional classroom instruction would not have allowed. Students learned first-hand about developing critical thinking skills by being pushed to consider the benefits and drawbacks created by the learning environments in American classrooms, which were different than the classroom norms in their home countries. The authors conclude with some suggestions for areas of emphasis in future research with similar student groups.

Section II offers four papers addressing the subtheme of "Enhancing Student Learning." In Chapter 4, Elson, Johns, and Petrie point out that there are very few service-learning research studies that investigate the impact on the recipient of services. Their study of Jumpstart demonstrates that children tutored by service-learning participants made greater gains than those tutored by non participants and that entire sites appeared to benefit by being associated with college students enrolled in courses that feature service-learning. While they caution that there are some regional effects and selection bias that need to be taken into account in the interpretation of the data, the results of their study are promising. They suggest that much is to be learned by examining service recipients and using service-learning in conjunction with early childhood education initiatives.

Chapter 5 presents the results of a study that Bradley and colleagues from across the nation. These authors investigated whether participation in a peer-to-peer service-learning project on seat belt use would make a different in high school participants' attitudes and behaviors. Both qualitative and quantitative data analyses clearly demonstrated impact. Students learned data collection and analysis skills, knowledge about automobile safety, self-discipline and leadership skills, and a displayed a host of prosocial behaviors. The more involvement in the design and presentation of materials, the stronger the outcomes. Engaging in reflection and a feeling of being challenged also moderated many of the effects. As hypothesized, there was also a strong increase in seat belt use. One finding was that though African American students demonstrated gains in their use of seat belts, the group had significantly lower usage than students from other subpopulations. Authors speculate why that may have occurred and urge additional research in this area.

In Chapter 6, Bernacki and Bernt discuss a longitudinal study that examined the relationship between service-learning and the attitudes and behaviors of college students during the first 2 years of undergraduate study at a Jesuit university. The study investigated the role service-learning involvement plays in the timing and depth of students' engagement in campus activities and the attitudinal changes that accompany such activity. Students were surveyed at three time points about their social, civic and religious attitudes and were interviewed each spring about their time use. Two years into the study, significant findings have already begun to emerge regarding students' faith orientations, their commitment to service and justice, and their participation in structured reflection/faith-based retreats.

Hart examines the connection between service-learning and literacy motivation in chapter 7. He argues that service-learning, as a prominent strategy for student engagement, should influence students' motivation to learn literacy strategies relative to their nonparticipating peers. In particular, Hart speculates that collaboration, real world connections, mastery goal orientation, and student autonomy are the components of service-learning that will have the strongest influence on outcomes. Using critical discourse analysis, his study of middle school students in an afterschool environmental club confirmed many of the hypotheses. He concludes by presenting a service-learning model of literacy engagement that emphasizes the synergistic connections between service-learning components.

The chapters in Section III address the important topic of "Engaging Communities in Learning and Institutional Change." In Chapter 8, Webster describes a study of a service-learning project in inner city Philadelphia. Webster points out that there are very few studies in the field that examine low-income minority communities, and particularly communities of color. Using a survey that measured risk and protective factors, social anxiety, and service attitudes, she found that none of the group differences were significant, though the findings did reveal a positive trend. In her discussion, Webster points out that the fact that the project addressed integrated pest management may have affected results, particularly in the area of social anxiety. She concludes that there is enormous potential for implementing service-learning as a strategy for engaging young people in their local communities and helping them to address problems in ways that are most meaningful to them.

Chapter 9 describes the experiences of a major metropolitan university in working with its local community to effect institutional change. Ersing, Jetson, Jones, and Keller describe the experiences of the University of South Florida in working with the community of East Tampa to create meaningful and effective partnerships. They describe an ongoing case study of a 3-year initiative in one urban neighborhood undertaken with faculty leadership, and limited financial and structural resources. Throughout this work there was a conscious effort to analyze this approach as a pathway toward building a program of community engagement through engaged scholarship. The authors articulate eight guiding principles that emerged: reciprocal, strength-based, sustainable, incremental, strategic, enterprising, dissemination-oriented, and creative. They conclude with steps for institutionalizing approaches to increase community engagement.

Section IV addresses one specific area of emphasis in service-learning research, that of teacher education. In chapter 10, Vickers discusses her experiences through the University of Western Sydney, Australia, in transforming a teacher education program. In the program in which this research was based, all secondary teacher-education students undergo an "alternative" practicum based on the principles of academic service-learning. This experience is not intended merely to provide extra hours of practicum for preservice teachers but instead to function as a disruption of students' more regulated classroom-based experiences. The students are all required to submit written reflections on their experiences at the end of their placements. This chapter provides an analysis of these student reflections, supplemented by some interview material. The analysis indicates that this disruption can create a space for transformational learning, allowing opportunities for student teachers to develop the capacity to connect with marginalized students and support their learning goals.

Chapter 11, written by Harwood, McClanahan, and Nicholas, presents the results of a study of service-learning in teacher education in the United States. Using surveys, focus groups, and reflective essays, the authors analyze the ways in which preservice teachers make sense of their experiences and develop knowledge and skills related to their chosen profession. Reflection was found to be a particularly powerful tool for these nascent teachers, helping them to understand adolescent behavior and dilemmas within classroom practice. The authors also clearly demonstrate the value in triangulating data and conducting indepth studies of attitudinal and behavioral changes over time.

Finally, Section V is titled "Building Our Understanding of Engaged Scholarship" and consists of two chapters by Sherril Gelmon. First she addresses the concept of "engaged scholarship"—scholarship that documents various aspects of faculty, staff and graduate student work with and in multiple communities. She presents a summary of both current context and future directions for engaged scholarship. In the second chapter Gelmon discusses the recent formation of the International Association for Research on Service-Learning and Civic Engagement, which has assumed responsibility for the annual research conference and its related publications, including this research series.

One of the goals of the International Service-Learning Research Conference since its inception has been to provide a venue for established researchers to share their work, and to provide a supportive environment where junior faculty and graduate students can present developing or completed research and receive feedback from their peers and scholarly mentors. Nicole Webster (chapter 8) was selected as one of four "Emerging Scholars" for the 2006 conference, showcasing junior faculty who demonstrate strong potential as researchers and scholars of community engagement and service-learning. The involvement of several doctoral students in the papers presented here is also noteworthy, including Matthew Bernt (chapter 6), Alisha Lund-Chaix (chapter 1), and Margaret Sallee (chapter 3). Jessica Petrie (chapter 4) also recently completed her doctoral work.

SECTION I

INTERNATIONAL AND
CROSS-CULTURAL PERSPECTIVES

CHAPTER 1

CONTEXT AND CULTURE

Models of Engagement Around the World

Margo Fryer, Robert Wallis, Kalawathie Sattar, John Annette, Richard Battistoni, and Alisha Lund-Chaix

ABSTRACT

The study of community engagement offers many different perspectives, which often are derived from local context and culture. Substantial variations are found when one travels to different countries and especially when one becomes immersed in various cultures, organizations, social issues, settings, and population groups. This chapter is an edited transcript of a conversation about international perspectives, with representatives from Australia, Canada, South Africa, the United Kingdom, and the United States, that took place as a plenary discussion at the Sixth International Service-Learning Research Conference in 2006.

The study of community engagement offers many different perspectives, which often are derived from local context and culture. Substantial variations are found when one travels to different countries and especially

From Passion to Objectivity: International and Cross-Disciplinary Perspectives on Service Learning Research, pp. 3–20

when one becomes immersed in various cultures, organizations, social issues, settings, and population groups. One of the featured plenary sessions at the Sixth International Research Conference on Service-Learning, held in Portland, Oregon, in October 2006, was a discussion of models of engagement around the world.

Richard (Rick) Battistoni, professor of political science and public/community service studies at Providence College in Providence, Rhode Island, moderated the panel. The four panelists were:

- Margo Fryer, chair of National Steering Committee, Canadian Association for Community Service Learning, Director of UBC Learning Exchange and UBC-Community Learning Initiative, and assistant professor, School of Community and Regional Planning, University of British Columbia, Canada;
- Robert (Rob) Wallis, national president, Australian Universities Community Engagement Alliance and pro vice-chancellor (Rural & Regional), Deakin University, Australia;
- Kalawathie (Bella) Sattar, director of Centre for Quality Promotion and Assurance, Durban University of Technology, South Africa; and
- John Annette, pro vice master and dean of FCE, University of London, United Kingdom.

This chapter is an edited transcript of their conversation.

Rick: *As we mark the 20th anniversary of efforts in the United States to engage higher education institutions with the issues and concerns of the communities of which they are a part, the 2006 International Service-Learning Research Conference decided to convene a distinguished group of international scholar-practitioners, to give us an appreciation of the different models of campus-community engagement that exist around the world. Let me begin by asking each of you, what motivates you, particularly within your own sociopolitical context, to do this work of engaging campuses with communities?*

Rob: An internal driver for some universities in Australia is the ultimate paybacks in terms of student recruitment and research opportunities. Engagement can produce enhanced student learning opportunities (for example internships, work placements), holiday employment, and access to professionals for guest lectures, mock interviews, and the like. Engagement can bring about effective research opportunities. As well, engagement is seen as enhancing the relevance and reputation of universities and providing access to increased resources such as scholarships, infrastructure, personnel, and government funds.[1]

Margo: Similarly, a major internal driver in Canada is our desire to improve the student experience and make students' learning more powerful. Once you start hearing students say things like, "This community service-learning project was the highlight of my university career," you get motivated to create more of these community-based, experiential learning opportunities. Those of us who are working to advance community service-learning in Canada see it as an important way to enhance students' grasp of core theoretical concepts and to develop critical thinking skills.

In addition, many Canadian universities and colleges have a focus in their vision or mission statements on developing students' capacity for engaged citizenship. Some use terms such as "global citizenship," others talk about "social responsibility," while still others emphasize "caring." While the language may be different, I think there is a common underlying thread that is connected to ideals and values that have deep historical and cultural roots in Canada. For example, after the Second World War, Canada built a pretty strong social safety net; our publicly funded, universal health care system is a cultural and political icon. The drive to build community service-learning in Canada is grounded in this tradition of caring for each other, which, I think, is related to factors such as our relatively harsh climate and our rural history. We have needed each other to survive. But in the current, more urbanized and multicultural context, we are aware that some of these social and cultural ties have weakened, and we see community service-learning as one way to strengthen them.

Rob: In Australia, to some extent the mission driven aspect of engaged scholarship is a manifestation of public policy. For many Australian universities, there are legislative requirements for the university to "serve," "engage," or "collaborate" with the local community. For example, the mission of Victoria University in Melbourne's western suburbs is to "transform the lives of individuals and develop the capacities of industries and communities within the western Melbourne region and beyond through the power of vocational and higher education."[2]

Similarly, the mission of the regionally based University of Ballarat is to be, "The leading regional university within Victoria renowned nationally for its excellence in technical, further and higher education, research, knowledge transfer and community and industry engagement."[3]

Bella: While community engagement has always been embedded in the mission statements of most higher education institutions in South Africa, until fairly recently not all institutions have given emphasis to it in a coherent manner. At the universities of technology, work-integrated learning has always been a particular underlying pedagogical focus.

Within this approach to teaching and learning, a spectrum of practices has developed that includes community engagement. Academic departments recognized the value of work-integrated learning but realized that this had to be contextualized for relevant programs. Therefore, some academic programs developed an approach that has greater alignment with community engagement and service-learning rather than with work-integrated learning and cooperative education.

The JET Education Services[4] (formerly Joint Education Trust), an independent nonprofit organization, approached my university in 2002 with regard to our participation in the Community-Higher Education-Services-Partnership (CHESP) project. This was an opportunity to strengthen and give emphasis to community engagement overtly and not simply within the context of work-integrated learning. As the director of the Centre for Quality Promotion and Assurance, it was also an opportunity to participate in national projects with CHESP pertaining to the management of the quality of community engagement. I was thus able to integrate my quality assurance function with my keen interest and commitment to community engagement.

John: There is an increasing interest in civic engagement and community involvement in the United Kingdom (U.K.). The challenge to higher education in the U.K. is to provide opportunities for students to develop the values of social responsibility through volunteering, to develop accredited community-based learning and research in partnership with communities, and to engage in knowledge exchange partnerships, which benefit the economic and social development of local and regional communities.

This challenge should be seen in the context of the rethinking of higher education that has followed from the Dearing Commission review of U.K. higher education. In 1997, a major Royal Commission under Lord Ron Dearing was established to examine the future of British higher education. One of the main aims of higher education, according to the *Dearing Report on UK Higher Education in the Learning Society* is to contribute to a democratic, civilized, and inclusive society.[5] The emphasis on civic and community engagement highlights the need for the curriculum in higher education to prepare graduates to become active citizens and to participate not only in formal politics but also play a leadership role in civil society.

Rick: *We have similar pedagogical and institutional forces driving the work here in the U.S. Still, many critics, particularly community critics, would argue that colleges and universities are only giving lip service to this responsibility to serve the public good. What is your response?*

Rob: In Australia, despite a trend to corporatization and reduced public funding of higher education, many university leaders still see public good outcomes as important in their institutions' missions.

Margo: This is important in Canada as well. I think many of us in Canada who are working to advance the growth of university-community engagement, and especially community service-learning, are highly motivated by the perspective that universities have a responsibility to be more actively engaged in the critical social, environmental, and economic challenges the world is facing. There is a sense that universities have enormous resources to offer, but these resources are disconnected from the "real-world" and therefore underutilized. So, this is one of the most predominant drivers, this conviction that universities have a responsibility to make their research, teaching, and service more relevant to, and engaged with, important societal issues.

This is related to the perspective that universities and colleges need to be more accountable to the public, since most higher education institutions in Canada are publicly funded. Even though cities in Canada are often at the top of lists of the best places to live in the world, there is no shortage of critical issues to attend to. For example, Canada has a per capita ecological footprint that needs to be reduced, the effects of colonization on aboriginal people have not been effectively redressed, and there is a growing gap between rich and poor.

Bella: Working with communities in South Africa in this way is a challenge. For many years before and after 1994, the relationship between universities and communities was one of *doing to the community* rather than *doing with the community*. These communities were, quite frankly, disenchanted with having to be available for anyone to bestow charity upon them whenever they wished. If not carefully designed and managed, community engagement initiatives can disempower the community.

Through structured community engagement activities, long-term relationships have been established between universities and communities around the country and many of these *have* been mutually beneficial. The outcomes of some of these relationships serve as role models in promoting community engagement in the country. Some of these relationships were established before 1994. It is important to note that not all universities in South Africa are at the same stage of development with regard to community engagement initiatives. This may be ascribed to a number of contributing factors including leadership at the university for community engagement, support from CHESP, the lack of a shared understanding of community engagement, inadequate resources, and so forth. Support for universities of technology through the CHESP initiative was only forthcoming from late 2002 onward.

Rick: *Are there any other "internal drivers" of this work that you want to mention?*

Margo: A third important internal driver in Canada is our learning about the various forms of the scholarship of engagement being developed and described in the United States, and especially the success of service-learning. While this "cultural contagion" could be seen as more of an external than internal force, I think of it as an internal driver because, as we develop this fledgling enterprise in Canada, we are trying to internalize the lessons learned through the experiences of our colleagues around the world, especially those in the United States. At the same time, we are aiming to develop new models for community service-learning and community engagement generally, that are grounded in and reflective of the Canadian context.

Rick: *You've spoken eloquently about the internal motivations for your work. What are the external drivers or driving forces for the work? Government mandate? Government support and encouragement? Nongovernment organizations (NGOs) or other associations without government mandate/ support?*

Bella: There are a number of driving forces for community engagement in South Africa. At the forefront is the national agenda and in this regard, the green paper and the white paper have been key to the development of community engagement in higher education. The Green Paper on Higher Education Transformation[6] criticizes higher education for not laying the foundations of a critical civil society and not contributing to a "democratic ethos and a sense of citizenship perceived as commitment to a common good."[7] In addition, the green paper found that higher education institutions were not responsive to the needs of South African society in particular and the challenges of Africa in general. The green paper evolved into the white paper, and subsequently the goals of the white paper were integrated into the National Plan for Higher Education.[8] At a national level, one of the goals of the national plan is to, "promote social responsibility and awareness among students of the role of higher education in social and economic development through community service programs." At the institutional level, higher education institutions are required to, "demonstrate social responsibility and their commitment to the common good by making available expertise and infrastructure for community service programs." These seminal papers sent a clear signal that community engagement is a core function of higher education together with teaching and research. As I indicated earlier, community service has always featured in the mission statements of universities, but universities gave attention to it in diverse ways.

John: There is also official support for community engagement in the U.K. The current New Labour government has espoused a program of civil renewal represented by its *Together We Can Program* that links the public, private, and voluntary and community sectors to work for the common good. Unlike the United States, most of the mission statements of universities and colleges of higher education in the U.K. do not use the rhetoric of civic engagement and do not talk about promoting citizenship or corporate citizenship and social responsibility. Despite the lack of a major movement for developing the civic role of higher education in the U.K., there are an increasing number of academics who are now arguing for higher education to participate more fully in civil renewal.[9] According to Bernard Crick, "Universities are part of society and, in both senses of the word, a critical part which should be playing a major role in the wider objectives of creating a citizenship culture. I am now far from alone in arguing this."[10]

Bella: Official support in South Africa, albeit not financially, also comes from our administrative body, the Department of Education. An external driver is the Higher Education Quality Committee (HEQC), an independent statutory body for conducting accreditation and advising the Ministry of Education through the Council on Higher Education.[11] This committee released its criteria for institutional audit in 2004 and these include criteria on service-learning and community engagement. In the same year, the HEQC also released its criteria for program accreditation that included the minimum criteria for service-learning if included in the curriculum. The HEQC approach to quality assurance is one of fitness for purpose in the context of the institutional mission and goals as well as fitness of purpose within the context of national goals. Therefore, all public institutions are required to provide evidence of the outcomes of their response to the national goals.

Rob: In Australia, the Commonwealth Government has major policy and financial influence in higher education, even though individual universities are set up under state government legislation. Recently, the Commonwealth Government of Australia, through its two most recent ministers (Nelson and Bishop) for education, science and training, has adopted a strongly interventionist approach to university governance, goals and operations. In particular the commonwealth is adamant that the "one size fits all" approach to the 39 public universities in Australia is no longer appropriate. There is thus an imperative for universities to diversify their missions, niches, and regions of operation.

While certain older universities (the "Group of 8") have focused on high-quality research and have urged the government to divide universities into research intensive and teaching intensive institutions, others have stressed differentiation in the sector can be best achieved through a focus on community engagement. While almost all Australian universities have joined the recently established organization that deals with university community engagement, Australia Universities Community Engagement Alliance (AUCEA),[12] it is true to say that some universities are embracing the whole endeavor more enthusiastically than others in response to a number of external drivers.

Rick: *In the United States, the development of service-learning in higher education was fueled by funding from the government, particularly through the Corporation for National and Community Service. What role does government funding play in encouraging community-based learning and research in your countries?*

Rob: In June 2005, the then Education Minister Dr. Brendan Nelson challenged Australian universities to propose a workable model that would financially support so-called third-stream activities, based on the scheme that exists in the United Kingdom.[13] Universities eagerly debated the pros and cons of such a proposal and saw it as a way of legitimizing and supporting engagement strategies. On January 27, 2006, Julie Bishop was appointed to the cabinet as minister for education, science and training and immediately extended the challenge for universities to justify support for such a funding scheme.

The outcomes from such discourse have included Minister Bishop specifying that the only third-stream activities the government would consider supporting would be those for which sizable direct or indirect economic benefits could be measured and achieved.[14] She gave examples of knowledge transfer in which universities develop patents and licenses that bring about economic gain for their industry or business partner. As well, Minister Bishop suggested partnership-based research that brought immediate or long-term direct economic gain would be included: for example, tourism-research initiatives. A third category of engagement activities that could be supported would be those that supported indirect benefits to society. As an example, Minister Bishop used the University of South Australia project based in Northern Adelaide that sought to reduce disadvantage in several communities.[15] The minister pointed out that such outcomes saved governments significant sums through improved community health, reduced rates of incarceration, and an improvement in the democratic process.[16]

Proponents of community engagement in Australian universities have been ambivalent in regard to third stream funding. On the one hand, a possible increase in resources for engagement activity has been applauded. On the other hand, there are those who view engaged scholarship as necessarily integrating research and student learning and that having a separate fund suggests engagement is an isolated, add on activity that is ranked as subordinate to other university core functions.

Margo: At present, there is little or no government funding available for community service-learning in Canada. Until recently the Liberal party was the dominant force in Canadian federal politics. During their tenure, various governmental entities encouraged significant discourses related to the importance of having an engaged citizenry and a strong civil society. However, these discourses were not particularly linked to activities in the postsecondary or higher education sector. In the current federal political climate, it is not clear whether CSL (community service-learning) might receive federal support. There is currently a minority government, led by a conservative party with a small-government agenda. It is being kept in power by the support of a party dedicated to achieving the separation of the province of Quebec from the Canadian federation. It remains to be seen whether the initiation of a funding program with goals related to citizenship or the strengthening of the national fabric of the country would be supported by the federal government. Under Canada's constitutional division of powers, postsecondary or higher education is the responsibility of provincial governments, so there may be some potential for government support from this level of government, but at this point in time, there are no funds specifically allocated for CSL programs.

John: This is an area where we've seen more government support in the U.K. than Margo is describing for Canada. One of the main external drivers for developing the civic and community engagement of higher education has been the funding councils. In England, especially, this is the Higher Education Funding Council for England or HEFCE, a non-departmental public body.[17] Since the 1960s, student volunteering has been an exciting and important part of U.K. higher education. Today leadership is provided by Student Volunteering England[18] and also the new organization of professionals who support student volunteering, Workers in Student Community Volunteering. This has been assisted by the Higher Education Active Community Fund, a fund for assisting universities and colleges of higher education in England to promote volunteering and community partnerships established by HEFCE.

Rick: *In addition to government encouragement and funding, NGOs and philanthropic foundations have also driven efforts in the United States. Has this been true in your context as well?*

Margo: In Canada, we are in the early stages of developing a national awareness of, and commitment to, the scholarship of engagement. St. Francis Xavier University in Nova Scotia was the pioneer of service-learning in Canada. It received funding in 1999 from the Montreal-based JW McConnell Family Foundation for its service-learning program and in 2001, hosted the first national meeting of people doing community service-learning in Canada. This meeting of about 10 people was the beginning of what has become the Canadian Association for

Community Service-Learning,[19] affectionately known as CACSL (and pronounced like "castle").

The McConnell Foundation, one of Canada's largest private foundations, was impressed by the service-learning program at St. Francis Xavier and when it heard about the emergence of a Canadian coalition of community service-learning practitioners, the foundation contacted us and we began talking about how to grow CSL in Canada. In the fall of 2004, CACSL received a 5-year grant from the McConnell Foundation to provide technical advice and support for universities and communities who are developing community service-learning programs and to promote the growth of CSL by educating people about CSL and creating national and regional networks of programs, practitioners, and researchers. In January 2005, the McConnell Foundation created a funding program for university-based CSL programs and has provided 5-year funding to 10 universities across Canada. The support of the McConnell Foundation has been absolutely crucial to the increasing strength of CSL in Canada.

Bella: JET Education Services, an independent nonprofit organization, has to a large extent been a driving force to give effect to the national goals on community engagement in South Africa. During 1997 and 1998 JET conducted a survey of community service in South African higher education institutions and the outcomes of the surveys informed the development of the CHESP initiative which was launched in 1999 with support from the Ford Foundation. Since then, capacity building workshops and other support have been provided through this initiative. Some institutions have developed policies and strategies for community engagement including the inclusion of community engagement in academic programs.

At a community engagement conference jointly hosted by JET and the HEQC in June 2006, the minister of education indicated that she would await the recommendations from the conference deliberations to inform the extent of her department's support for community engagement.

John: Community-based learning involves students working in partnership with local communities and learning through a structured program that includes reflection. While this development has resulted in the significant growth of exciting and challenging volunteer activities, there has also been an increase in the certification of volunteering and the development of an increasing number of academic programs that accredit the learning involved. Throughout the U.K., we can find examples of universities recognizing the challenge of establishing partnerships to work with local and regional communities. Increasingly, we can also find evidence of the development of community-based learning and research programs as a response to this challenge.[20]

What is important about community-based learning is that it is multidisciplinary, so it can be integrated into a wide variety of academic fields and learning experiences. These could include environmental and global study and the opportunity for students to undertake community service-learning while studying abroad. The Development Education Association[21] is leading the way in promoting education for global citizenship and the skills to engage with global civil society. HEFCE has supported these developments through the Fund for the Development of Teaching and Learning programs, the establishment of Centres for Excellence in Teaching and Learning in this area. The Higher Education Academy has encouraged this work through its subject centers to promote innovation in teaching and learning.

Rick: *A little over 10 years ago, at the first National Gathering in Providence of an organization that is now called Educators for Community Engagement, John McKnight challenged us to consider our local communities as the primary motivators of our work. At the time, while many of us were talking about our "community partners," McKnight didn't think we could use this language, because he believed local communities and their concerns were not driving our work. I think this has changed, at least somewhat, in the United States. To what extent are communities and community development driving the work in your universities?*

John: The provision of the opportunity for students to participate in community service-learning requires partnerships with the university's local communities. This emphasis on partnership working with local communities is especially true of those who advocate learning through community-based research. The Higher Education Innovation Fund (HEIF), also supported by HEFCE, has provided key funding and strategic direction for universities to think creatively about establishing university wide community partnerships and to create innovative knowledge transfer or exchange partnerships with local and regional communities. Universities UK published in 2002 a series of research-based studies which examined the regional role of higher education institutions. This has been supplemented by the work of HEFCE in promoting the achievements of HEIF 1 and 2. We now await the outcomes of a new national program funded by the various "national" funding councils in England, Scotland and Wales to establish "Beacons for Public Engagement," partnerships between universities, the research councils, and the funding councils to promote the public engagement of higher education in the U.K.

In the U.K., the CSV (Community Service Volunteers)[22] has been promoting and facilitating education for citizenship and community-based learning and research in higher education by working in partnerships with over 150 programs in higher education institutions. This network is now relaunching itself as HECP, the Higher Education Community Part-

nership. The aims of this national multidisciplinary and community linked network are to promote community-based learning and research and knowledge transfer partnerships through university-community partnerships that develop students' skills, educate for active citizenship, and meet community needs.

HECP has been established to act as a network to promote partnerships working with local and regional communities, community-based learning and research, and community-based knowledge transfer partnerships. This is a new association that promotes all aspects of partnership activities between higher education institutions and their local and regional communities in the U.K. This association has developed out of the CSV Council for Citizenship and Learning in the Community, which promoted student volunteering, civic engagement and new ways in which students could learn through these activities. We would like to expand the association and broaden its scope to work with a wider range of external and international partner organizations and networks.

Rick: *Are there any other "external drivers" influencing campus-community partnerships?*

John: An important new area of development in the U.K. has been how professional education (business, engineering, medical, teaching, etc.) has begun to address not only ethical issues but also *civic professionalism*, by providing community-based learning and research opportunities for its students in the U.K. and also abroad to address issues of poverty, social justice and global citizenship.

It should be noted that one area in U.K. higher education where there is an increasing interest in learning for active citizenship is in departments of lifelong learning and continuing education. This is important given the fact that increasingly students in higher education study part-time and are mature students. A number of universities have been part of the Active Learning for Active Citizenship program for adult learning in the community, supported by the Civil Renewal Unit of what is now the Department for Communities and Local Government. The Universities Association for Lifelong Learning has now established a network to support the work in higher education lifelong learning for active citizenship and community partnerships.

Rob: In summary, external drivers in Australia and elsewhere for universities engaging more with communities include possible funding opportunities and responses to government requirements to increase diversity in the sector. As well, communities are recognizing the valuable contributions universities can make to activities such as regional economic development, community capacity building and improved initiatives in terms of sustainable development.

Rick: *We've learned what motivates you and your colleagues, both internally and externally, to do the hard work of linking universities with communities. What barriers or obstacles do you face in advancing the agenda of increased engagement between educational institutions and communities?*

Margo: The primary barrier to community-university engagement is, I think, the same in Canada, as in other jurisdictions—namely, academic culture and tradition. The tendency for the academy to be isolated from the "real world," the notion that the best science is value-free, pure, driven only by the curiosity of the independent scientist, the fact that the reward structure recognizes research more than teaching, and that service to the university community is only minimally valued and service to the external community not at all. These are all barriers to the institutionalization of CSL and other forms of community engagement.

Bella: Similarly, the tendency in South Africa to attach greater value to research than to teaching is a serious barrier to community engagement. Until and unless universities accord the same status to teaching as they do to research, community engagement as an approach to learning will not receive the attention and recognition that it should. Community engagement must be promoted as a scholarly activity that informs teaching and learning, as well as research. There is also a need for a mindset change vis-à-vis cooperative education and community engagement. The two may not be mutually exclusive at some operational levels but have inherent, fundamental differences. In South Africa, the universities of technology could learn a lot from the CHESP initiatives in service-learning.

John: There are three main types of barriers to the public engagement of higher education in the U.K. that are not unique to that country. The first, as my colleagues have noted, is the emphasis on "academic research." In the case of the U.K. this is defined by the HEFCE Research Assessment Exercise that evaluates and ranks academic departments in universities according to their levels of international research excellence. To a large extent this devalues "applied research" and therefore a good deal of community-based research. It also emphasizes the importance of research over both teaching and learning as well as knowledge transfer or exchange activities in gaining status and promotion in the university.

Rob: There are a series of internal (i.e., within university) barriers to advancing the agenda of increased community engagement in Australia. As with the previous sentiments, these include the view that engagement and service are seen as of lesser importance compared with teaching and research for promotion and the tenure track. Other impediments include the lack of champions at a sufficiently senior level within a university who can influence its university's strategic thinking to embrace community-based learning and scholarly engagement. Despite the recent creation of many senior positions which include "Engagement" within their titles or duties, the reality is that many give much higher priority to development, external relations, and marketing than to community engagement.

Rick: *I think we could go on forever talking about how the culture of higher education inhibits this and other forms of engaged research and pedagogy. This remains true in the U.S., despite valiant efforts to address the privilege that "pure," "objective" research maintains in our institutions. But what about other obstacles to realizing your vision of campuses fully engaged with their communities?*

Bella: While the tendency of many academic staff and faculty, in South Africa and certainly elsewhere, is always to cite finance as a key obstacle. This is not necessarily true as there is a lot one can accomplish with existing financial resources. Having extra money with which to do the work is a bonus. Just getting recognition for the work would be fantastic. The lack of a clear national funding formula for community engagement is a concern for South African universities as there is a lack of clarity on how government will fund it, if at all. The situation is exacerbated at universities of technology as work-integrated learning does not receive funding from the government and many community engagement activities have their genesis in work-integrated learning. Therefore, there is a danger that these initiatives will slowly dissipate.

Margo: In this regard, in Canada the other barrier is one I mentioned earlier, and that is the lack of substantive government funding for CSL and other forms of community engagement. As we all know, this kind of activity is very labor intensive and thus, expensive.

Rob: Along these lines, external barriers to increased engagement in Australia include inadequate resourcing and lack of government incentives to collaborate with other universities. For instance, the Commonwealth Government has established a Collaboration and Structural Reform Fund.[23] However, Minister Bishop has recently announced that strong priority will now be given to structure reform within the higher education sector as opposed to collaborative proposals.[24]

John: In the U.K., another obstacle to advancing the engagement agenda is the challenge of creating equitable partnerships with community organizations on a sustainable basis. Too often the partnerships are seen in terms of short and medium term gains for both partners instead of long-term partnerships which over time establish a basis of equity. A third barrier in the U.K. is the emphasis in creating knowledge transfer or exchange partnerships placed on working with employers and the business community and not local and regional community organizations in civil society. More recently the Leitch Report on skills and employability has stressed the role of employer engagement with universities as a key new role for higher education. There is a danger that this will marginalize the growing work that has been done in establishing the role of partnerships between universities and their local and regional communities.

Margo: Related to this is the lack of capacity both within universities and within local communities. Many faculty members in Canada have little or no experience working in community settings or working in collaboration with people with diverse backgrounds and agendas. Many community organizations are so focused on meeting the day-to-day needs of their constituents and keeping the organization afloat that it is challenging for them to think about how to create service placements or projects that will stimulate students' learning and complement particular courses, or how to use students' energy and a long-term partnership with a university to achieve strategic goals.

A similar capacity problem is the lack of understanding about how university-community collaborations can effect meaningful organizational, cultural, and social change. I think this kind of international conversation is a great venue for raising questions about how social and cultural change can be effected and how context affects change processes. For example, who is a legitimate change agent in which contexts? What change strategies are most effective in which situations or times? How do you find the right balance between continuity or stability and change? As well, there are deeper questions about which goals or end points the change process is intended to achieve and who decides what those goals are.

Rob: Other barriers in Australia include managing unrealistic community expectations and the great variation in language and definitions used in the discourse on community engagement.

Bella: Similarly, one of the obstacles to the development and implementation of a quality management system for community engagement in South Africa is the fuzziness around the terminology used. There is a reluctance to clearly define community engagement and then to stick with the definition. The danger is that the goalposts keep shifting and the establishment of standards is extremely challenging. Defining community engagement is fertile ground for exhaustive (and exhausting) philosophical debate, which ultimately does not contribute much to the quality management agenda. In the South African context, risk management is also a serious issue and could pose an impediment to community engagement.

Margo: The final set of challenges I have observed is related specifically to the Canadian context. We live in a very large country, spanning five (and a half) time zones. We are officially a bilingual country, with a longstanding Francophone separatist movement in Quebec. Our population is relatively small. These factors all have implications for our ability to build momentum for CSL and community engagement. For example, last year CACSL had a national CSL research conference in Montreal. We were really excited that 40 people came. This seems pretty pathetic compared to the 400 attendees at this conference, but this actually reflects exactly the tenfold difference in the population of Canada as compared to the United States. So it is challenging to create a critical mass of practitioners and researchers. It is hard to include the diversity of the voices we would like to include. It is hard even to schedule teleconferences! But it is very inspiring to be here at this conference where we are learning so much from our colleagues from around the world. These barriers are not insurmountable. And the work is vitally important.

Rick: *I think it's fitting to end on this positive note. Let me say on behalf of all of my colleagues here that we have been inspired by the exciting work going on in all of your countries. Thank you for sharing your thoughts on this vitally important work and the cultural factors influencing it.*

NOTES

1. For more details see Wallis (2006a, 2006b, p. 32).
2. See the Victoria University (2005) mission statement.
3. See the University of Ballarat (2007) mission statement.
4. See JET Education Services, http://www.jet.org.za/
5. To review the complete report see NCIHE (1997).
6. For more details see Department of Education (1996).
7. To review the complete report see National Commission on Higher Education (1996).
8. To review the complete report see National Commission on Higher Education (1997).
9. For more information, see Annette and McLaughlin (2005).
10. See Crick (2000).
11. See Higher Education Quality Council, http://www.che.ac.za/heqc/heqc .php
12. See Australia Universities Community Engagement Alliance, http://www .aucea.net.au
13. For more details see PhillipsKPA (2006).
14. For a complete statement see Bishop (2006).
15. For more details see University of South Australia (2004).
16. For a complete statement see Bishop (2006).
17. See Higher Education Funding Council, http://www.hefce.ac.uk
18. See Student Volunteering England, http://www.studentvol.org.uk/
19. See Canadian Association for Community Service-Leaerning, http://www .communityservicelearning.ca/en/
20. For more information see Annette, Buckingham-Hatfield, and Slater-Simmons (2000) and Annette (2000).
21. See Development Education Trust, http://www.dea.org.uk/
22. See Community Service Volunteers, http://www.csv.org.uk/

23. For more details see Department of Education, Science and Training (2007).
24. For more details see Armitage (2007).

REFERENCES

Annette, J. (2000). Education for citizenship and experiential service-learning. In D. Lawton, J. Cairns, & R. Gardner (Eds.), *Education for citizenship* (pp. 77-93). London: Continuum.

Annette, J. (2003). International service learning. *Frontiers: Journal of International Education.*

Annette, J., Buckingham-Hatfield, S., & Slater-Simmons, E. (Eds.). (2000). *Student-community partnerships in higher education.* London: CSV Publications.

Annette, J., & McLaughlin, T. (2005). Citizenship and higher education in the UK. In J. Arthur & K. Bohlin (Eds.), *Citizenship and higher education* (pp. 74-95). Abingdon, Oxon, United Kingdom: RoutledgeFalmer.

Armitage, C. (2007, April 11). Bishop plan to cut unis. *The Australian* (Higher Education Supplement). Retrieved April 11, 2007, from http://www.theaustralian .news.com.au/story/0,20867,21535498-12332,00.html

Bishop, J. (2006, June 16). Knowledge transfer and engagement forum. Keynote address. Sydney. Retrieved April 11, 2007, from http://www.dest.gov.au/ ministers /media/bishop/2006/06/b001160606.asp

Crick, B. (2000). *Essays on citizenship.* London: Continuum.

Department of Education. (1996). *Green paper on higher education.* Retrieved April 13, 2007, from http://www.info.gov.za/greenpapers/1996/highereduc.htm

Department of Education, Science and Training. (2007). Retrieved April 13, 2007, from http://www.dest.gov.au/sectors/higher_education/publications_resources/ profiles/collaboration_structural_reform_fund.htm

Mayo, M., & Rooke, A. (2006). *Active learning for active citizenship: An evaluation report.* London: Crown Publication. Retrieved August 13, 2007, from http:// www.communities.gov.uk/index.asp?id=1502441

National Commission on Higher Education. (1996). *An overview of a new policy framework for higher education transformation.* Retrieved from http://www.polity .org.za/pol/home

National Commission on Higher Education. (1997). *Education White Paper 3: A programme for higher education transformation.* Pretona, South Africa: Author.

National Committee of Inquiry Into Higher Education. (1997). *"Dearing Report," The Reports of the National Committee of Inquiry into Higher Education.* United Kingdom: Higher Education in the Learning Society.

PhillipsKPA. (2006). *Knowledge transfer and Australian universities and publicly funded research agencies.* Retrieved April 11, 2007, from http://www.dest.gov.au/NR/ rdonlyres/36818C20-9918-4729-A150-464B662644B3/12630/ Knowtran_FinalCompilation_005_web1.pdf

University of Ballarat. (2007). *Mission statement.* Retrieved April 13, 2007, from http://www.ballarat .edu.au/pr/resources/UB_2020_Vision_summary.pdf

University of South Australia. (2004). *UniSA wins funding for northern Adelaide health and well-being project*. Retrieved April 11, 2007, from http://www.unisa.edu.au/news/2004/160804.asp.

Victoria University. (2005). *Mission statement*. Retrieved April 13, 2007, from http://www.vu.edu.au/library/pdf/AR05Missionvalues.pdf

Wallis, R. (2006a, June). *What do we mean by "Community Engagement."* Paper presented at the Knowledge Transfer and Engagement Forum, Sydney, Australia. Retrieved April 11, 2007, from http://www.aucea.net.au/cgi-bin/articles/display.pl/a:442/Knowledge_Transfer.html

Wallis, R. (2006b, November 29). Engagement key to regional success. *The Australian* (Higher Education Supplement), p. 32.

CHAPTER 2

APPLES, ORANGES, AND KUMYS

Models for Research on Students Doing Intercultural Service-Learning

Martha Merrill and Margaret D. Pusch

ABSTRACT

Researchers used 5 intercultural theories to interpret student-learning outcomes in 9 international/intercultural service-learning programs. The 5 theories include contact theory, acculturation, the developmental model of intercultural sensitivity, intensity factors, and reentry theory. The theories are explained and then used in the interpretation of results from a qualitative study of alumni/ae of International Partnership for Service-Learning semester-long programs. This study was conducted to determine the impact of participation within the International Partnership for Service-Learning (IPSL) and Leadership programs on the students' intercultural competence and the impact on their subsequent life choices such as careers and further education.

From Passion to Objectivity: International and Cross-Disciplinary Perspectives on Service Learning Research, pp. 21–40

INTRODUCTION

Every beginning researcher knows that one does not compare apples to oranges. In order to have valid research results, the populations compared must be similar. Service-learning researchers know that they cannot compare service-learning outcomes for college students with those for high school students, or outcomes for an "alternative spring break" project with a semester-long, service-learning placement that involves continuing interaction with a client population. However, to state the obvious: apples and oranges are both fruits. Even when one compares apples to oranges, the researcher still is comparing items within the same broad paradigm. In these cases, researchers are still discussing students, service in context, and learning outcomes as they are defined in the United States, and familiar classrooms. Researchers can conduct qualitative research or quantitative research, "snapshot" studies or longitudinal research, formative or summative studies, but they are always dealing with familiar categories.

When service-learning researchers begin to study international service-learning, they may begin to encounter a set of unfamiliar issues. While it seems that apples are being compared to apples, there may really be "kumys" involved. Thus, completely different categories of analysis are needed, and different student descriptors or different categories of predictable outcomes must be used. In order to conduct valid research on service-learning that takes place in a cultural context other than the student's own, it is necessary to be familiar with intercultural research and theory, and specifically with the research on acculturation and cultural competence, in addition to service-learning research and educational or learning outcomes research and their categories.

For the purposes of this chapter these different categories are called "kumys." Kumys is not a fruit: it is fermented mare's milk, and it is the national drink of the Kyrgyz, a formerly nomadic people in Central Asia. When thinking about the lifestyle of nomads one realizes that most fruits and vegetables could not be part of their diet. Being a nomadic people, the Kyrgyz do not stay in one place long enough to plant, water, weed, and prune fruits and vegetables. Therefore, traditional foods for the Kyrgyz are every part of the animals that the Kyrgyz herd, plus foods like tea and flat bread and dumplings that can be cooked over a flame and do not require an oven.

Just as the traditional Kyrgyz diet challenges the assumptions about a healthy diet that the sedentary eater takes for granted, studying international/intercultural service-learning draws on different categories of theories and requires a willingness to have some assumptions challenged. This chapter suggests that there are five essential theories that apply to investigating student results in service-learning abroad. These are:

1. *Contact theory* (Allport, 1954) and the many analyses of the situations in which contact with "others" does and does not alleviate prejudice;

2. *Acculturation* (Ward, Bochner, & Furnham, 2001)—the affective, behavioral, and cognitive paradigms of adapting, more specifically described as "stress, coping, and adjustment" (affective); "culture learning" (behavioral); and "social identification theories" (cognitive);

3. *Developmental model of intercultural sensitivity* (DMIS) (Bennett, 1993)—a model of change that addresses ethnocentrism and ethnorelativism;

4. *Intensity factors* (Paige, 1993)—the factors in the interaction between the individual and the environment that make the intercultural encounter more or less intense for specific individuals; and

5. *Reentry theory* and the factors that affect it in practice (Martin & Harrell, 2004), including reentry styles (Pusch, 1998), especially for researchers doing longitudinal studies.

These theories in no way cover the waterfront of intercultural research or theories. However, considering a few of these ideas suggests the "kumys" that need to be taken into account when international/intercultural service-learning is the research topic.

THE THEORIES

Contact Theory

It is sometimes assumed that simply by going to a new culture, students will become more interculturally sensitive and will develop a more relativistic perspective in their beliefs (see Perry, 1970/1999, for a definition of and discussion of the concept of relativism). Engle and Engle (2002), express criticism of the assumption that what they call "The Magic" will work its wiles when a student is abroad. These authors stated:

> The implicit assumption, again: life abroad will simply work its magic ... we assume that our students will progress linguistically in ways impossible on the home campus; they will develop intercultural skills and new sensitivity to the other; they will see links between in-class learning and their first-

hand exposure in the field; they will grow personally because they are challenged to adapt as never before, and, in a startlingly new cultural context, required to call into mature question much of what they have previously simply assumed to be true. (Engle & Engle, 2002, pp. 26-27).

Gordon Allport, in his classic work, *The Nature of Prejudice* (1954), made it clear that "magic" has little to do with increased sensitivity to "the other." As Thomas Pettigrew summarized in his 1998 article:

> Allport (1954) held that positive effects of inter-group contact occur only in situations marked by four key conditions: equal group status within the situation; common goals; inter-group cooperation; and the support of authorities, law, or custom. (Introduction).

Pettigrew noted that "equal status" may be difficult to define, but a researcher can appreciate that students working together in a classroom might be more likely to change their opinions of their hosts than would a group from a wealthy country that travels to a less wealthy country to put a roof on a school for "them." With regard to "common goals," Pettigrew cited researchers who used the example of an athletic team. Its members have the common goal of winning, and need each other to do so, so they come to appreciate each other's strengths. Additionally, Allport hypothesized that the attainment of the common goal must require inter-group cooperation. If subgroups compete, then the prejudice between the groups will not be reduced. Finally, authorities, law, or custom must sanction the cooperation.

Since 1954, hundreds of studies have tested Allport's hypotheses in various contexts. Pettigrew and Tropp (2000) summarized what they call "recent meta-analytic findings," saying that there was a small but significant reduction of prejudice for a great variety of contact situations that did not meet the standard conditions previously held essential. However, when the theory's key conditions were met, there were typically far larger decreases in prejudice. They wrote that increased prejudice will occur when negative factors such as anxiety and threat are involved. As discussed later in this chapter, Paige's intensity factors are important in this regard.

Acculturation—Affect, Behavior, and Cognition

Ward et al. in a comprehensive survey of "the major theoretical approaches to understanding and explaining intercultural contact" titled *The Psychology of Culture Shock* (2001), categorized those approaches as "Affect, Behaviour, and Cognitions." By "affect" they meant "the stress and coping perspective ... making particular reference to those factors that facilitate and impede psychological adjustment ... such as self-efficacy, emotional resilience, and social support, as well as culture-specific variables" (p. 2). "Behaviour" presupposes culture learning. The authors stated that "effective intercultural interactions are often hampered by the fact that participants are unaware of the subtle, culturally-defined rules and regulations that govern social encounters. These include verbal and nonverbal forms of communication, as well as etiquette, the use of time, and strategies for resolving conflict" (p. 2). "Cognitions" includes "both inward-looking cognition, i.e., how one views oneself in terms of social and cultural identity, as well as outward-looking perceptions, i.e., how an individual perceives and makes judgments about members of other ethnic, cultural, or national groups" (pp. 2-3) These latter perceptions are influenced by the conditions that Allport hypothesized.

Developmental Model of Intercultural Sensitivity

Most educators, and perhaps particularly service-learning educators, hope that students will change, grow, and develop as a result of their learning and their experiences. In this regard, the developmental model of intercultural sensitivity (DMIS) is particularly important, precisely because it is a model of development—a model of change. The stages in the DMIS are divided into two segments: ethnocentrism, which includes denial, defense, and minimization, and ethnorelativism, which includes acceptance, adaptation, and integration (M. Bennett, 1993).

Ethnocentric States

"Denial" indicates an inability to construe cultural differences, which may be due to living in isolation in a homogeneous group or due to intentional separation from different others. Any recognition of difference is reduced to broad categories such as "foreigner," "Asian," or "Black."

Those in "defense" recognize cultural differences but tend either to denigrate them and engage in defending their own culture, or to see their own culture as superior to all others. There is the possibility of defense/reversal that can occur when someone becomes deeply involved in another culture and begins to see that culture as superior to his/her own. It is important to note that in both of these states, extreme dualistic thinking is common.

"Minimization" is a state in which there is recognition and acceptance of superficial cultural differences (clothing, food, quaint practices) in the context of seeing all human beings as essentially the same and having common values. The measure for sameness is being like "us." This sameness can be expressed in terms of physiological similarity (basic needs and the like) or transcendent universalism (everyone is a child of God, whether they know it or not). While minimization is a somewhat more benign form of ethnocentrism, the tendency is still to judge other groups from one's own cultural perspective. It can be seen as a stage of transition to becoming ethnorelative.

Ethnorelative States

"Acceptance" is a state in which people recognize and appreciate differences in behavior and values and see those differences as viable alternative solutions to achieving satisfaction in human existence. It is characterized by an ability to interpret various phenomena within the context in which they occurred and develop categories within which they can be compared. Values, beliefs, and other ways of indicating that one is "good" or "bad" are seen within the cultural contexts in which they arose. Behavior is analyzed within the cultural context.

"Adaptation" to difference requires the development of communication skills, and the use of empathy or frame of reference shifting that allows one to be understood and to function effectively across cultures. A more sophisticated step is what Bennett termed "pluralism," the internalization of more than one complete worldview and the ability to both interpret and respond within that frame with little conscious effort (behavioral adaptation). There is an intentionality to adaptation; it is an expansion of one's capabilities and options for behavior and valuing, not a substitution of one set of cultural behaviors with another (assimilation).

"Integration" is not only the internalization of bicultural or multicultural frames of reference but of seeing oneself as "in process" or "self-creating," and accepting that identity is not based in any one culture. People in this state may see themselves as marginal. Constructive marginality was a term devised by Janet Bennett (1993) to indicate that this was not a pathological state but a way of being that allowed one to have rich experiences in any culture rather than having one's reference point always based in a particular culture. People with this orientation are "at home" anywhere. They can function in ways that are consistent in any culture while maintaining a position "at the edge."

The Intensity Factors

Paige (1993) proposed that there were a number of factors that made an intercultural experience more or less intense for a specific student. Those factors included:

- **Cultural difference:** The degree of actual difference between two cultures and how negatively the students evaluate those differences; this influences their attitudes and ability to adapt.

- **Ethnocentrism:** The more ethnocentric the student is, the more difficulty he or she will have in accepting the other culture. Conversely, the less accepting of difference the host culture is, the more difficult it will be for the student to become engaged with members of the host culture.

- **Language:** The less language ability the student has, and the more essential language is to functioning well in the host culture, the more difficult it will be for the student to function in the culture; as a result, the experience will be more stressful.

- **Cultural immersion:** Students who are deeply immersed in the culture will have a higher level of anxiety, since they are repeatedly confronted with difference, ambiguous situations, questions about how to behave, and the need to learn.

- **Cultural isolation:** If the student has little or no access to fellow students from home, there will be a higher level of anxiety.

- **Prior intercultural experience**: If this is the first time the student has been out of his or her own culture, the intensity of the experience will be higher than it will be for the student who has been abroad before and has developed coping strategies, an understanding of the adjustment process, and other intercultural skills.

- **Expectations:** If the student's expectations of the host culture and of his or her own ability to function in it are unrealistically positive, disappointment can be a serious factor and intercultural adaptation can be adversely affected.

- **Visibility and invisibility:** Being physically different from the host nationals and thus being very visible can make the intercultural experience more intense. Conversely, having to keep parts of one's identity hidden, such as being homosexual, can also increase the intensity of the experience.

- **Status:** Feeling that one is not getting appropriate respect can raise the intensity of the experience. Conversely, receiving attention that does not seem warranted to the student-sojourner, can be equally distressing.

- **Power and control:** When sojourners feel they have no power and control in intercultural situations, especially over their own circumstances, the intensity of the experience increases. This factor consistently emerges as a major problem. The behaviors that allow one to control a situation in the home culture—language, relationships, professional and other roles—all are likely to be missing or changed in the new society.

Reentry Theory

Martin and Harrell (2004) wrote: "Intercultural re-entry has been defined as the process of reintegration into primary home contexts after an intercultural sojourn (an intensive and extended visit into cultural contexts different from those in which one was socialized)" (2004, p. 310). Martin and Harrell pointed out that the definition was subsequently modified because more individuals now have multiple experiences in different cultures, and reentry for voluntary sojourners can differ from reentry for those for whom leaving was forced, such as political exiles or labor migrants. However, this definition is useful for examining the reentry experiences of college students. They are often on their first extended sojourn out of the country and have gone abroad by choice, although with a growing number of institutions requiring study abroad of all students, this may not always be the case.

Pusch (2004) maintained that, "re-entry is the hardest and, for learning, the most productive time of study or, indeed, any stay abroad. It takes the complete cycle of departure/sojourn/return to solidify the learning" (2004, p. 121). Part of the issue here is that for many sojourners, the difficulties of reentry are unexpected: it is going home, so everything should be the same. In actuality, however, friends and family and the home society have changed while the sojourner was gone, and the sojourner has also changed. How profoundly the sojourner has changed is often not obvious until "familiar" ideas and situations are encountered and they are seen through the new lenses of experiences in another culture.

In summary, a researcher of intercultural service-learning needs to take into account, at a minimum, the concepts of: Allport's contact theory and its critiques; Ward et al.'s "ABC's" of acculturation (affective, behavioral, and cognitive dimensions); Bennett's developmental model of intercultural sensitivity; Paige's intensity factors; and intercultural reentry. The ways in which these concepts elucidate researchers' understanding of student responses to an intercultural service-learning experience is the subject of the next section.

RESEARCH ON THE ACTIVITIES OF THE INTERNATIONAL PARTNERSHIP FOR SERVICE-LEARNING AND LEADERSHIP

The International Partnership for Service-Learning and Leadership, founded in 1982, sponsors 16 undergraduate service-learning programs in 14 countries, plus a master's degree program that takes place in Mexico, Jamaica, and the United Kingdom. Between 2001 and 2004, the partnership received funding from the Ford Foundation to research the effects of its undergraduate programs. The study sought to understand the characteristics of partnership alumni, the effects of partnership programs on students, the impact of the partnership and of service-learning in general on the agencies where partnership students work, the impact of the partnership on the colleges and universities hosting the partnership, and to develop an evaluation protocol for partnership programs (Tonkin, 2004, xiii). This chapter discusses the alumni study. The students in the study had lived in Guayaquil and Quito, Ecuador, Mexico, Jamaica, South Dakota, (with the Lakota and Dakota Native American peoples), India, France, the Philippines, and England between 1986 and 2001.

Methodology

The study was conducted with 17 partnership alumni, representing a broad range of colleges and universities as well as multiple types of international service experiences. The alumni assembled in New York City in April 2003 with four research team members (Tonkin, 2004). Research team members conducted individual interviews and focus groups during the course of a single day (approximately 9 hours), interviewing students individually during a morning session and conducting group interviews in an afternoon session. This process was designed to minimize cross-communication (and thus standardization of their narratives) among the participants in the early stages and to maximize it at the end.

A data collection protocol used in the data-gathering process was developed around six major domains, which, taken together, represented a broad range of intellectual, social, and cognitive areas. Questions addressed students' intellectual development, affective and moral development, definitions of service, cross-cultural awareness, social integration, and assessment of their experience. Interviews and focus groups were tape-recorded with consent. Transcripts of the interviews were sent to all members of the four-person research team, who used them to conduct further analysis. Data from transcribed interviews were analyzed using an inductive process, whereby emerging themes, patterns of behavior, and categories were identified and developed using methods of categorization and unitization.

IPSL undergraduate programs "integrate academic study with substantive volunteer service, creating a powerful dynamic between direct cultural exposure and academic learning. Interaction with the community teaches you how the culture functions. Time in the classroom teaches you why it functions as it does. By testing theory with practice, IPSL students find their learning takes on greater depth and meaning" (IPSL Web site). Students attended a local university where an IPSL program director guided their academic work, providing a unifying course on "Societies and Institutions," arranging their service assignments of 15-20 hours per week, and seeing that they were housed with host families or in some other appropriate situation with local residents. One program was in South Dakota and students lived and served on one of several Lakota and Dakota reservations. This was a very "foreign" experience within the borders of the United States.

Interpretation of Data Using Intercultural Theory

Exploring the impact of the International Partnership for Service-Learning programs on subsequent life decisions and change in intercultural competence of participating students produced rich contextual information about how students fared during and after their period abroad. What emerged confirmed the life-changing impact of the programs.

Motivation

Students entered the program for a range of personal reasons, from learning about their heritage and attempting to explore and understand their own cultural background, to learning about an unfamiliar culture within their own national borders by going to the Lakota/Dakota reservations in South Dakota. What these experiences tended to have in common was an interest in coupling a focus on service with academic and cultural learning. Students wanted to be fully engaged in the life of the community and to have some structure within which to serve, study, and live. Students also shared a need to experiment, to be involved directly, to connect the experience to theory or ideas, and to reflect on everything that was being encountered. They all knew what they wanted in an educational experience and how they would go about extracting the learning from their situations.

The "classroom" part of the program was essential to understanding the local environment and the cultural challenges it presented. Students tended to rely on reflection to sort out their own place, their own identity, and their sense of what this experience meant to them in the long term. Ultimately, this led to an internalization of the learning, sometimes immediately. However, in some cases, it was years before the individuals realized the full richness of what was learned. David,[1] in reference to later work on his dissertation, said that something he began to learn 12 years ago finally came clear: "I didn't really grasp the weight of [it] until maybe even last year." Reflection did not always happen immediately and the transformative learning that tends to occur in service-learning programs may not emerge until years later.[2] Anita, unhappy with her agency placement, was frustrated by the lack of attention to her plight and continually asked for help to change her agency assignment or to alter the nature of her assignment. In the end, she remained in her placement, only to discover, years later, that it deeply influenced her choice of career.

Service Placement

Almost everyone had some complaints about his or her service placement. The complaints focused on the lack of organization within agencies, the perceived inability of agencies to use the volunteers constructively, the lack of direction, and the students' own inability to make a "real" contribution. There was a sense that the service portion of the program was too "loose." In the end, however, most of the students realized that the placement was a cultural immersion experience, that they were learning the culture by sorting things out and finding their way within a structured environment. In addition, they took pride in how they had helped: one tutored a high school student who had special needs and later returned to attend the student's wedding; another documented the work of musicians in Jamaica and helped them come to the United States to perform. A third student brought a new perspective into a Tribal Historical Preservation Office as well as contributing some expertise in environmental studies; and a fourth found a role as an assistant cooking instructor for mentally challenged individuals. Talking about what they did and how they felt about their experiences a number of years after the fact, the students realized that they had made a contribution in a way they had not immediately understood. The impact on those in the host culture took on new meaning, and the impact on their own future direction became clear.

Culture Learning and Adaptation

The alumni in this study adapted to and learned the culture in various ways, both subtle and practical. They became very sophisticated in their views of the world and in their ability to function competently within a foreign culture. Most reached the point of being able to internalize more than one world view and their behavior shifted into different frames of reference without much conscious effort, revealing both an ethnorelative perspective (J. Bennett, 1993) and behavioral adaptation, based in culture learning (Ward et al., 2001). This process was expressed by David when he said:

> When you are waiting at a bus stop and you want the bus to stop, there's a ... way that Jamaicans hail a bus; it's not the same as a taxi here. So it's the little things you pick up on. Just being ... a White person on the bus gave you some respect because you're not in a car, you're in the public transportation, and people would see you. I mean they'd see you taking the bus one day, and they'd see you the next day. So you feel good about that.

He began to acquire the overt patterns of behavior of the Jamaicans, which not only made his life smoother but also made those around him more comfortable and more accepting. These were subtle changes in personal behavior that began with observation, followed by application, and eventually became "natural" (Pusch, 1994). David had to adapt not only to fit in but also to make this a more rewarding experience. With that behavior shift came a shift in world view; "You switch—your mind switches over." The experience in Jamaica was intensified by being white in a Black society, but at some point in David's stay, he forgot he was White much of the time because the people perceived he was in "tune" with the culture. Another student from Africa reported that she was not seen as "Black enough," which was equally stressful.

A heritage student was interacting with relatives and discovering how they thought about life and their spiritual beliefs, and why certain goals and behaviors were so critically important.

> I had to interact with my aunts and uncles who are much older than me, who are different... You know over here I was running around doing this or that, busy, busy according to some schedule. Over there, things don't happen that way. They're much less regular, people don't do things on time and you have to get used to it. You know you have to adjust because things will get done but not according to your schedule ... I felt just very comfortable with the people there.

Again, the pattern of observing and adopting new behaviors emerged, as did the ability to reflect on one's own behavioral shifts and patterns of thinking. Her search for her own cultural roots led to "understanding my parents and their struggles a lot better ... I understood them better as people and not just as parents." She was able to discuss her experience drawing on the knowledge she gained, the emotion that surfaced during the experience, and the ability to apply her learning to better comprehend her parents' experience.

Elizabeth, who lived on a reservation in South Dakota, talked about gaining a sense of and being affected by a "kind of historical trauma," and how little she knew of the history of the Indians and the degree to which American society is rooted in Indian practices. For example:

> The Constitution is based after the Iroquois tribe's political arrangement or something like that. I was constantly struck and still am by just how much our institutions are built on, you know, like the American Indian presence is everywhere. It just isn't talked about.

She was also impressed by the family structure and how important it was to have "a real concrete sense of which people you come from:

> I mean people qualify their relationship to everyone, for the most part. And everyone is your auntie or your grandma or your cousin ... and immediately kind of looking for what that connection is... It was illegal for them to leave the reservation until the fifties or something so people have been in the same place for quite a long time ... and just to be able to see that history all over, in the landscape ... the names of towns and even the chief camps ... and that family still sort of lives in that area ... environmentalists always stress the interconnectedness of everything ... but it put it on a human level, the idea that we are all related ... taking care of burial grounds and burial places ... the idea that we need to take care of this place because we love it and learn from it all the time, and need it to still be there to teach us who we are ... the idea that you're related to and have a responsibility to the people who are in the earth, it really just brought it to a different level for me.

The recognition of patterns of behavior different from their own, and the ability to make adjustments in one's own behavior, emerged over and over again as themes. Students made statements that indicated a high level of adaptation as defined in the DMIS (M. Bennett, 1993) and an ability to learn from the small or everyday behaviors, to gain some level of effectiveness in the culture (Ward et al., 2001), and to develop important connections with people and with institutions.

The new behaviors were an outward manifestation of the slow internalization of a new set of values: a greater orientation to being people-rather than task-centered, an increased concern for building and maintaining relationships, a sense of responsibility for the collective and an ability to change one's own goals and objectives because of new ways of perceiving the world and their place in it. They had become more mindful, they learned to withhold judgment, and to be flexible, both important intercultural skills. The word "openness" was frequently used in the responses to questions: openness to the new cultures, ideas, and ways of learning and openness to what they were learning about themselves and who they were becoming through these experiences. For most, this did not become clear until they returned home.

In addition, the ability to move beyond empathy to pluralism was evident in these alumni. They had acquired and employed at least a second worldview (some acquired more than two) and were able to talk about the shifts they made between them. Some appeared to have reached the level of internal integration Bennett described with the ability to evaluate situations contextually, as they continually analyzed situations from more than one cultural perspective and discussed those perspectives.

An illustration came from one respondent, Nancy, who said:

> I know that people come from different frames of reference ... and when you are considering your stance on situations, you really need to be cognizant of where others are coming from. Thinking about the well-being of not only you as the individual, but everybody involved.

Culture Shock

It is often difficult to remember the transition process one experienced after the adaptation to a new culture is complete, and especially after some time has passed. This difficulty was evident in the discussions. There was often denial that culture shock had occurred until students were asked about when they felt comfortable in their host cultures and if there were any frustrations. Comfort or a sense of fitting in was not achieved until the students hit their stride in their work with community agencies, became more competent in the use of an unfamiliar language, found ways to become less obvious as a foreigner, and no longer felt they were constantly being thrown into new situations. The intensity of the experience was greater if the differences between the home and host culture were relatively dramatic. Every culture these students entered was very different from their own and they had to deal with ambiguity for a long period as they became more adept at anticipating situations and responding to them appropriately (Paige, 1993; Ward et al., 2001).

Some alumni were very aware of being a minority (White in Jamaica, Black in London), standing out because of their appearance. This, at least in one case, had a profound impact because it was a new experience. Being comfortable meant "forgetting" that one looked different because he or she was interacting successfully and being accepted by the host people. While this level of acceptance occurred among people they encountered on a daily basis, it was never possible in the larger community where the students always stood out. Being noticed, however, became more comfortable as time went on. David said:

> I wanted to experience other cultural situations and other people, so I was interested and open to that experience, but being open to that experience is

different than actually being in that experience. And I mean, when you are a minority, it was a powerful experience. It was a scary experience. It was a reflective experience. It was many things for me.... When the tables are turned like that it really makes you think about how other people feel when they are in that experience.

Others felt they would fit in because they were American-born members of the host culture but quickly learned that appearance was, literally, only skin deep. While they looked like other people, they had different patterns of behavior that made them stand out. One student mentioned that she was surprised at how little she knew about where she came from, and how much she had to learn; "It's probably more of a life-long process." In some ways, this adjustment was more difficult because heritage students expected to fit in easily and they are unable to do so (Paige, 1993).

Class issues loomed for some. Students were struck by the gaps between the desperately poor and the affluent. Living with middle- or upper-class families placed them in the position of living well while working with those who were in serious need. There was some frustration, if not guilt, about their comfortable lives.

Gender issues were raised, especially for *gringa* women in a Latin culture. One male student said he felt it was more difficult for women and he was always impressed at how well they managed the experience in a Latin culture. In general, women found ways to deal with the attitudes toward women and were less and less affected by them as time went on.

Of the intensity factors for sojourners that Paige identified, five emerged as the most applicable: the degree of difference between the home and host cultures, the level of cultural immersion, visibility and invisibility due to physically different characteristics, ethnocentrism on the part of the sojourner and the hosts, and language. Others, such as power and control over their own circumstances, may have been present early in the experience, but as time went on these former students gained control over their lives and this no longer posed a problem (Paige, 1993).

All in all, the frustrations raised were ones to be expected and the former students saw them as something they "got over" as they became more familiar with the culture. They clearly failed to remember the more subtle process of psychological adaptation. They remembered what they had learned about the culture, but forgot the discomfort of the learning.

Most research on study abroad shows that host-sojourner interactions are, if they occur at all, disappointing (Ward et al, 2001). This was never voiced by partnership alumni. The partnership program facilitated interaction between sojourners and hosts to a remarkable degree by embedding students in the community through agency service and local living arrangements. The conditions of those placements had most of the factors that Allport (1954) cited as critical to positive relations between hosts and sojourners:

(1) equal status is enjoyed by everyone in the situation (they may not have equal status in society or in the world but conditions for equal status were established for the situation in which they were together); (2) everyone involved is committed to an active, goal-oriented effort; (3) there is no competition between the those involved in the situation; and (4) the contact and conditions of the contact are sanctioned by "the authorities.

While partnership students did not have "equal status" with those who ran agencies or taught at the partner universities, they had student status which conveyed a purpose for their presence and an agreed-upon status within the service agency. All the conditions Allport indicated were essential to successful relationships in a cross-cultural situation existed, to some degree, and contributed to success in overcoming the greatest hurdle for study abroad students—getting to know people in the host culture.

Much of the research on study-abroad students has focused on listing the problems students encountered, one of which was the fact that students must simultaneously engage in culture learning and study in an unfamiliar academic system, unsure of what is expected of them (Pettigrew & Tropp, 2000). Although Partnership alumni had some complaints about academic content, there were no complaints regarding the manner in which the teaching was approached. In fact, alumni were more apt to praise than to complain and cited specific professors and their effort to forge a connection among their service, academic work, and experience in the community. In the end, students probably did experience culture shock, but they were able to deal with their frustration and adapt well enough to get along well in the culture, make friends, and return home to be "shocked" again.

Reentry

It is the authors' contention that re-entry is the hardest and for learning, the most productive time of study or any stay abroad. It takes the complete cycle of departure/sojourn/return to solidify the learning. When asked about their return experience, the alumni were almost uniformly certain that it was the most difficult aspect of the entire program.

Jeremy said he definitely had the hardest time coming home. His return was delayed by five months of travel in Latin America and a long period of working in Spanish restaurants in the Dallas-Fort Worth area where he let his hair grow and became careless about his appearance.

This earned him a reputation that he did not particularly like, but it was part of trying to figure out how to fit back in at home. It took him a long time to find his niche.

Laurel said she was overwhelmed by so many white people. At a deeper level, she noticed that poverty seemed to be different in the United States; it was an individual experience. In India, the poor still had cohesive families. She felt the poor in the United States suffered emotional as well as economic poverty.

Tamara noted that her return was fine in the short run, but after a week or so, she was ready to return to England. She felt she needed to make sure everyone was all right at home and then she was ready to go away again. Emily was, at first, elated to see her family and then she became disgusted by the materialism in the United States.

Laurel said she was scared.

> I felt like everyone would look at me and know that I was different ... you wonder, do they know I've been in India for six months? ... You wonder, where am I, how am I going to fit back in, and you miss the food and the lifestyle in India.... You know even around my own family ... I didn't feel the same, but you have to give it some time and allow yourself to assimilate into that role that you want. Or even if you don't right away, it will happen eventually.

Elizabeth said reentry was difficult when she returned to South Dakota State University, the host university, from the reservation. Going back to her home college was not as difficult because friends had a lot of questions and were interested in her experience. Their interest not only made her feel good, but also was helpful in her reentry. Going home to her family was also a good experience. She had a new appreciation for them, so being able to spend time with them and to explore her family history was a pleasure. Elizabeth used the skills she had employed going into the new culture in her reentry and that was most effective in easing her reentry but also in connecting her Indian and non-Indian life. She became even more aware, however, of the huge division between Indian and non-Indian communities.

In general, the reactions of these alumni to returning home were not unusual. Rarely did students (or anyone else) expect to have difficulty returning, so it was interesting that some of these former students were a bit apprehensive about their return. It was harder than they anticipated and all of them were still working through their reentry in some way. Reentry tended to be a lifetime event. There will always be a "before" and an "after" to the time when they were in another culture. Their visits abroad had a continuing impact and the realization that having this experience has led them in new directions was one of them.

DISCUSSION AND CONCLUSIONS

Memories, some more than a decade old, are often unreliable resources in evaluating study abroad, or any other experience. This was especially true with regard to recalling the experience of transition to a new culture, labeled somewhat inaccurately as "culture shock." It made sense that culture shock symptoms emerged in the context of the service portion of the IPSL program. It was there that students had the most contact with the local culture and had the most difficulty with decoding and adapting to the culture. Instead of recognizing their discomfort and demands for changes, more structure, and assistance, students found that by labeling these experiences as culture shock, they tended to blame the agencies for being disorganized, unable to use their skills appropriately, and to provide them with meaningful work. This sentiment culminated in a lack of belief in the value of their contribution to the agency and any substantive impact on the clients they were serving. Ultimately, they saw the service as a crucial part of their learning overall and, when they had either discovered a way or simply endured long enough to feel useful, found a great deal of satisfaction in the service experience. This indicated that they had gone through a process of adaptation and cultural learning that resulted in a realistic view of the culture, and an ability to function in it coupled with a greater sense of usefulness in the service. They continued, however, to express dissatisfaction with their inability to make a lasting contribution to the welfare of the agency clients.

It was hard for partnership program participants to see the long-term impact of the program and their part in it. Their impacts have been eloquently stated by Victor Maridueña Varela, a former director of service agencies in Ecuador, who pointed to the constant presence of students, year after year, doing small things that meant something to the people with whom they worked, that made a difference, if only by demonstrating that there was a group of people who care.

Reentry remained an immediate memory because it tended to be a very unique and life-long experience, unlike culture shock, which is a recognized phenomenon whose symptoms are widely known (Pusch, 2001). Those who returned recognized their own change and the impact of the other culture experience in their career choices, relationships, attitudes, and assessment of social, political, and economic conditions and events. Thus, the IPSL and the service-learning process had an impact on the lives of these former students. Their greatest problem was finding a way to process what they had learned on a continuing basis. Elizabeth was fortunate in having interested friends, in being able to use her skills in cultural learning during the return, and in maintaining contact and returning to the reservation. She was in a constant state of entry and reentry and learned to not only manage this process but to connect her two worlds. David was successfully keeping the experience fresh with continuing contact, due largely to his dissertation research. He stated, however, that by constantly having new experiences with Jamaica, he has "layer upon layer of experience ... you can still see through, you see the top and somewhere you can still get through to the bottom."

Just as kumys is essential to a summer in Kyrgyzstan, intercultural theory is essential to understanding service-learning in a culturally different environment. The IPSL study clearly demonstrated the usefulness of these theories, not only in exploring the student experience of service-learning abroad, but in establishing programs and support systems that anticipate the issues that arise from the cross-cultural nature of the programs and in the ongoing assessment of student progress, student complaints, and of the programs themselves.

NOTES

1. All names are fictitious, used to make the reading of student comments easier.
2. David is writing a dissertation on artists in Jamaica and realized how they connect everything in their lives.

REFERENCES

Allport, G. W. (1954). *The nature of prejudice*. Reading, MA: Addison-Wesley.

Bennett, J. (1993). Cultural marginality: Identity issues on intercultural training. in M. Paige (Ed.), *Education for the intercultural experience* (pp. 109-136). Yarmouth, ME: Intercultural Press.

Bennett, M. (1993). Towards ethnorelativism: A developmental model of intercultural sensitivity. In M. Paige (Ed.), *Education for the intercultural experience* (pp. 21-72). Yarmouth, ME: Intercultural Press.

Engle, J., & Engle, L. (2002). Neither international nor educative: Study abroad in the time of globalization. In W. Grunzweig & N. Rinehart (Eds.), *Rockin' in Red Square: Critical approaches to international education in the age of cyberculture* (pp. 25-40). London: Lit Verlag.

International Partnership for Service-Learning and Leadership Web site. (n.d.). Retrieved August 24, 2007, from www.ipsl.org

Martin, J. N., & Harrell, T. (2004). Intercultural re-entry of students and professionals: Theory and practice. In D. Landis, J. M. Bennett, & M. Bennett (Eds.), *Handbook of intercultural training* (pp. 309-336). Thousand Oaks, CA: Sage.

Paige, R. M. (1993). On the nature of intercultural experience and intercultural education. In M. Paige (Ed.), *Education for the intercultural experience* (pp. 1-20). Yarmouth, ME: Intercultural Press.

Perry, W. G. (1999), *Forms of ethical and intellectual development in the college years: A scheme.* San Francisco: Jossey-Bass. (Original word published 1970)

Pettigrew, T. F. (1998). Intergroup contact theory. *Annual Review of Psychology, 49.* Retrieved August 24, 2007, from http://www.questia.com/app/direct/SM.qst

Pettigrew, T. F., & Tropp, L. R. (2000). Does intergroup contact reduce prejudice? Recent meta-analytic findings. In S. Oskamp (Ed.), *Reducing prejudice and discrimination* (pp. 93-114) Mahwah, NJ: Erlbaum.

Pusch, M. D. (1994). The chameleon capability. In R. D. Lambert (Ed.), *Educational exchange and global competence* (pp. 205-210). New York: CIEE.

Pusch, M. D. (1998). Going home: Styles of re-entry. In D. Lynch, A. Pilbeam, & P. O'Connor (Eds.), *Heritage and progress* (pp. 248-255). Bath, England: SIETAR Europa.

Pusch, M. D. (2001). *Research on re-entry and reintegration into the home community.* Unpublished paper, Antioch University.

Pusch, M. D. (2004). A cross-cultural perspective. In H. Tonkin (Ed.) *Service- learning across cultures: Promise and achievement—A report to the Ford Foundation.* New York: The International Partnership for Service-Learning and Leadership

Tonkin, H. (Ed.). (2004). Preface. In *Service-learning across cultures: Promise and achievement—A report to the Ford Foundation* New York: The International Partnership for Service-Learning and Leadership.

Ward, C., Bochner, S., & Furnham, A. (2001). *The psychology of culture shock* (2nd ed.). Philadelphia: Taylor & Francis.

CHAPTER 3

AN EASTERN PERSPECTIVE ON WESTERN EDUCATION

The Experiences of International Students Engaged in Service-Learning

Margaret W. Sallee and Susan C. Harris

ABSTRACT

Thousands of international students currently study in the United States and many struggle to understand the new culture in which they are immersed. Service-learning, a pedagogy that integrates community service and academic coursework in mutually beneficial ways, provides an opportunity for international students to learn more about American culture, yet few studies document the experiences of international service-learning students. This chapter explores the experiences of 41 Taiwanese and South Korean international graduate students enrolled in teaching English as a foreign/second language program who were engaged in service-learning in urban schools in the United States. Participants gained insight into American culture and the differences between Asian and American approaches to education in ways that traditional classroom instruction would not have

From Passion to Objectivity: International and Cross-Disciplinary Perspectives on Service Learning Research, pp. 41–62

allowed. The lessons learned through their experiences offer suggestions to service-learning practitioners who may develop programs for international students at their own institutions.

Despite a recent dip in international student enrollment as a result of policy changes and other concerns following the terrorist attacks of September 11th, 2001, the number of international students studying at American universities has increased steadily since the 1950s. Fifty years ago, approximately 34,000 international students came to the United States to study; today that figure stands at nearly 565,000 students per year (Institute of International Education, 2006).

Service-learning is frequently touted as a way to help domestic undergraduates rethink some of their basic assumptions about society by immersing them in a social context that is often different from their own. Most international students come from countries that differ considerably from the United States. Can engaging in service-learning help international students gain a deeper understanding of the United States? How does being from another country shape the experiences and perspectives of service-learning students working in an American community? These are questions addressed in this chapter. The authors draw on data collected in a qualitative study of Taiwanese and Korean graduate service-learning students enrolled in the teaching English as a foreign/second language (TEFL/TESL) program at a large urban university with one of the largest international student populations in the United States.

The chapter begins by providing a brief overview of the East Asian educational system, then turns to a discussion of the differences between civic education and service-learning. To help understand international students' service-learning experiences and the differences they identified between the United States and their country of origin, the authors draw on the work of Hofstede (1986) who created a typology to categorize differences between cultures. The remainder of the chapter discusses participants' experiences as they were engaged in service. The chapter concludes by offering suggestions for service-learning practitioners who work with international students and identifying directions for future research.

THE TAIWANESE AND SOUTH KOREAN EDUCATIONAL SYSTEMS

Unlike the United States, where education varies dramatically from state to state, and from school district to school district, the governments of Taiwan and South Korea have ministries of education that regulate education. Not only do they prescribe a central curriculum that all teachers must follow, but they also approve the use of specific textbooks (Butler, 2005; Sorensen, 1994). Although there is some variation in quality, particularly between urban and rural schools, the centralized curriculum leads to a more uniform education for each country's citizenry.

Students follow the same curriculum in elementary school and middle school. At the age of 15, Taiwanese and South Korean students are channeled into either an academic or a vocational high school based on their results on high school entrance exams. Similar separation takes place through the use of exams for college admission. As a result, the majority of students' secondary education is geared toward passing high school and university admissions exams. Due to the social pressure to succeed academically, many students attend "cram schools," or extracurricular academic instruction designed to supplement the material taught in their regular classrooms. Students and parents in both countries seek out cram schools in an effort to bolster students' chances of admission to the most prestigious high school or university (Lee, 2004; Sorensen, 1994).

Teachers act as the gatekeepers to educational success for students. Given their important role, teachers in both countries are highly respected and teaching is viewed as a high-status occupation (Hofstede, 1986; Sorensen, 1994). Teachers' knowledge is not to be questioned. Their role is to impart knowledge to students. Just as children are meant to show respect to their parents, so are students charged with showing respect for their teachers. This emphasis on respect stems in part from East Asia's adherence to Confucianism, which calls for citizens to embody the characteristics of loyalty, filial piety, benevolence, and reciprocity (Kuan & Lau, 2002; Liu, 1999; Morris, Kan, & Morris, 2000). Filial piety directs youth to respect and never question their elders. Such a value is immediately apparent in the traditional methods used for instruction in Asian schools. A teacher's responsibility is to convey the material to students who are expected to be passive receivers of knowledge. Traditional learning takes place through rote memorization, not through class discussion or critical thinking.

Both the Taiwanese and South Korean educational systems are defined by competition. From an early age, students compete with one another to earn the highest scores and entrance into further education. Rarely do East Asian classrooms employ active learning strategies, such as group work or class discussion. As such, the educational experiences of East Asian youth differ considerably from the experiences of youth in the United States.

CIVIC EDUCATION, CIVIC ENGAGEMENT, AND SERVICE-LEARNING

Teaching students to pass entrance exams is not the sole focus of East Asian education. Both explicitly and implicitly, schools are also charged with giving students the tools to become ideal citizens. This education occurs through the type of knowledge imparted to students along with instruction in civic education, or the necessary skills to participate in the country's civic, community, and political life (Cogan, Morris, & Print, 2002).

What is required of a citizen in one country will differ from what is required of a citizen of another. As Mei-Hui Liu (1999) argues, civic education is an effective means for transmitting ideology and for inculcating nationalistic and patriotic values into citizens. The ideology that drives the country determines the tools for citizenship that students are taught. Such ideology is not limited to Asia, but can be found in countries around the world. For example, in the United States, school children are reminded of their citizenship by reciting the Pledge of Allegiance each day. As they progress through school, they learn the history of the United States and are taught to embrace democracy. Civic education arms students with the knowledge, skills, and values to be good citizens.

Much of East Asian civic education includes values and knowledge transmission. There is less emphasis on teaching students practical skills for participating in either the political system or in the community. For example, civic education in Taiwan emphasizes awareness and understanding of the political process, but does not encourage actual participation (Liu, 1999). In both Taiwan and Hong Kong, civic education is designed to train students to be obedient and to not question authority (Liu, 2002; Morris & Morris, 2002).

In her case study of two schools in Taiwan, Liu (2002) found that teachers believed that citizenship could be developed through persuasion and indoctrination. In other words, students simply needed to be told what to believe. Morris and Morris (2002) found that teachers in Hong Kong taught civic education through a reliance on discipline and an emphasis on school rules. One teacher argued that "punishments and discipline were far more effective than the use of notice boards telling students how to be a good person" (quoted in Morris and Morris, 2002, p. 59). Civic education in these schools relies more on teaching students how not to act than teaching them to assume active roles in society.

Students in Asia do not engage in community service to the same extent as their peers in the United States. Part of this difference might stem from the relative homogeneity of culture and of education in these countries. The ministry of education in Taiwan and South Korea each create a centralized curriculum for all schools, thus providing a similar education for students across the country, and ignoring differences at the local level. Since teachers are obligated to follow a centralized curriculum, they have little ability to incorporate activities that promote service to the community into the curriculum. In the United States, many students and their parents look to volunteerism as a way to improve their chances of being admitted into college. In East Asia, admission to college rests on performance on standardized tests. Neither civic education nor civic engagement is tested and, therefore, for many students and parents, is not highly valued (Liu, 1999). Consistent with this rationale, Zhao, Kuh, and Carini (2005) found that international students do not engage in community service to the same extent as their domestic peers. Given East Asia's educational system that relies on the transmission of knowledge and uses standardized test scores as measures of student learning, international students have not been socialized into the process of engaging in educational activities outside of the classroom.

CULTURAL DIMENSIONS OF TEACHING AND LEARNING

Hofstede's (1986) research on cultural differences identifies five dimensions to explain variations between societies: individualism/collectivism; power distance; uncertainty avoidance; masculinity/femininity; and short- versus long-term orientation. Individualism/collectivism refers to the degree to which individuals are integrated into groups. In individualist societies, people tend to care only for themselves and their immediate families. In collectivist societies, people are integrated into cohesive networks, often including extended family. These networks welcome and protect them in exchange for unquestioning loyalty.

Power distance refers to the degree to which less powerful people in a society accept inequality and consider its unequal distribution to be normal. This concept suggests that inequality is endorsed by followers as much as leaders. A society's power distance level determines the degree to which families instill a sense of obedience versus initiative in their children.

Uncertainty avoidance addresses the way in which a society programs its members to react to unstructured (i.e., unknown or unusual) situations. Cultures that engage in strong uncertainty avoidance try to minimize the possibility of unstructured situations by promoting strict adherence to laws and rules as well as through the acceptance of an absolute truth. Those who come from countries with low uncertainty avoidance are more tolerant of a variety of opinions and accept the existence of multiple truths.

Masculinity/femininity refers to the distribution of emotional roles between men and women. Cultures that are masculine strive to achieve a great distinction between men's and women's responsibilities. They expect men to be assertive, ambitious, and competitive and expect women to act as caretakers. In contrast, feminine cultures permit men to adopt less aggressive and more caring behaviors and allow men and women to fulfill overlapping roles.

Short-term versus long-term orientations delineate the importance various cultures place on honoring the past versus planning for the future. Countries with a short-term orientation tend to value respect for tradition and fulfilling social obligations. Countries with a long-term orientation look more toward the future by emphasizing thrift and persistence (Hofstede, 1986; Hofstede & McCrae, 2004).

None of these dimensions establishes clear distinctions. Rather, a country may fall anywhere along the continuum between either of the two extremes, such as individualism and collectivism. However, Hofstede's dimensions identify fairly significant differences between the average score of respondents in the United States and the average score of respondents in both Taiwan and South Korea. For example, while the United States rates high in individualism, Taiwan and South Korea rate high in emphasis placed on collectivism. Hofstede's findings, particularly the differences between the United States and East Asia on the dimensions of individualism/collectivism, power distance, uncertainty avoidance, and short-term versus long-term orientation, can help explain the differences that international students identify between the educational systems of the United States and their country of origin.

METHODOLOGY

Participants in the study were international graduate students enrolled in the TEFL/TESL program at a large private urban university. All participants had some experience teaching in their home country, though experience ranged from helping for a month in a cram school to being a classroom teacher for several years. The TEFL/TESL program requires students to observe and teach in classrooms in elementary and secondary schools. Students have the option of making their own arrangements or enrolling in the university's primary service-learning program and working as a teaching assistant while observing classroom activities.

Over four semesters, 41 students, all of whom were enrolled in the service-learning program, elected to participate in the study. Of this sample, 37 were from Taiwan and 4 were from Korea, and all but one were female. Students spent 2 hours a week for 6 to 8 weeks engaged in service in public elementary schools and high schools with large numbers of English language learners. Participants performed a variety of services in the classroom, including tutoring individual students, working with small groups of students, and teaching the entire class.

Each week, participants responded to questions prepared by the co-authors that were designed to help them reflect on their experiences in the classroom and on differences between the Asian and American educational systems (see the Appendix). Upon completing their service, 37 participants completed semistructured exit interviews, lasting between 20 and 45 minutes, with at least one of the authors. All interviews were tape recorded and later transcribed.

RESULTS

The international students used their journals and interviews to explore perceived similarities and differences between Asian and American approaches to education. Their comments reflected a tension between a loyalty to their personal experiences and professional training in their countries of origin and an attraction to many of the markedly different approaches they observed in American classrooms. For many of the students, the different teaching styles represented larger differences between Western and Eastern cultures. They used their service-learning experiences to reach conclusions about the divergent values that drive the two societies. This section of the chapter focuses on three differences that were particularly salient for participants: teacher-centered versus student-centered classrooms; active versus passive classroom participation; and teachers as authority figures versus teachers as friends.

Teacher-Centered Versus Student-Centered Classrooms

Most students were struck by the differences in the ways that Asian and American teachers managed and instructed their students. From their first day in the classroom, the majority of students discovered that American teachers tended to employ student-centered teaching, which stood in stark contrast to their own experiences as students and as teachers in the teacher-centered classrooms of Asia. Asian classrooms tended to elevate teachers to a position of high authority. Students were expected to quietly listen to the teacher and absorb knowledge. One participant defined a teaching-centered classroom as follows:

I grew up in a teacher-centered classroom, where the teacher is the expert with high authorities and she/he pours down all knowledge to the students. That is, what students do is [sit in] the chairs and tak[e] notes whatever the teacher says. There are few interactions between the teacher and students, which leads to the consequence that students ... lack ... critical thinking and autonomy of learning.

This participant identified several key features of a teacher-centered classroom. First, the teacher was an expert who "pours down all knowledge" to students. She emphasized that students were expected to take notes and not to ask questions. As she pointed out, since Asian teachers seldom created opportunities for interaction between teacher and students, there were few chances for questions, either for students to clarify the teacher's lecture or to help students develop critical thinking skills. This observation of Asian classrooms as teacher-centered was echoed in other students' responses. Another participant described a Taiwanese classroom this way:

In the East, most of the classrooms are teacher-centered. Students obey what the teachers say and what the teachers teach. It is the most common teaching and learning methods that the teachers give the lecture in front of the class and the students are busy in taking notes in class. The teachers seldom interact with students; furthermore, students are shy to ask questions and even shy to answer the teachers' questions.

Perhaps these elements were most salient for participants due to their experiences in American classrooms, which did not resemble the ordered environment of their Asian counterparts.

Participants described American classrooms as ones where the teacher did not rely on lecturing as the preferred format of instruction. Rather, teachers' roles transformed from being the all-knowing sage imparting wisdom to a facilitator who created conditions to allow students to learn. One student described the classroom she observed:

The role of the teacher is an assistant and she always gives the students instructions first and ha[s] them do activities. I think it is a good way for students to develop their positive learning and be responsible for themselves. In addition, children like to [do] group work and cooperative activities, from which students are motivated and learn how to work with others as well.

Unlike Asian classrooms where teachers lecture and students listen, in this American classroom, the teacher provided opportunities for students to engage in hands-on learning through group work. Another student commented on the benefits of group work:

(The teacher) form[s] the students into a small group and she provide[s] the activity, ask[s] the students to participate in the class and they can discuss ... the questions and they learn how to solve the problems for their learning.

Both students' comments suggest that the teacher provided background knowledge to students to help them complete the class activity. In these classrooms, students were expected to engage with the material and with each other to discover the appropriate answer and complete the task.

When contrasting Asian and American classrooms, many students highlighted the differences in teachers' flexibility in structuring their time. Since both the Taiwanese and South Korean governments mandate a centralized curriculum, teachers in these countries were constantly under pressure to stay on schedule and rarely had the luxury of straying from the prescribed curriculum. In addition, since Asian students were under pressure to pass high school and university entrance exams, teachers experienced additional pressure to teach all of the materials that students need to succeed.

Some students defended the use of teacher-centered instruction due to these two limitations. One student's comments illustrated this defense:

When we get into junior high or senior high school, the goal for us is to pass high school entrance exams. And then college entrance exam. So in class, the teacher just teach[es] and we just have our exams, yeah. So there is ... not too much communication between [teacher and students] ... because the time is limited. The teacher want[s] to teach us in such a limited time.

Another student's comments reiterate this point:

In Taiwan ... I have to follow the timetable and schedule. So limited time stops me to give students more time to finish their jobs or even I have to push them to do faster sometimes. Furthermore, I have to be meaner because I don't have time to talk to them patiently.

In contrast, although American teachers used textbooks approved by the local school board, they often had more flexibility in structuring their school day. While American students are required to take performance assessment exams, only recently have these exams acquired any significance for students' educational achievement. Although some states have enacted legislation mandating that students pass a statewide test to receive their high school diploma, Asian students still appear to experience far greater anxiety and pressure surrounding test-taking. One student found that her teaching experience in an American classroom led her to think differently about the role that she needed to play as an instructor for American students:

I integrated different kinds of teaching principles into my lessons, and also, I made adjustments all the time according to students' needs and feedbacks, which taught me that teaching is a flexible and dynamic work, and there are always unexpected situations coming out. So, a good teacher should have the ability to confront all kinds of obstacles and fix it as soon as possible for the sake of enhancing the teaching and learning at the same time.

In the American student-centered classroom, this international student recognized that teachers need to be responsive to students' needs and adjust their lesson plans accordingly. Such attentiveness would be more difficult in a traditional, teacher-centered classroom where the teacher lectures and seldom checks students' comprehension. This student and many others commented on the benefits they saw of student-centered approaches, but few were able to reconcile these practices with the test-centered culture of Taiwan and South Korea.

Active Classroom Participation

All of the participants commented on the degree to which American students volunteered to participate in the classroom. They frequently contrasted the eager American students, clamoring to answer the teachers' questions, with the more reticent Asian students who not only would not volunteer to answer teachers' questions, but were in fact fearful that they would be called on. In the United States, teachers frequently design activities and pose questions to help students develop critical thinking skills. In contrast, Asian teachers tend to focus on memorization to help students pass exams. American children are generally praised for offering a solution whereas Asian children are chastised if their response is incorrect. These two courses of action lead to different rates of student participation between the United States and Asia

Students were amazed at the ways in which American children wanted to participate in the classroom. One student contrasted her experience in the American classroom with her memories of teaching in Taiwan:

As for American kids ... the most impressive to me is their willingness to volunteer. The kids love to show themselves in public. I remember the first time when the teacher wanted volunteers to read the letters they wrote to the whole class, I saw a lot of hands in the air! I could not say it was a culture shock, but it did surprise me. In my home country, only few students would want to volunteer in such cases, even none would. Generally, they would just wait until the teacher called their names. I think Eastern students are really shyer or more passive than Western students. Maybe it is because we are taught not to show off, and this kind of behaviors might be considered as showing off.

This quote highlights several issues. First, the American students were eager to share what they wrote with other students. The teacher was not calling on students to give the correct answer to a math problem. Rather, this was an activity in which there was not one correct answer. Also, as the student pointed out, Asian students are less likely to volunteer to participate because to do so was equated with showing off. Many of the participants remarked that Asian students are expected to be modest. Willfully volunteering to share their work is equated with trying to distinguish oneself from the crowd.

Throughout their journals, many of the students pondered this striking difference between American and Asian classrooms. One student highlighted one potential reason for the differences by pointing to the different emphases of education in the two cultures. She wrote:

In Taiwan, the students who are good at exam[s] are regarded as smart and good students. While in the U.S., they value the students who participate in activity actively or share opinions.

As previously discussed, Taiwanese and South Korean classrooms place great emphasis on test performance. Consequently, the students who were most rewarded are those who score highest on tests. In contrast, participants perceived that students who were most rewarded in American classrooms were those who were most willing to participate.

While engaged in service, participants were also taking courses in the university's TEFL program and learning new pedagogical techniques, many of which were in direct contradiction to the techniques they had utilized in their teaching practices in their home country. Many of the students commented on the way in which Asian teachers emphasized memorization as a learning tool for students. One student summed it up as follows:

The general teaching [in Taiwan is] just really, really traditional.... Teacher just told me that there is no second way. Just memorize everything.

Other students shared stories from their own education in which students who did not give the correct response were publicly shamed by the teacher. To answer incorrectly signaled that a student had not completed his or her reading, or at least inadequately learned the material. Several students described teachers who, upon getting an incorrect response from a student, would ask increasingly difficult questions. As a result, participants suggested that many students were hesitant to volunteer to answer questions in the classroom, out of fear of being publicly shamed.

Whereas Asian classrooms emphasized students producing the correct answer, American teachers simply wanted students to participate. The goal in American classrooms was not for students to generate the correct response, but to help students develop critical thinking skills. Adjusting to these norms proved to be a challenge for some participants. In the following excerpt, one student describes her experiences teaching in an American classroom and the feedback she received from the classroom teacher afterward:

> When I asked the questions, I expect students to answer me the correct answer and if they didn't answer the correct answer, I will be a little frustrated because I know they didn't get it. But [the classroom teacher] told me that thinking process is more important than the correct answer. So ... he recommend me to ask students why they think [their response is the correct answer], instead of just "Oh it's not correct, the correct answer is blah blah blah." And I guess that's pretty important ... I will try that in my future teaching.

This student's response echoes those of many of her classmates. Many of them described their own frustration as students, being subjected to the scorn of their teachers if they answered a question incorrectly. Yet, they also seemed to replicate that same behavior themselves as teachers. American pedagogy, however, emphasizes different skills and creates a more supportive learning environment for students. This participant's mentor teacher provided her with concrete suggestions of ways to encourage students to develop their critical thinking skills.

Teacher as Authority versus Teacher as Friend

The international students spent a great deal of time puzzling over the different ways that American teachers related to their students compared with their Asian counterparts. Often, they described Asian teachers as authority figures while American teachers were friends. While many remarked on the fact that American students did not fear their teachers, they saw this closer relationship as responsible for perceived chaos in the classroom.

In East Asian classrooms, the teacher is the sole authority figure. One student described the teacher as follows:

> In Taiwan the teacher is the only authority in the class and the teacher is in control of everything. So everything the teacher say[s] is the only right thing ... If you try to negotiate with the teacher, it's like you reject ... it shows that

you don't want to do it. So, we are afraid to negotiate or argue with the teacher.

Several students remarked on the ways in which American students were able to negotiate with their teachers. This was in sharp contrast to their experiences in Asian classrooms, where such behavior is strictly forbidden as it displays disrespect. This student also highlighted the fact that Asian students were afraid of their teachers. As another student suggests, this fear may stem from the fact that, until very recently, corporal punishment was allowed in Taiwanese schools:

> In our country, [corporal punishment is] very popular. So ... when the teacher kept the stick out, then everyone sit quiet. But here [in the U.S.], you have to ... say many words and then yell at them. And make them scared so the teacher can focus on you.

As this student expressed throughout her journals and interviews, fear and control was the primary way to get children to respond to teachers and parents. For this student, as for several others, it was critical for teachers to maintain their status as an authority figure in order to control the classroom.

Not all students shared this opinion. After spending time volunteering in American classrooms, many came to appreciate the different ways that American teachers related to their students. One student contrasted Asian and American teachers as follows:

> Usually [in South Korea], the teacher is like king, and ... students should show our ... respect towards teachers. But in here, I feel like the teacher, you know, sometimes show their ... respect toward students.... They are willing to help their students as much as they can.... But you know they still have their authority.... They can be like my models.... I should be like them.... Sometimes they are like their students' friends, but you know sometimes they are ... more.... For example, when they gave their advice for the students, they feel like, okay, teacher. Or, you know, more authority.

This student described a classroom in which teacher and students showed respect for one another. In a typical Asian classroom, the teacher was elevated "like a king," to whom students were expected to show deference. However, in the classroom where she served, she had the opportunity to interact with teachers who shared their respect for students. At times, they served as friendly mentors for students while at other times, they acted as greater authority figures.

Many students were particularly drawn to the close relationships American teachers had with their students. Participants used phrases such as "friends," "buddies," and "like a family" to describe the teacher-student relationship in the classroom. Many students denounced the ways in which Asian teachers acted toward their students, as this student does here:

> In my country, teachers seldom compliment their students and tell students what they feel. Instead, they take it for granted toward students' good behaviors. Also, they are unwilling to tell students their true feelings because it makes them feel that they show their weakness to students. It's pathetic. From my point of view, sharing my thoughts and feelings with students can make me feel closer to my students and shorten the gap with students.

Like many of her classmates, this student remarked on the ways in which American teachers try to "shorten the gap" between teacher and students, by treating students more as equals in the learning process.

Because of their complex status as professional teachers and former students in a system that establishes a clear "gap" between teachers and students, and as service-learning students who were encouraged by their university instructors and K-12 teacher-supervisors alike to establish egalitarian relationships with the children, the students grappled with their own roles in the classroom as teachers, volunteers, authority figures, and friends. The students' reflections identified some the cultural factors that facilitate or constrain friendly teacher-student relationships:

> Because I go there twice a week and an hour for each time, therefore, sometimes I need to catch up what the learning agenda of the class in a short time. So, I would ask the little boy about it. He is just like a little assistant to me. And now, with the times I spent more there, the kids in the same group of hers have already become familiar with me, we are just as friends. It's totally different from my country. In my country, the students usually afraid of talking to someone they don't really know or even they have already known the person, especially they see the person as a teacher, they still keep in a distance. By doing so, it would be a little bit hard to have a good interaction between a teacher and the students.

Although many participants spoke highly of the strong bond children were able to form with teachers—and with them—they did not always see the compatibility of teacher as authority and teacher as friend. Instead, they continued to rely on their experiences from their home country to shape their impressions of what a teacher should be. Many felt that teachers who acted as students' friends were unable to establish order in their classrooms. One student described her mentor teacher as follows:

> Sometimes she was like their friend, but ... most of the time she didn't control the classroom very well. The class was crazy.

For many of the students, it seems that the drawback of establishing a friendly rapport with students was risking losing some element of control. It was never entirely clear what "out of control" meant to participants. Some of them described classrooms in which students were free to roam about during lessons and often chatted with one another. In contrast to the strict discipline employed in Asian classrooms, where students are expected to sit quietly and listen to the teacher, such classrooms would indeed appear to be out of control.

DISCUSSION

Students' comments depicted two contrasting classroom environments. They described U.S. classrooms that favored student-centered learning in which teachers encouraged students to actively participate in classroom activities designed to promote critical thinking. In contrast, they described Taiwanese and South Korean classrooms as those in which the teacher reigned supreme and students obediently absorbed the knowledge necessary to pass entrance exams. These cultural differences reflected the countries' locations on Hofstede's various cultural dimensions. For example, the fact that East Asian countries favor lecture as a method of instruction derives in part from these countries' respect for elders and tradition—qualities that are inherent in the dimensions of short-term orientation. In addition, societies with high power distance endorse gaps in power between individuals in society. In the teacher-centered classroom, the teacher has high status and is charged with filling students with the correct information. Students are less powerful and therefore mandated with accepting what they are told. Similarly, they learn that it is disrespectful for them to question their teachers and often refrain from asking questions in class.

However, this lack of classroom participation may also be due to students' hesitation to distinguish themselves from their peers. As one of the students commented, to volunteer to answer a question in an Asian classroom is tantamount to showing off. In Eastern cultures, citizens are expected to blend into the crowd and to avoid distinguishing themselves from their peers. Volunteering to answer a question in an American classroom does not carry the same negative connotations. In fact, American students are rewarded for their willingness to participate, regardless of whether their response is correct or not. However, the fear of answering a question incorrectly in Taiwan or South Korea keeps many students from volunteering. In contrast to the United States, both Asian countries scored high on Hofstede's dimensions of uncertainty avoidance, meaning that people do not want to put themselves in situations where they cannot be certain of the outcome. This explains the preference for lecture as a method of instruction in Asian classrooms as well, since teachers and students both know what is expected of them.

The type of knowledge that is emphasized varies across the cultures as well. In East Asian countries, teachers tended to ask students to repeat what they have just learned whereas American teachers asked students questions to develop their critical thinking skills. This, too, points to a difference in levels of uncertainty avoidance as well as in individualism versus collectivism. Promoting critical thinking skills may lead to differences in the way people think, thereby producing greater gaps between people, leading to a more individualist culture, as in the United States. Employing critical thinking in the classroom rests upon the notion that there are multiple answers to a question, another hallmark of cultures with low uncertainty avoidance. Although many of the students expressed interest in promoting critical thinking with their students upon their return to their home countries, the great differences in culture may mean that such attempts will fail.

The different relationships between teachers and students also illustrate Hofstede's dimensions of power distance and uncertainty avoidance. In Asian classrooms, teachers derive their authority from their elevated status and their control of students. Some students hypothesized that American teachers were unable to control their classes due to the fact that they did not have enough authority over students. Acting as students' friends may make both teachers and students feel better, they conjectured, but it creates problems for maintaining order. In the American classrooms, teachers were willing to "give up" some of their authority by occasionally negotiating with students on minor matters, such as homework assignments. Such behavior was not problematic in American classrooms where uncertainty avoidance is quite low. In fact, this is one of the hallmarks of student-centered classrooms: spaces where teacher and students work together to create conditions that are optimal for learning.

LIMITATIONS OF THIS STUDY

This study has several limitations. First, all journals and interviews were completed in English. Although participants were enrolled in a teaching English as a foreign language master's program and nearly all were at least proficient in English, students may not have been able to fully express their ideas to the interviewers. Students often paused during interviews to search for the right words and many frequently commented on this fact. Cost barriers prevented the researchers from hiring additional assistants to conduct the interviews in either Mandarin or Korean.

Although students may have been able to express their ideas more easily in their native tongue, there were benefits to having interviews conducted by the coauthors. Participants had gained familiarity with the first author through repeated contact throughout the semester as she conducted two trainings and provided feedback on weekly journals. She was a fellow graduate student and more of a peer than an authority figure to the students, which may have allowed them to be more candid in their comments.

Though the researchers' relationship with participants may have made them more comfortable in interviews, there is also the possibility that students felt coerced to participate in the study. During the initial orientation, the first author introduced the study and asked for students' participation. She emphasized that choosing not to participate would have no effect on their final evaluations. While some students chose to opt out, it is also possible that other students felt compelled to participate despite their reluctance.

Finally, students spent a limited amount of time engaged in service. Depending on the semester, students spent 2 to 3 hours a week for 6 to 8 weeks engaged in service. Although students were able to identify differences between Asian and American classrooms based on their service-learning experiences, students' understanding of American approaches to education may have benefited from prolonged engagement in the community.

SUGGESTIONS FOR PRACTITIONERS

Since international students are a small, but sizable, presence on most campuses, chances are that some will participate in service-learning programs. As a result of the experiences conveyed in this chapter, the authors offer the following three suggestions for service-learning practitioners who work with international students. While the focus here is on suggestions for students from East Asian cultures, the suggestions may be modified for work with students from across the globe.

1. **Understand the cultural background of students:** Knowing about the students' cultural background is crucial for developing service-learning assignments that introduce new and challenging social contexts for students. However, it is also important to consider learning objectives and pedagogies, and the implications for students who plan to return to their countries of origin. It is one thing to encourage American students to learn more about what it means

to be good citizens and to become more civically engaged. It is another to encourage international students to do the same, when they plan to return to countries that discourage or, in some cases, forbid such behavior. Work with international students forced the authors to consider the global-political implications in a way that has not been apparent in work with domestic undergraduate students. The practitioner should recognize the additional difficulties students may experience by engaging in service.

2. **Prepare students for the differences between the U.S. culture and their home country:** While it is helpful for practitioners to gain an understanding of international students, it is perhaps more critical for students to have knowledge about U.S. culture before entering their service site. In the program described here, the authors tried to prepare students by holding two mandatory training sessions—one before they entered their service site and one midway through service. At the first training, a staff member discussed students' responsibilities and answered any questions students might have. The second training typically proved to be more helpful since students had been at their service site for at least three to four weeks. At the second training, students had an opportunity to share their experiences with one another. This allowed students to compare their experiences with their peers and to use the group meeting as an opportunity to generate strategies for challenges they faced. Although training sessions were exclusively for international students, mixed training sessions with both domestic and international students may be effective as well.

3. **Establish clear guidelines for community partners and students before beginning service:** During the first training session, students were told that they must speak with the teacher about having the opportunity to teach the class, which was a requirement of the course. However, the cultural background of these international students hindered many of them from feeling comfortable approaching the classroom teacher. Occasionally, there were other challenges that students were hesitant to discuss with their mentor teachers. Based on student feedback, the authors generated a letter that was distributed to both students and teachers before beginning their service. The letter spelled out many of the program's expectations in the hopes that students and teachers would use the letter as a way to start a conversation about expectations for service. The authors also used the letter to provide a brief introduction to East Asian cultures so that classroom teachers might more readily understand participants and their hesitation to become involved.

Though these three suggestions did not provide problem-free service experience for all participants, they did help the majority of international students more readily engage in the local community.

CONCLUSION

There are multiple areas for study of international programs that feature service-learning. Future studies of international student programs might examine the role of critical reflection in service-learning. How can educators encourage critical reflection from international students whose own education and approaches to teaching have openly discouraged critical thinking? Are there additional challenges that international students might face in employing critical reflection or can it be an effective tool for helping them to learn about United States culture?

The norms of service-learning clash with those of civic education in many Asian countries. Service-learning encourages engagement in the community and critical reflection on societal inequities whereas civic education simply teaches students the values and norms of what is required to be an ideal citizen. Should U.S. educators employ service-learning with international students if its goals clash with students' backgrounds and belief systems? At what point are we educating students and at what point are we indoctrinating them?

The chapter discussed the many differences that international students identified between the Asian and American educational systems. Like the majority of students who engage in service-learning, study participants found themselves involved in a community that differed considerably from their own. However, unlike typical undergraduate service-learning students, participants were professionals with varying degrees of experience in the same type of service site and yet with distinctly different experiences in these settings. Though participants had experience in classrooms in their home countries, many of the norms and practices they encountered in the American classrooms differed from their past experiences.

Participants were encouraged to reflect on these differences and to try to draw connections between practices in the classroom and cultural norms. As international students considered the strikingly different classroom environments, they learned about American culture and educational practices through their experiences in the classroom. The new experiences and their assignments for reflection led them to think critically and challenge their ideas about teaching. Their experiences simultaneously expanded their perspectives about techniques they might use as teachers while challenging them to use these very strategies as students themselves. They learned first-hand about the benefits of developing crit-ical thinking skills by being pushed to consider the benefits and draw-backs created by the learning environments in American classrooms. This challenged them on multiple levels: as service-learning students, encour-aged to think differently as a result of new experiences; as students who have been educated in a system that actively discourages critical thinking; and as professionals who must reconcile this new way of teaching with the approach that is essentially mandated in their own culture. Much like domestic service-learning participants, engaging in service provided international students with the opportunity to learn more about the United States from a new perspective while considering the ways in which their future practices might change as a result of the knowledge they gained through their experience.

APPENDIX: WEEKLY JOURNAL AND INTERVIEW QUESTIONS

1. Describe your initial experience at your JEP assignment. Include a detailed description of the responsibilities and activities involved in your particular assignment. What are your initial impressions of the school? Of the teacher? Of the students? How do your experi-ences during Week One compare to your expectations prior to beginning your assignment?

2. What languages are used in the classroom or other parts of school, by whom, and when (i.e., in what social situations, for example, official classroom activities, interactions with teacher, play with peers, etc.). Do the students appear more comfortable/competent in one language compared to another?

3. Describe the relationship between the teacher and the students in the classroom. How does the teacher interact with the students and manage the classroom? Please give specific examples.

4. Choose a lesson you observed and comment on how that lesson might be different if taught in your country/school. What about the lesson was culture-specific?

5. Describe your experiences working with students in the classroom. You may choose to discuss either working one-on-one with an indi-vidual student (or several students) or an experience leading the entire class. How did the students respond to you? If you have experience teaching in your home country, how did that experi-ence differ from your past experiences?

6. Reflect on your experiences volunteering in the community and classroom thus far. How have your perceptions of the neighbor-

hood and its residents changed, if at all? Have you learned anything new about American kids and American culture? If so, what?

7. Many of you have written about how active and willing to participate the kids in the classrooms are. Reflect on your own role as
"active participants," both as teaching assistants and participants
in service-learning, and compare it to your experiences in education in your home country. Are your experiences in your home
country the same or different from your experiences in the United
States? If they are different, what might account for those differences?

8. Please reflect on your 8 weeks of volunteering in the classroom.
Have you learned anything new about yourself? Will your experience in the American classroom change the way you teach in your
home country? Why or why not?

Questions for Interview

1. Please describe your experiences in the classroom. How did you
spend your time? Did you observe the teacher, work with small
groups of students, or lead the entire class?

2. What surprised you the most from your experience in the classroom? That is, did anything unexpected happen during your
experience?

3. What did you learn from this experience?

4. Have your ideas about the United States changed since you have
been here? If so, how?

5. Have your ideas about Los Angeles and the community surrounding USC changed since your arrival? If so, how?

6. How would you describe American culture to a friend back home?

7. Will your teaching techniques change as a result of your teaching
experience in an American classroom? Why or why not?

ACKNOWLEDGMENTS

The authors would like to thank Tammara Anderson, Andrea Clemons,
Ann Marie Yamada, and four anonymous reviewers for their helpful feedback on drafts of this chapter.

REFERENCES

Butler, Y. G. (2005). Comparative perspectives towards communicative activities among elementary school teachers in South Korea, Japan and Taiwan. *Language Teaching Research, 9*(4), 423-446.

Cogan, J. J., Morris, P., & Print, M. (Eds.). (2002). Civic education in the Asia-Pacific region: An introduction. In *Civic education in the Asia-Pacific region: Case studies across six societies* (pp. 1-22). New York: RoutledgeFalmer.

Hofstede, G. (1986). Cultural differences in teaching and learning. *International Journal of Intercultural Relations, 10*, 301-320.

Hofstede, G., & McCrae, R. R. (2004). Personality and culture revisited: Linking traits and dimensions of culture. *Cross-Cultural Research, 38*(1), 52-88.

Institute of International Education. (2006). Open doors 2006. Report on international educational exchange: International students by academic level, selected years 1954/55–2006/06. Retrieved November 30, 2006, from http://opendoors.iienetwork.org/?p=89207

Kuan, H., & Lau, S. (2002). Traditional orientations and political participation in three Chinese societies. *Journal of Contemporary China, 11*(31), 297-318.

Lee, A. C. (2004). Changes and challenges for moral education in Taiwan. *Journal of Moral Education, 33*(4), 575-595.

Liu, M. (1999). Civic education in Taiwan: Patterns, problems, and prospects. *International Journal of Social Education, 14*(1), 30-41.

Liu, M. (2002). Civic education at the crossroads: Case study of Taiwan. In J. J. Cogan, P. Morris, & M. Print (Eds.), *Civic education in the Asia-Pacific region: Case studies across six societies* (pp. 93-117). New York: RoutledgeFalmer.

Morris, P., Kan, F., & Morris, E. (2000). Education, civic participation, and identity: Continuity and change in Hong Kong. *Cambridge Journal of Education, 30*(2), 243-262.

Morris, P., & Morris, E. (2002). Civic education in Hong Kong: A tale of two schools. In J. J. Cogan, P. Morris, & M. Print (Eds.), *Civic education in the Asia-Pacific region: Case studies across six societies* (pp. 46-69). New York: RoutledgeFalmer.

Sorensen, C. W. (1994). Success and education in South Korea. *Comparative Education Review, 38*(1), 10-35.

Zhao, C., Kuh, G. D., & Carini, R. M. (2005). A comparison of international student and American student engagement in effective educational practices. *The Journal of Higher Education, 76*(2), 209-231.

SECTION II

ENHANCING STUDENT LEARNING

CHAPTER 4

JUMPSTART'S SERVICE-LEARNING INITIATIVE

Enhanced Outcomes for At-Risk Children

Dean Elson, Lauren Johns, and Jessica Taisey Petrie

ABSTRACT

The research literature on the effect of service-learning (SL) on community outcomes is limited, and has focused predominantly on community organizations' perceptions of students' service and not on outcomes for service recipients. This chapter addresses this significant research gap by discussing the results of a quasi-experimental study that compared outcomes for low-income preschool children mentored by Jumpstart college students enrolled in SL courses to a matched group of low-income children mentored by Jumpstart students not enrolled in SL courses. The results indicated that gains in early language, literacy, and social skills were significantly greater for children working with SL students than children not paired with SL students.

From Passion to Objectivity: International and Cross-Disciplinary Perspectives on Service Learning Research, pp. 65–87

INTRODUCTION

Service-learning (SL) in higher education has been defined by Bringle and Hatcher (1995) as a "course-based, credit-bearing educational experience in which students (a) participate in an organized service activity that meets identified community needs and (b) reflect on the service activity in such a way as to gain further understanding of course content, a broader appreciation of the discipline, and an enhanced sense of civic responsibility" (p. 112). One of the fundamental characteristics of SL is the element of reciprocity whereby students and community members both benefit from their participation in the experience.

Multiple studies have shown that participation in SL courses at institutions of higher education (IHEs) benefit students, faculty, the institution, and community members (Eyler, Giles, Stenson, & Gray, 2001). While the research has been relatively robust in documenting the effect of SL course participation on college students, only a limited quantity of research has examined the influence of SL on the community organizations and members served (Melchior, 1998; Schmidt & Robby, 2002). Community outcomes most often have been measured through organizational *perceptions* of SL students' impact on the community instead of using *direct measures* of recipient outcomes (Bailis, 2006; Cruz & Giles, 2000). The study discussed in this chapter addresses this gap by examining the outcomes for at-risk preschool-age children enrolled in Jumpstart, a supplemental early education program, during the 2004-05 program year. The children were paired either with college student mentors participating in a related SL course or with student mentors who did not participate in a SL course.

This chapter first reviews the research on SL student outcomes and community outcomes. Next, the research on child outcomes that result from participation in high-quality early education interventions is summarized. After briefly describing the Jumpstart program, SL at Jumpstart is explained and a rationale is presented for why SL students would be expected to have a greater impact on child outcomes than non-SL students. Finally, the research questions, study design, methods, and findings are discussed, along with a presentation of the results, study limitations, and considerations for future research.

REVIEW OF RESEARCH

The research on SL has largely focused on the influence of course participation on student outcomes. It is important to note that the outcomes to be described are not purely the result of the presence or absence of SL; indeed, course quality matters (Billig, 2006). For example, the quality and quantity of course reflection activities are important for students (Ash, Clayton, & Atkinson, 2005; Astin & Sax, 1998; Astin, Vogelgesang, Ikeda, & Yee, 2000; Eyler & Giles, 1999; Ikeda, 1999). Several key SL program characteristics have been found to be highly correlated with outcomes for SL students. These include a strong link between SL activities and content standards, direct contact with those being served, cognitively challenging reflection activities, youth choice in planning and implementation of SL activities, and duration of at least one semester (Billig, Root, & Jesse, 2005). In her review of the literature, Billig (2005) reported that meeting authentic community needs, public demonstration of learning, and respect for diversity also are related to student outcomes.

Research has identified many positive outcomes of SL course participation for students. In their comprehensive review of the literature, Eyler et al. (2001) wrote that participation in SL courses positively affected student outcomes in the following areas: personal development, social benefits, advances in learning, career development, and improved relationships with their college or institution. The authors noted that the influence of SL courses on student grade point average was mixed (Eyler et al., 2001). Participation in SL courses has also been shown to affect student beliefs such as commitment to service, perceptions of others, satisfaction with courses, and awareness of community issues. Giles and Eyler's (1994) study of the changes in student social and personal responsibility as the result of SL experiences revealed significant increases in student beliefs that people can make a difference and that students should be involved in community service. Results also demonstrated an increase in student commitment to perform volunteer activities and continue service. In addition, students developed more positive perceptions of the people with whom they worked.

One study has been conducted using self-reported surveys to compare pre- and postcourse outcomes of Jumpstart corps members (CM) in SL courses to those who did not participate in SL courses (Lukianov, 2004). Lukianov's results indicated that the Jumpstart SL group showed significantly greater increases from fall to spring on over half of the early childhood best practices items than the Jumpstart non-SL group. Lukianov also found that Jumpstart SL students appeared to have a greater awareness and understanding of issues facing their community than non-SL respondents. It was hypothesized that SL participants' increased awareness could be attributed to the additional course reflection activities (Lukianov, 2004).

In a summary of the research on the effects of SL on community outcomes, Eyler et al. (2001) found host organizations and agencies believed SL students provided useful services while enhancing university relations with the community. Gray et al. (1998) showed that host organizations believed SL students were more effective than volunteers. Driscoll, Holland, Gelmon, and Kerrigan (1996) reported that community agencies where SL students were placed perceived that the students had an effect on the agencies' capacity to serve clients and to receive economic and social benefits. Ferrari and Worrall's (2000) analysis revealed that host organizations believed SL students were helpful, sensitive, friendly, empathetic, appropriate in their relationships, interested, and dedicated to their work. Melchior's 1998 national evaluation of Learn and Serve America found that agencies were pleased with the results of hosting SL students, would use SL students again, and believed that SL students improved agency capacity and services. Melchior also reported that host agencies believed that SL students who were tutoring and providing other educational services helped to increase the skill levels, engagement, and self-esteem of the students being assisted. Overall, these studies revealed that agencies hosting SL students believed that SL brought positive benefits to the communities in which they served.

In their evaluation of the impact of K-12 SL programs in California, Ammon, Furco, Chi, and Middaugh (2002) requested that grantees provide direct outcomes on community members. However, they found that grantees still reported on perceptions of outcomes for recipients of SL services, rather than actual outcomes. Only a limited number of studies have directly investigated outcomes for the recipients of SL student services. One such study of 260 elementary children who received tutoring services from SL students reported, compared to a nontutored group, the tutored children had higher 1-year gains in Stanford Achievement Test (SAT/9) scores in math and spelling (Schmidt & Robby, 2002). Children and their teachers gave high ratings to the tutors and believed that tutoring helped the children learn.

Scholars of SL have noted the gap in the SL literature concerning recipient outcomes (Bailis, 2006; Cruz & Giles, 2000). In the 2006 *Growing to Greatness* report, Bailis stated there have been surprisingly few "rigorous efforts to define and measure the difference service-learning makes for the people served" (2006, p. 67). One of the challenges of measuring outcomes for recipients that Bailis (2006) discussed was that there are immediate and long-term outcomes for young recipients of SL. Therefore "community impacts are often cascading, with immediate (primary) impacts on service recipients resulting in further (secondary) impacts down the road over varying periods of time" (pp. 69-70).

EARLY CHILDHOOD EDUCATION PROGRAM OUTCOMES

In stark contrast to the literature cited on the impacts of SL on those being served, there is a robust literature in the field of early childhood education (ECE) demonstrating the positive impact that early intervention can have on at-risk children's development, early success in school, and later success in life. The 2001 *Eager to Learn* report demonstrated that children who are living in circumstances that place them at greater risk of school failure (e.g., poverty, low level of maternal education, maternal depression, and other factors related to learning and development) were more likely to succeed in school if they attended well-planned, high-quality early childhood programs (Bowman, Donovan, & Burns, 2001). Recent research on state prekindergarten programs consistently found that high-quality programs led to positive gains in short-term developmental outcomes for young children (Barnett, Lamy, & Jung, 2005; Gormley, Gayer, Phillips, & Dawson, 2005). In addition, many compelling experimental studies of model preschools and public programs have been conducted (Barnett, 1995; Campbell & Ramey, 1995; Campbell, Ramey, Pungello, Sparling, & Miller-Johnson, 2002; Reynolds, Temple, Robertson, & Mann, 2001; Schweinhart, et al., 2005). These studies showed that high-quality programs and services for at-risk preschool children delivered by well-trained adults lead to less retention in grade, fewer referrals to special education, less juvenile delinquency and involvement in crime, and higher academic achievement and high school graduation, among other positive outcomes.

One key element of building preschool children's school readiness skills identified repeatedly by the research was *intentionality* in practice. Epstein (2007) interviewed 40 respected experts in the early childhood education field to provide educators with a new "roadmap" to quality programming. Epstein's approach focused on intentionality of planning and strategies for both child-guided and adult-guided experiences in the classroom. As Epstein made clear, past publications about appropriate practices in ECE programs emphasized the importance of highly organized and structured environments, which needed to be carefully prepared and managed by teachers. Recent research also revealed that children must be actively involved in their own learning. Epstein concluded that teachers must intentionally connect activities to the learning outcomes they have for their children.

Many low-income children, however, do not have access to the high-quality programs that develop important school readiness skills and are available to economically well-off families. Instead, low-income children are typically enrolled in programs with less qualified staff, higher staff-to-child ratios, larger group sizes, and less well-equipped classrooms—

factors associated with lower school-readiness skills among low-income preschoolers (Landry, 2005).

Jumpstart was created to help address this gap in quality of early educational experiences and to enhance the school readiness of low-income children. Jumpstart's mission is to work toward the day every child in America enters school prepared to succeed. Through implementation of a standard program using an intentional curriculum that focuses on early language, literacy, initiative, and social skills for at-risk children, Jumpstart addresses the limited access to high-quality preschool education that many children living in poor communities face across the country.

As a national AmeriCorps program, Jumpstart trains college and university student CMs to deliver a research-based program through one-to-one relationships with children from low-income backgrounds. The Jumpstart curriculum is based on research and best practices in early childhood education from the National Association for the Education of Young Children (NAEYC), the High/Scope Educational Research Foundation, and the Stony Brook Reading and Language Project's dialogic reading method. Dialogic reading is based on research indicating that children need to possess three basic skills to learn to read: print knowledge, emergent writing, and linguistic awareness. Studies of dialogic reading have demonstrated the positive impact of this reading methodology on the emergent literacy and oral language skills of children enrolled in Head Start, and indicated that dialogic reading is a key component in increasing young children's vocabulary and oral language skills (Lonigan & Whitehurst, 1998; Whitehurst et al., 1994).

To reach children in communities with large percentages of low-income children lacking access to high-quality preschool education, Jumpstart collaborated with 66 IHEs in 2004-05 to recruit college students from diverse backgrounds and academic interests. In that program year, the organization recruited more than 2,100 college and university students to work with preschool-age children in 24 states and Washington, DC. The majority of CMs were female (83%), in their freshman or sophomore year of college (59%), and identified as African-American, Hispanic or Latino, or Asian (53%). CMs committed to a school year (200 or 300 hours) or school year and summer (ranging from 450-675 hours) term of service; for many students, service with Jumpstart qualified as a federal work-study position on their campus. CMs implemented 2-hour Jumpstart sessions twice a week, using a curriculum that focused on language, literacy, initiative, and social skill development.

Each CM is assigned a "partner child" to whom he or she provides targeted, one-to-one attention both during Jumpstart sessions and during additional time spent within the child's classroom as part of the regular preschool day. All Jumpstart Corp members receive 60 hours of preservice and in-service training. In addition to professional development on citizenship and civic engagement, Jumpstart trains CMs on the basics of child development and developmentally appropriate activities for pre-schoolers. The training sessions emphasize early literacy and dialogic reading techniques, the importance of developing nurturing, positive relationships with children, and how to communicate and engage in appropriate interactions and activities with children.

JUMPSTART AND SERVICE-LEARNING

In 2001 faculty members at Jumpstart's partner IHEs connected the Jumpstart program to academic coursework in their disciplines. In 2003, Jumpstart began developing tools and professional development to support the work of faculty and staff. Faculty at Jumpstart's SL sites represented a wide variety of institutions—public, private, community colleges, historically Black colleges and universities—and disciplines. Currently, Jumpstart courses are offered in the fields of early childhood education, human development, psychology, and public service.

Jumpstart staff work with faculty members during the initial phases of course design to ensure that academic study in their discipline can enhance CMs' preparation for service beyond the training already received and to verify that service in the classroom will provide CMs with the opportunity to put course concepts into practice. Jumpstart does not require instructors to cover specific content areas, to adhere to a given format, or to offer particular assignments. Driven by faculty expertise and department/university requirements, the design of each course reflects the unique nature of the stakeholders involved (including IHE administration, faculty, students, and community partners). Jumpstart SL courses are required to incorporate regular reflection as an integral part of the course in addition to other, similarly rigorous assignments that highlight the connection between academic study and service in the community.

In the 2004-05 program year, 8 of the 57 Jumpstart sites across the country offered a SL course. SL courses were offered to Jumpstart CMs at California State University (CSU) Fresno, CSU-Fullerton, CSU-Northridge, San Francisco State University and City College of San Francisco, Southern Louisiana University, University of Michigan at Dearborn, University of Washington, and University of Wisconsin at Eau Claire. Participation in these courses was required as a part of CMs' service with Jumpstart at five of these eight sites. Six IHEs offered courses with an ECE focus; the other two offered courses on communication and language development and the social, economic, and political factors impacting families served through the federal Head Start program.

Examples of outcomes and assignments within the ECE courses included:

- *Observation and assessment of child development*: After receiving deeper instruction on successful observation techniques, CMs completed observations of their partner children and children in other classrooms served by Jumpstart. Guiding questions directed students to observe for particular areas of development studied in the course, allowing CMs to identify key developmental milestones in child development and to use these markers to understand the progress of their individual partner child.

- *Knowledge of key curriculum and instruction practices*: Following their study of discussions, artwork and other evidence that illuminated children's understanding of instructional concepts, CMs created a series of documentation panels demonstrating children's learning during sessions and placed them in the classroom for review by teachers, parents, and, most importantly, children.

- *Ability to create rich learning environments for children*: Based on their observations of classrooms, course readings, and experience planning and implementing curriculum activities, CMs worked in small groups to design a classroom environment evaluated using a research-based rating scale commonly used in the field.

Examples of outcomes and assignments within the non-ECE courses included:

- *Theoretical analysis of language and communication skills*: Using classroom observation notes and theoretical frameworks discussed in class, CMs analyzed language samples produced by partner children to discuss the skills evidenced and appropriate supports for children's learning.

- *Creation of community resource guides*: After studying services provided through Jumpstart and researching the specific assets and interests of the preschools where they were serving, CMs created guides outlining available resources of interest to families in the community and distributed these guides at partner preschools.

Instructors crafted courses designed to deepen knowledge gained during Jumpstart training and to hone CMs' abilities to observe, analyze, and reflect on their interactions with children. CMs in SL courses also built a greater awareness of ECE best practices, their partner children, and their families through a deeper knowledge of the community and its many available resources.

METHODOLOGY

In this section, the study purpose, hypotheses, research questions, study design, and data collection methods are discussed.

Study Purpose, Hypotheses, and Research Questions

This study investigated the effect of SL on outcomes for community members. More specifically, the study examined whether low-income preschool children who participated in the program made greater developmental gains from fall to spring of the program year if their CMs participated in a SL course compared to the gains of children whose CMs did not take a SL course. Although all CMs received training in developmentally appropriate practices and received support from local site managers throughout the year, it was hypothesized that enrollment in related SL courses would allow for greater reflection time among students about their service and a greater understanding of the connection between developmental theory and classroom practice. Lukianov's results showed that Jumpstart SL CMs achieved significantly greater gains in more areas of early childhood practice knowledge and had a better understanding of issues facing their community than non-SL CMs (2004). It was further hypothesized that SL courses would create greater opportunities for students to discuss challenges from direct service activities (e.g., child behaviors, supporting English language learners, interactions with family members, etc.) and help students to engage with faculty and site staff in conversations about modifying practices with children, thus allowing the participating CMs to be more effective. These hypotheses and the findings from the SL research literature led to the following research questions:

1. Do participating children at Jumpstart sites with CMs taking a SL course achieve greater gains than a comparison group of non-Jumpstart children from the same classrooms on a measure of overall development, and language, literacy, initiative and social relations skills specifically?

2. Do participating children at Jumpstart sites with CMs taking a SL course achieve greater gains than participating children at Jumpstart sites where CMs do not take a SL course?

Research Design

The 2004-05 national evaluation of the Jumpstart program employed a quasi-experimental design with pre-post assessments of language, literacy, initiative, and social skills. The sample was comprised of low-income preschoolers receiving the Jumpstart supplemental educational intervention and a comparison group of children, matched by age and gender, who did not receive Jumpstart services but were enrolled in the same preschool programs as participants.

The children's classroom teachers were instructed to complete a child assessment measure (described below) on twice as many children in the fall as Jumpstart could accommodate for intervention. For example, if the local Jumpstart site was going to serve 15 children at a local early childhood program (community-based center, Head Start program, or public preschool), teachers were expected to complete assessments on 30 eligible children.

Teachers used six key eligibility criteria, aimed at identifying children likely to benefit most from supplemental intervention, when selecting children for assessment. Children had to be between the ages of 36- and 59-months-old at the start of the program year; had good to excellent attendance in their preschool program; had limited (but not extremely limited) development in the targeted skill areas; exhibited no highly disruptive classroom behavior; and were not receiving or likely to receive special-needs education services in the program year. Children who did not speak English could be considered for the program if there were CMs who could communicate well in the children's primary language. For every child who met the eligibility criteria, teachers were asked to find another child in the classroom who also met the eligibility criteria and who was the same gender and within three months of age as the first child. This pairing method was intended to increase the likelihood of a matched comparison group at the local, regional and national level.

To create an assessment that could be conducted by the preschool teachers on every child in Jumpstart and a comparison group, Jumpstart modified the High/Scope Educational Research Foundation's *Preschool Child Observation Record (COR), Second Edition*. Jumpstart chose the COR because it had been normed on a population of low-income children from Head Start programs and shown to have good test properties for a diverse group of children. The reliability of the COR is quite high, with total Cronbach's alphas of .91 and above.

Jumpstart's *School Success Checklist* is comprised of 15 of the original 32 COR items that assess children's language, literacy, initiative, and social relations skills. The *School Success Checklist* had a Cronbach's alpha of .949. The *Checklist* does not require direct observation, but instead relies on the teachers' experiences with the children.

Children were rated on each item on the *School Success Checklist* by teachers using a 5-point scale. Two subscales of developmental skills were derived from the checklist: language-literacy (8 items), which includes, for example, the abilities to listen to and understand speech, identify sounds and letters, and demonstrate knowledge about books; and initiative-social relations (7 items), which includes, for example, the abilities to understand and express feelings, express choices, initiate play, and relate to adults and children. (The Appendix provides a copy of the 15 items and rating scales.)

To eliminate ceiling effects, the child selection process was designed to enroll children who did not score 4 or 5 on 8 or more of the 15 items at baseline. In addition, local program sites were advised not to select only those children at the lowest end of the score range (i.e., 8 or more items with ratings of 1 or 2) to reduce the potential for bias among teachers' ratings at the end of the year. This "middle of the range" approach was relatively successful across the 57 Jumpstart sites. Analyses of children's scores at baseline showed that participants working with CMs at SL sites scored an average of 2.26 on the total scale compared to an average of 2.34 for participants partnered with CMs not at SL sites.

In the 2004-05 program year, preschool teachers from approximately 200 early childhood centers rated the skills of preschool children on the *School Success Checklist* and then repeated the assessment in the spring. Local Jumpstart site managers collected the assessments from partner preschools and sent them to Jumpstart's assessment consultants. The independent consultants were hired to enter the checklist ratings and produce selection reports using the fall checklist results. The selection reports sorted all children within the preschool centers by starting score (lowest to highest mean score). Local Jumpstart staff then worked with the partner preschool teachers to randomly select children for the program from the selection report. The comparison group was comprised of the children who were not offered the program.

The national sample included 1,627 Jumpstart participants and 1,918 comparison children. There were no significant group differences between participants and comparisons by age (mean = 49 months), gender (51% male), or language group (approximately 70% spoke English only) in the national sample. Children in the participant and comparison groups received similar regular preschool experiences from fall to spring, but Jumpstart participants received supplemental services via Jumpstart sessions for 5 to 6 months. (The national evaluation and SL study did not include children from summer programs).

The national sample was further examined for the characteristics of the participating children working with CMs in SL courses, compared to participants working with CMs not engaged in SL (see Exhibit 4.1). Anal-

Exhibit 4.1. Characteristics of the 2004-05 Jumpstart Participants

Participant Group Demographics	Children Paired With Students Enrolled in SL Course	Children Paired With Students not Enrolled in SL Course
Number of children	293	1334
Mean age (S.D.)	50.0 months (5.18)	48.7 months (6.28)
Gender	54.1% boys 45.9% girls	49.8% boys 50.2% girls
Language	79.0% English-speaking-only 21.0% Not English-speaking-only	90.6% English-speaking-only 9.4% Not English-speaking-only

yses revealed there were significant differences by age ($t = 3.39$, $df = 1625$, $p = .001$) and language group ($\chi^2 = 31.32$, sig. $= .000$), but not gender. Children working with CMs at SL sites were significantly older than children of CMs not at SL sites (mean: 50.0 months versus 48.7 months, respectively). In addition, children working with CMs at SL sites were significantly more likely to be non-English-only speakers (21%) compared with children working with CMs not at SL sites (9%).

RESULTS

To analyze pre- to postprogram changes for both groups on the total scale, language-literacy subscale, and the initiative-social relations subscale, standardized percentage gains were calculated. The standardized percentage gain assumed that a one point (1.0) gain from any point on the scale between fall and spring could be calculated as a 25% gain because a child at the lowest point on the scale (rating of 1) can only improve by as much as four rating points (to the highest rating of 5). Using the standardized percentage gain, independent samples t tests were run on the total scale, language-literacy subscale, and initiative-social relations subscale to test the research hypotheses.

As shown in Exhibit 4.2, the percentage gain on all three scales for Jumpstart participants at SL sites was 32% compared to a 29% gain for comparison children at SL sites. The t test results indicated that Jumpstart participants at sites with SL courses achieved significantly greater percentage gains than their non-Jumpstart classmates on the language-literacy subscale ($t = -2.27$, $df = 835$, $p = .02$) and the total scale ($t = -2.26$, $df = 835$, $p = .02$), but not significantly greater gains on the initiative-social relations subscale ($t = -1.96$, $df = 835$, $p = .05$).

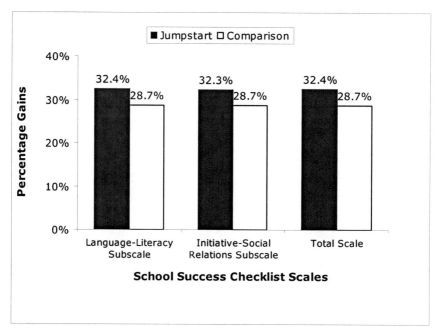

Exhibit 4.2.   Differences in assessment scores between Jumpstart and comparison children at SL sites.

As shown in Exhibit 4.3, the results also indicated that Jumpstart participants at SL sites achieved significantly greater percentage gains than Jumpstart participants at sites without a SL course on the total scale ($t = 3.72$, $df = 1{,}625$, $p = .000$), the language and literacy subscale ($t = 3.44$, $df = 1{,}625$, $p = .000$) and the initiative-social relations subscale ($t = 3.64$, $df = 1{,}625$, $p = .000$).

DISCUSSION

Jumpstart's national child assessment results have consistently demonstrated that all preschool children made gains in teacher ratings of developmental progress from fall to spring, but that Jumpstart participants made significantly greater gains than comparison children. This study found the same outcome when examining the eight Jumpstart sites that offered a SL course for students in 2004-05. Children who were partnered with students in SL courses achieved significantly greater gains than the matched comparison group of children from the same classrooms. The study also investigated whether there were enhanced program effects for participating children at SL sites. The analysis demonstrated that signifi-

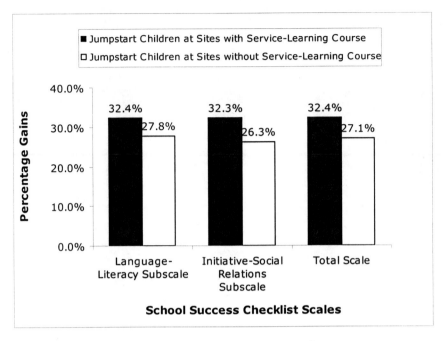

Exhibit 4.3.   Participant gains at SL sites versus non-SL sites.

cantly greater gains were found for participating children at SL sites than for participating children at non-SL sites.

One unexpected finding was that the average gains for comparison children in SL sites were greater than the gains for participating children in non-SL sites. This finding may have been due to the fact that five of the eight SL sites were in Jumpstart's Western region and four of those five sites were located in California. Analyses of regional results have shown that gains for children in the Western region, and in California in particular, were higher for both participants and comparisons than for participants in other Jumpstart regions. This may be due to the fact that the program model has changed in California in recent years such that comparison children are also participating in Jumpstart sessions. Follow-up studies of California sites and what has been termed the Jumpstart in-classroom model will be important to learning more about the relative impact of the service delivery model and the intersection with Jumpstart SL.

The results of the study should be considered with caution due to design and methodological limitations. Although classroom teachers completed *School Success Checklist* ratings in the fall before they knew who would be enrolled in the program, the teachers knew which children had received the intervention when completing the spring checklist. This knowledge may have led, intentionally or unintentionally, to positive bias in ratings for participants over comparisons. Although there was no reason to expect that teachers would give significantly higher ratings to participants in SL sites than the teachers who were rating participating children at non-SL sites, there were no independent validation checks of teachers' ratings of the children's skills. Post-hoc analyses revealed that there were significant differences in participants' baseline scores (2.26 mean at SL sites versus 2.34 mean at non-SL sites, $t = -2.14$, $df = 1,625$, $p = .03$). This result indicated that children at SL sites were significantly further behind at the start of the program year. Regression analyses of past Jumpstart evaluations have shown that baseline scores were predictive of spring scores. Therefore, it could have been anticipated in this study that significantly greater gains would be found for program participants at SL sites at the end of the year. In addition, the analysis for this study was limited to t tests whereas more in-depth statistical procedures would likely yield better estimates of effects by controlling for preprogram scores and other child characteristics.

Second, the study relied on a quasi-experimental design. In most program locations, random assignment of children to Jumpstart and comparison groups was not possible. This was in part due to local Jumpstart sites placing a high degree of importance on collaborating with preschool center staff in making selection and enrollment decisions. Without a truly randomized design, the degree of selection bias is uncertain and therefore it is unclear how the differences in groups may have affected the results. In fact, the estimates of the program's effect on children may be confounded with the effects of unmeasured child and/or family characteristics.

The potential selection bias of the college students who were hired for Jumpstart and those that enrolled in Jumpstart SL courses must also be acknowledged. Since Jumpstart is a work-study position, most students who apply most likely have chosen Jumpstart among a range of other work-study jobs on campus. Five of the eight SL courses in 2004-05 were mandatory, meaning all the Jumpstart members at a given university had to participate in the SL course. Students at Jumpstart sites with mandatory SL courses may have been more committed because they signed up for the job and the course. On the other hand, the students in the nonmandatory classes could have been even more committed members than other Jumpstart CMs because they went beyond the basic requirements of the job. It is also possible that the students in the nonmandatory classes took Jumpstart SL courses because the courses satisfied requirements for an ECE major, which signifies a greater commitment to the ECE field than the average CM. Future analyses should explore whether Jumpstart children paired with CMs who are enrolled in mandatory or optional SL courses achieve greater gains in key outcome areas.

Finally, the study was not able to directly test whether course content, SL student learning outcomes, and commitment to service mediated or moderated the relationship between SL course participation and child outcomes. Therefore, it is unknown whether significantly greater gains for Jumpstart children paired with SL students can be attributed to SL course content, quality, or student learning, or the extent to which these factors may contribute to improved outcomes for service recipients. Future analyses should combine Jumpstart CM and child outcomes data to test the hypothesis that SL student course content and outcomes correlate with increased outcomes for Jumpstart children.

Despite the study's limitations, the results present a compelling case for continuing its support for SL and conducting additional investigations of outcomes for children as well as students. As Jumpstart's SL courses represent a wide range of disciplines and teaching methods employed as part of course implementation, additional research is necessary to better understand precisely which factors of course design may be responsible for children's gains. This information will help Jumpstart improve its training and technical assistance and further clarify its definition of quality course design by using data to indicate which program variables are particularly salient to the type of service experience executed by CMs.

APPENDIX: JUMPSTART SCHOOL SUCCESS CHECKLIST[1]

1. Listening to and understanding speech

1.   Child responds with actions or words to a suggestion, request, or question.
2.   When listening to a story, rhyme, or narrative, child anticipates and fills in a word or phrase.
3.   When listening to a story, rhyme, or narrative, child comments on or asks a question about it.
4.   Child contributes to an ongoing conversation.
5.   Child sustains a dialogue by taking three or more conversational turns.

2. Using vocabulary

1.   Child talks about people or objects close at hand.
2.   Child talks about absent people or objects.

3. Child uses vocabulary related to a particular subject.
4. Child uses two or more words to describe something, such as "That's a big, furry dog."
5. Child asks about the meaning of a word.

3. Using complex patterns of speech

1. Child uses words and phrases.
2. Child uses a sentence of four or more words.
3. Child uses two or more simple sentences in a row.
4. Child uses a compound subject or object in a sentence, such as "I'm going to make a car and a garage for it."
5. Child uses a clause that starts with "when," "if," "because," or "since" in a sentence.

4. Showing awareness of sounds in words

1. During play, child makes the sound of an animal or vehicle, or some other environmental sound.
2. Child joins in saying or repeating a rhyme or a series of words that start with the same sound.
3. Child rhymes one word with another or makes up a phrase or sentence that includes a rhyme.
4. Child says that two words begin with the same sound.
5. Child creates a pair or series of words that start with the same sound.

5. Demonstrating knowledge about books

1. Child shows interest when a book is read aloud.
2. Child holds a book right-side up, turns the pages, and looks at them.
3. Child asks another person to read a book to him or her.
4. Looking at the pictures in a book, child tells the story or makes up a story related to the pictures.

5.   Child points to the words in a book or follows a line of text while telling or reading the story.

6. Using letter names and sounds

1.   Child says or sings some letters.
2.   Child names three or more alphabet letters he or she is holding, looking at, typing, or making.
3.   Child makes the sound of a letter in a word he or she is looking at, writing, or typing.
4.   Child names 10 or more letters over time.
5.   Child says a word and identifies the beginning letter or letter sound.

7. Reading

1.   Child uses the same word to name more than one object.
2.   Child says what a picture or symbol represents.
3.   Child calls attention to print.
4.   Child recognizes a written word.
5.   Child reads aloud a simple phrase or sentence.

8. Writing

1.   Child writes using pictures, squiggles, or letter-like forms.
2.   Child uses clay, wire, or sticks to make a recognizable letter.
3.   Child writes two or more recognizable letters.
4.   Child writes a string of letters and reads them or asks to have them read.
5.   Child writes a phrase or sentence of two or more words.

9. Making choices and plans

1.   Child indicates a choice by pointing or some other action.
2.   Child expresses a choice in one or two words.
3.   Child expresses a choice with a short sentence (e.g., "I'm gonna play with the truck.")

4. Child makes a plan with one or two details (e.g., "I'm going to work in the block area with the fire truck.")
5. Child makes a plan with three or more details (e.g., "I'm going to paint my mom a picture of our new truck and I'm gonna use two brushes and the green paint.")

10. Solving problems with materials

1. Child expresses frustration when encountering a problem with materials.
2. Child identifies a problem with materials and asks for help.
3. Child tries one way to solve a problem with materials.
4. Child tries two ways to solve a problem with materials.
5. Child tries three or more ways to solve a problem with materials.

11. Initiating play

1. Child engages in exploratory play (e.g., fills and empties a bucket with sand.)
2. Child makes something with materials (e.g., rolls playdough into a long string and then connects the ends.)
3. Child engages in pretend play.
4. During play with other children, child adds an idea that changes the play in some way.
5. Child joins with other children in playing a game with rules.

12. Resolving interpersonal conflict

1. In a conflict with another child, child responds with yelling or physical action.
2. Child requests adult help in resolving a conflict with another child.
3. Child identifies the problem in a conflict with another child.
4. With adult help, child offers a solution to a conflict.
5. Child negotiates the resolution of a conflict with another child.

13. Understanding and expressing feelings

1. Child expresses an emotion.
2. Child comforts another child (e.g., patting, hugging, giving something to an upset child.)
3. Child talks about an emotion (e.g., "I'm mad—don't take my truck!")
4. Child represents an emotion through pretend play or art.
5. Child identifies an emotion and gives a reason for it (e.g., "Sari is sad today because she misses her Mommy.")

14. Relating to adults

1. Child participates in a conversation initiated by a familiar adult.
2. Child participates in a conversation initiated by an unfamiliar adult.
3. Child initiates an interaction with an adult.
4. Child sustains an interaction with an adult.
5. Child involves an adult in an activity and sustains the involvement.

15. Relating to other children

1. Child responds when another child initiates an interaction.
2. Child initiates an interaction with another child (verbally or non-verbally).
3. Child sustains an interaction with another child (e.g., a conversation of 5 or more exchanges or extended nonverbal interaction.)
4. Child invites another child to play.
5. Child shows loyalty to another child (e.g., plays repeatedly with the same child, consistently saves a seat for the same child.

NOTE

1. Jumpstart's *School Success Checklist* is adapted from the High/Scope Educational Research Foundation's Preschool Child Observation Record (COR), Second Edition.

REFERENCES

Ammon, M. S., Furco, A., Chi, B., & Middaugh, E. (2002). School/district and community impacts of K–12 service-learning. *Service-Learning in California: A Profile of the CalServe Service-Learning Partnerships (1997-2000)* (Chapter 6). University of California-Berkeley Service-Learning Research and Development Center. Available: http://servicelearning.org/filemanager/download/61/chap6.pdf>

Ash, S. L., Clayton, P. H., & Atkinson, M. P. (2005). Integrating reflection and assessment to capture and improve student learning. *Michigan Journal of Community Service-learning, 11*(2), 49-60.

Astin, A. W., & Sax, L. J. (1998). How undergraduates are affected by service participation. *Journal of College Student Development, 39*(3), 251-263.

Astin, A., Vogelgesang, L., Ikeda, E., & Yee, J. (2000). *How service-learning affects students. Higher Education Research Institute.* Los Angeles: University of California. Available: www.gseis.ucla.edu/heri

Bailis, L. (2006). A framework for further research: The community impacts of service-learning. In J. C. Kielsmeier, M. Neal, & A. Crossley (Eds.), *Growing to greatness report* (pp. 67-72). Saint Paul, MN: National Youth Leadership Council. Available: www.nylc.org

Barnett, W. S. (1995). Long-term effects of early childhood programs on cognitive and school outcomes. *Future of Children, 5*(3), 25-50.

Barnett, W. S., Lamy, C., & Jung, K. (2005). *The effects of state prekindergarten programs on young children's school readiness in five states.* New Brunswick, NJ: National Institute for Early Education Research/Rutgers University.

Billig, S. (2006). Lessons from research on teaching and learning: Service-learning as effective instruction. In J. C. Kielsmeier, M. Neal, & A. Crossley () *Growing to greatness 2006: The state of Service-Learning Project* (pp. 25-32). Saint Paul, MN: National Youth Leadership Council. Available: www.nylc.org

Billig, S. H. (2005). Celebrating the good news: Research shows service-learning works. *The Generator, 23*(2), 30-32.

Billig, S. H., Root, S., & Jesse, D. (2005). The relationship between the quality indicators of service-learning and student outcomes: Testing professional wisdom. *Improving service-learning practice: Research on models to enhance impacts* (pp. 97-115). Greenwich, CT: Information Age.

Bowman, B.T., Donovan, M. S., & Burns, M. S. (2001). *Eager to learn: Educating our preschoolers, executive summary.* Washington, DC: National Research Council.

Bringle, R., & Hatcher, J. (1995). A service-learning curriculum for faculty. *Michigan Journal of Community Service-learning, 2,* 112-122.

Campbell, F. A., & Ramey, C. T. (1995). Cognitive and school outcomes for high risk African-American students at middle adolescence: Positive effects of early intervention. *American Educational Research Journal, 32,* 743-772.

Campbell, F. A., Ramey, C. T., Pungello, E., Sparling, J., & Miller-Johnson, S. (2002). Early childhood education: Young adult outcomes from the Abecedarian project. *Applied Developmental Science, 6*(1), 42-57.

Cruz, N. I., & Giles, D. E. (2000). Where's the community in service-learning research? (Fall special issue). *Michigan Journal of Community Service-learning*, 28-34.

Driscoll A., Holland, B., Gelmon, S., & Kerrigan, S. (1996). An assessment model for service-learning: Comprehensive case studies of impact of faculty, students, community, and institutions. *Michigan Journal of Community Service-learning, 3*, 66-71.

Epstein, A. S. (2007). *The intentional teacher: Choosing the best strategies for young children's learning.* Washington, DC: National Association for the Education of Young Children.

Eyler, J. S., & Giles, D. E., Jr. (1999). *Where's the learning in service-learning?* San Francisco: Jossey-Bass.

Eyler, J. S., Giles, D. E., Jr., Stenson, C. M., & Gray, C. J. (2001). *At a glance: What we know about the effects of service-learning on college student, faculty, institutions and communities, 1993-2000: 3rd Edition.* Nashville, TN: Vanderbuilt University.

Ferrari, J. R., & Worrall, L. (2000). Assessments by community agencies: How "the other side" sees service-learning. *Michigan Journal of Community Service-learning, 7*, 35-40.

Giles, D. E., & Eyler, J. S. (1994). The impact of a college community service laboratory on students' personal, social and cognitive outcomes. *Journal of Adolescence, 17*, 327-339.

Gormley, W. T., Gayer, T., Phillips, D., & Dawson, B. (2005). *Developmental Psychology, 41*(6), 872-884.

Gray, M. J., Ondaatje, E. H., Fricker, R., Geschwind, S., Goldman, C. A., Kaganoff, T., Robyn, A., et al. (1998). *Coupling service and learning in higher education: The final report of the evaluation of the Learn and Serve America, Higher Education Program.* Santa Monica: CA: The RAND Corporation.

High/Scope Educational Research Foundation. (2003). *Preschool child observation record* (2nd ed). Ypsilanti, MI: High/Scope.

Ikeda, E. K. (1999). *How does service enhance learning? Toward an understanding of the process.* Unpublished doctoral dissertation, University of California, Los Angeles.

Landry, S. (2005). *Effective early childhood programs: turning knowledge into action.* San Antonio: University of Texas Health Sciences Center and James A. Baker III Institute for Public Policy, Rice University.

Lonigan, C. J., & Whitehurst, G. J. (1998). Relative efficacy of parent and teacher involvement in a shared-reading intervention for preschool children from low-income backgrounds. *Early Childhood Research Quarterly, 13*(2), 263-290.

Lukianov, A. (2004). *The effects of service-learning on college student development in the Jumpstart program.* Unpublished master's thesis, California State University, Fresno.

Melchior, A. (1998). *National evaluation of Learn and Serve America school and community based programs, final report.* Boston: Center for Human Resources-Brandeis University and Abt Associates

Reynolds, A. J., Temple, J. A., Robertson, D. L., & Mann, E. A. (2001). Long-term effects of an early childhood intervention on educational achievement and juvenile arrest: A 15-year follow-up of low-income children in public schools. *Journal of American Medical Association*, *285*(18), 2339-2346.

Schweinhart, L. S., Montie, J., Ziang, Z., Barnett, W. S., Belfield, C. R., & Nores, M. (2005). *Lifetime effects: The High/Scope Perry Preschool study through age 40.* Ypsilanti, MI: High/Scope Press.

Schmidt, A. & Robby, M.A. (2002). What's the value of service-learning to the community? *Michigan Journal of Community Service-learning*, *9*(1), 27-33.

Whitehurst, G. J., Arnold, D. S., Epstein, J. N., Angell, A. L., Smith, M., & Fischel, J. (1994). A picture book reading intervention in day care and home for children from low-income families. *Developmental Psychology, 30*, 679–689.

CHAPTER 5

EVALUATING THE IMPACT OF PEER-TO-PEER SERVICE-LEARNING PROJECTS ON SEAT BELT USE AMONG HIGH SCHOOL STUDENTS

Pilot Study

Richard Bradley, Janet Eyler, Irwin Goldzweig, Paul Juarez, David Schlundt, and Deon Tolliver

ABSTRACT

The Teen Service-Learning Evaluation Project (TSLEP) explores the potential of service-learning interventions to increase seat belt use and improve safety knowledge and attitudes among high school youth, particularly minority youth. The research also examines the impact of different characteristics of service-learning on personal and social development and safety knowledge and behavior of students involved in implementing the projects.

From Passion to Objectivity: International and Cross-Disciplinary Perspectives on Service Learning Research, pp. 89–110

Seat belt use in the 6 participating schools was measured through pre-post observations at school parking lot exits. Knowledge and attitude outcomes were measured through a pre-post survey. Additional data were gathered through interviews with students and teachers. Over the course of the project a significant increase in seat belt use was observed for youth and adults in the participating schools. Quality of service experience, the student's level of involvement, and reflection were all predictors of personal development, social commitment, and school engagement, and of safety related knowledge and attitudes.

INTRODUCTION

Meharry Medical College (MMC) is the nation's largest private, independent historically Black institution dedicated solely to educating health science professionals. The mission of MMC is to improve the health and health care of minority and underserved communities by offering excellent education and training programs in the health sciences. MMC places special emphasis on providing opportunities to people of color and individuals from disadvantaged backgrounds, regardless of race or ethnicity and conducting research that fosters the elimination of health disparities.

One area of particular interest for MMC has been the disparity in the rates of use of passenger restraints among African Americans. A 1999 MMC report found a disparity in seat belt use between African Americans and the overall population and concluded that an increase in the use of seat belts among African Americans could: (1) save 1,300 African American lives each year; (2) prevent 26,000 African American injuries annually, and (3) save $2.6 billion in societal costs each year. The disparities in seat belt use among African Americans are confirmed studies by Wells and Williams (2002) and Briggs et al. (2006). Research by MMC documents that young African Americans and Hispanic males are at the highest risk of preventable death and injury due to low rates of seat belt use (Schlundt, Easley, & Goldzweig, 2005). Statistics released by the CDC indicate that African American students (13.4%) and Hispanic students (10.6%) were more likely than white students (9.4%) to rarely or never wear seat belts (2006).

THE MEHARRY-STATE FARM ALLIANCE

The Meharry-State Farm Alliance (MSFA) was formed in 2002 to decrease preventable deaths and injuries among African Americans due to motor vehicle crashes by promoting appropriate and consistent use of seat belts and child safety seats. MSFA has conducted research focused on seeking to better understand cultural barriers—such as knowledge, attitudes, and behaviors of African Americans—related to the observed lower rates of use of passenger restraints in this population, as compared to observed rates of use among White Americans, with the objective of increasing use of passenger restraints among African Americans.

This study builds on this work as well as the literature review by Fell, Baker, and McKnight (2006), and findings of service-learning research which suggest that engaging students actively in the learning process with an important community goal in mind may have an impact on their knowledge, attitudes, and behavior and on the community.

DESCRIPTIONS OF PROJECT SITES AND PROJECTS

A-MI (Urban, 95% Minority)

Original objectives for this curriculum-based science project included: (1) students would begin to demonstrate how important seat belts are when riding in a vehicle; (2) students would begin to develop a positive attitude toward using a seat belt when riding in a vehicle; (3) students, parents, and the community would become more aware of seat belt use among African Americans; and (4) students would design more user-friendly seat belts that people would be likely to use more often.

After learning about the physics behind passenger restraint systems in their science class, students involved in the project conducted a 1-month survey of seat belt use among parents dropping their children off for pre-school (located in the same building). During this period they talked with preschoolers about the importance of seat belt use. Students also conducted research projects on seat belt use, including surveys of parents about their attitudes towards and use of seat belts. They visited the General Motors Test Facility to learn more about seat belt design and to observe a "mock crash," and sponsored a design contest to come up with designs for seat belts that would be more "user-friendly." Finally, students held a schoolwide campaign to come up with a seat belt use slogan for their school—the winning slogan was "Don't touch the ignition until your seat belt's in position."

B-MI (Urban, 85% Minority)

The seat belt safety project at B-MI high school was under the direction and facilitation of the Children's Hospital of Michigan-Redford Adolescent Health Center. Original objectives were to have students: (1) increase their personal knowledge and use of seat belt use; (2) reflect on how participation in the project impacted their own use of seat belts; (3) develop peer leadership skills; (4) develop skills in the art of collaboration; and (5) learn the importance of the value of community service.

This cocurricular project was designed and implemented by members of the school health center's student health advisory group (SHAG). Activities included presentations on seat belt and infant restraint systems at the school's annual career day, a pre-prom program, "Teens Behind the Wheel," and seat belt checks at a nearby women's health center.

C-OH (Rural, Low Income—Mostly Appalachian White)

This cocurricular leadership class seat belt safety project was designed to: (1) teach students in Grades K-12 the importance of wearing a seat belt by integrating seat belt safety into health classes; (2) develop a high school leadership team that would advocate the importance of wearing a seat belt; (3) integrate lessons on the importance of seat belt safety into K-12 language arts; (4) place important seat belt safety information into the hands of all school district students and parents; and (5) plan service-learning projects related to seat belt safety which would involve K-12 students.

Activities included developing a high school leadership team that advocated for increased seat belt use among their peers; campaigns to increase awareness of the importance of seat belt use among students at all grade levels; including student presentations in individual classrooms; and letter writing to local legislators urging them to support primary seat belt legislation. A planned poster campaign was deferred to fall 2006.

D-MI (Urban/Suburban, 85% Minority)

This curriculum-based health occupations seat belt safety project had as its objectives: (1) to increase the knowledge and awareness of safety belt and car seat issues in teens and teen parents; (2) to increase the use of safety belts and car seats among teens participating in this program; and (3) to decrease injury morbidity and morality rates due to motor vehicle crashes involving teens and young children. Project activities included a community baby shower for new teen moms; an assembly program with a "safe prom" focus for seniors at the high school; and having a booth on auto safety that included information about the use of seat belts and child safety seats as well as an opportunity for students (and parents) to wear goggles that simulate driving while impaired.

E-OH and F-OH (Suburban, 15% and 20% Minority Respectively)

Projects at these sites were coordinated by the family and consumer science teacher (FCS), who teaches at both high schools. Objectives included: (1) to increase the use of seat belts among students at both high schools; (2) to increase student awareness of the risks associated with not using seat belts; (3) to plan and implement service-learning projects and campaigns related to seat belt use; and (4) to integrate the seat belt safety projects into the FCS curricula for 10th and 11th grade students enrolled in FCS classes at each high school. Students at each high school conducted research on the importance of seat belt use, prepared informational public service announcements for their high schools, wrote letters to state legislators asking them to support primary seat belt legislation under consideration by the legislature, and prepared and distributed seat belt safety brochures (along with key chains supplied by State Farm) to all juniors and seniors.

Schools A, B, and D were selected by staff from the Meharry-State Farm Alliance, because they were urban schools with a high enrollment of African American students. Schools C, E, and F were selected because of teachers' known expertise in service-learning.

SERVICE-LEARNING AND STUDENT IMPACTS

Service-learning is defined as "an educational strategy that involves students in meaningful service to their communities and/or society, while engaging them in some form of reflection or study that is related to their service (Corporation for National and Community Service)." It has its roots in the field of experiential education and the educational philosophy of John Dewey.

Service-learning has been widely used by educators in K-12 and post-secondary settings for the past 30 years. Well-designed service-learning projects connect with, reinforce, enrich and enhance what students learn in the classroom by providing them with hands-on opportunities to apply classroom content and skills in addressing real-world problems. Components of high-quality service-learning projects likely to have the greatest impact on students include: (1) strong connections with the curriculum integration, (2) cognitively challenging reflection, (3) student voice, (4) respect for diversity, (5) meaningful service, (6) process-monitoring and progress-monitoring, (7) duration of at least one semester, and (8) reciprocal relationships among all partners (Billig, 2007). The quality of the placement including important, challenging, and interesting work also contributes to positive outcomes (Conrad & Hedin, 1989; Eyler & Giles, 1999).

Numerous studies point to the impact of engaging young people in service on reducing risk-taking behavior (Benson, 1993; Follman, 1998). Schaffer (1993, as cited in Bhaerman, Cordell, & Gomez, 1998) and Duckenfield and Swanson (1992) found that service-learning is an effective strategy for the prevention of substance abuse and dropping out of school. Conrad and Hedin (1982, 1987, 1989, 1991) and Weiler, LaGoy, Crane, and Rovner (1998) found that students engaged in service gain in social and personal responsibility and sense of educational competence. Melchior (1999) and Berkas (1997) found that students engaged in high quality service-learning programs showed an increase in the degree to which they felt aware of community needs, believed they could make a difference and were committed to serve now and later. Follman (1998), Melchior (1999), Melchior and Bailis (2002), Meyer and Billig (2003), and Meyer, Billig, and Hofschire (2004) found that service-learning was positively associated with impacts such as attendance, school engagement, attitudes toward school, motivation, and improved achievement scores.

Bradley and Rodgers (2005) have also linked service-learning to developmental theories and two learning theories that could be used, either individually or in combination to design and evaluate the effectiveness of service-learning programs: (a) psychosocial development (Chickering & Reisser, 1993; Erikson, 1963, 1964, 1968, 1982); (b) cognitive development (Gilligan, 1982; Kolhberg, 1981; Perry 1970); (c) personality type (Jung, 1971); and (d) multiple intelligences (Bruner, 1986; Gardner, 1983, 1997; Vygotsky, 1968) also gave indirect support for the pedagogy of service-learning, noting that learning involves the creation of meaning in individualized settings through hands-on learning experiences outside the classroom.

Service-learning has also been linked to helping students move from risk to resiliency. Resiliency is defined as "the ability to spring back from and successfully adapt to adversity" (Billig & Kraft, 1997). Benard (2004) has suggested that two sets of factors are involved in promoting resiliency: personal strengths (social competence, autonomy, having a sense of purpose) and environmental factors (caring relationships, high expectations for learning, opportunities for participation and contribution).

The Teen Service-Learning Evaluation Project (TSLEP) was designed to explore the potential of service-learning as an intervention to increase seat belt knowledge, awareness and usage among teens in selected high schools. Juarez, Schlundt, Goldzweig, and Stinson (2006) have outlined a conceptual framework linking service-linking and seat belt safety campaigns, suggesting that "a peer-to-peer (service-learning) approach" is an effective alternative to traditional public health education campaigns.

Because well-designed service-learning programs integrate student academic learning with service meeting real community needs (e.g., increasing seat belt use among African Americans) provide these kinds of experiences known to promote resiliency, service-learning may be an effective strategy for addressing the disparities in seat belt use among African American teens, many of whom attend urban high schools and are considered to be at-risk, not only academically, but also personally.

RESEARCH QUESTIONS AND METHODOLOGY

Three primary research questions examined in this project are explored in the pilot study:

1. What are the impacts of peer-to-peer educational service-learning projects on seat belt use among the general student population at participating high schools?
2. Does the service-learning experience add to the learning experience of students directly involved in designing and implementing the project?
3. Are particular characteristics of the students' service-learning experience associated with personal, social, school connectedness, and safety-related outcomes of the students involved in service-learning?

A quasi-experimental, pretest/posttest design was used to assess the impact of service-learning on student knowledge, awareness and usage. Six high schools in Ohio and Michigan participated in the pilot project.

The program was to have begun in the fall of 2005. However, because of delays in instrument design and subsequent Institutional Review Board (IRB) approval, the project did not begin until March, 2006. Each participating school received a grant of $1,500 to support its service-learning project. While the application process was the same for each high school, each school and the teacher/advisor—in collaboration with his/her students—were free to develop its own project and implementation strategy, consistent with the school curriculum, state standards, and student interests.

Two surveys were developed for use: (1) the Teen Seatbelt Usage and Safety Service-Learning Survey (Version C), a pretest for all students and posttest for students *not* involved in implementing the actual service-learning project, and (2) the Teen Seatbelt Usage and Safety Service-Learning Survey (Version D), a posttest for students *directly* involved in planning and implementing the service-learning project. Focus groups with students involved with the projects were also held at the six participating high schools.

Participants in the service-learning group responded to a series of specific items on the post Teen Seat Belt Usage and Service-Learning Survey that assessed their level of involvement in the design and presentation of activities during the project. They were asked whether they found the experience interesting and/or challenging and whether the project provided them important tasks and responsibilities (placement quality). They documented the frequency with which they engaged in oral and/or written reflection about their project. They also responded to questions that asked them to assess the impact of the service-learning experience on personal development and civic engagement outcomes such as increased personal efficacy or a greater sense of involvement in their school and community.

Teacher feedback was collected by means of a written instrument: The Seatbelt Safety Project—Teacher Report Form. This form asked teachers for specific information about the types of reflective activities they used, observed changes in student classroom knowledge and skills, observed changes in student behaviors and attitudes, ways in which students involved in the project increased their interpersonal skills and responsibility to the community, length of the project, number of students involved, and number of hours spent on training/preparation and number of actual service-hours.

Actual rates of seat belt use were assessed through direct observations of vehicles in and out of school parking lots before and after school. A staff member from MMC was assisted by students at participating high schools in collecting this data.

Data Collection Procedures

The total number of students directly involved in planning and implementing seat belt related service-learning projects was 199. Recruitment of students who participated in the design and implementation of service-learning projects was left up to the teacher/advisor at each school site.

Preproject parking lot observations of seat belt usage were conducted in mid-March and postproject observations in mid-May, using hand-held PDAs, utilizing software designed and used for similar studies of this type by MMC. Survey data were collected in the same time frame. Observation data were randomly collected on student and adult drivers and their passengers, entering and leaving school parking lots and/or student drop-off areas.

Exhibit 5.1.   Number of Seat Belt Observations

School/State/Classification	Pre (Feb.-Apr.)	Post (May)
School A-MI (U)	237	133
School B-MI (U)	75	361
School D-MI (S)	218	205
School C-OH (R)	276	220
School E- OH (S)	430	502
School F- OH (S)	736	816
Total	1,972	2,237

Note: U = Urban; S = Suburban; R = Rural.

Evaluators also made site visits corresponding to the timing of the pre- and postparking lot observations to meet with implementing teachers and student teams. The first visit served to clarify project expectations; the second to conduct focus groups with student teams and meet with teachers.

Seat belt usage findings were analyzed using a general linear model treating data as a two (intervention versus control) × two time 1, time 2) factorial design. The total number of students completing the pretest of the Teen Seatbelt Survey (Version C) was 407 (199 students directly involved with planning and implementing the service-learning project and 208 students in the comparison group). Four hundred seventy-five students completed the posttest of Version C.

For the purposes of this study, only the results of survey data from the service-learning participants (Version D) are reported. Posttest surveys of service-learning participants were analyzed using linear regression to detect an impact of quality, level of participation and reflection on personal development, school and civic responsibility, and safety related knowledge and behavior. Because of relatively low return rates and difficulties in linking pre-/postsurveys for these students, data for only 52 participants directly involved in the project were available for analysis. Schoolwide data were not analyzed due to difficulties in linking pre-/post-surveys (students were asked to create their own IDs, but many did not use the same ID from pre- to post-) and in getting postsurveys returned—one school did not turn in its data and another site developed its own post-survey.

Qualitative data from students and teachers were collected by means of focus groups (students) and interviews (teachers). Only teacher data are presented here.

RESULTS

This preliminary report on results from the pilot study includes (1) the impact of projects on observed seat belt use for participating schools; (2) faculty perceptions of student learning; and (3) initial findings for the effects of the quality of individual student experiences, the level of participation and reflection activity on student outcomes for students involved in planning and implementing service-learning projects.

Qualitative data were obtained from teachers in two ways: (1) through postproject report forms completed by the teachers (teachers at schools A, C, and D) and (2) interviews with teachers at all schools. Benefits observed by teachers are summarized below.

Changes in classroom knowledge and academic skills: students broadened their use and awareness of data gathering, graphing, and statistical analysis through the research involved; learned to use medical terminology within a scope of practice in order to interpret, transcribe, and communicate information, data, and observations; improved their writing skills in completing science fair projects related to vehicle safety and seat belt use; learned to organize, write, and compile technical information and summaries; improved their critical thinking skills (gathering and analyzing information, drawing logical conclusions) as they developed seat belt designs; improved their oral communication skills through presentations to parents and community; learned to apply active listening skills using reflection, restatement, and clarification techniques and to interpret verbal and nonverbal behaviors to augment communication; and gained skill in applying their math, writing, research, communication, teamwork, and networking skills.

Changes in attitudes about learning, school, and self as a learner: students made connections between what they were learning in school and the outside world; wanted to help others learn about the importance of wearing a seat belt to prevent injuries and save lives; became engaged and committed to the importance of seat belt use; and became more dependable and trustworthy.

Changes in attitudes about the value of the subject: students began to internalize the value of teamwork and the dedication and commitment it takes to complete a project; became much more aware of the importance of wearing a seat belt and obeying traffic laws; and became passionate regarding seat belt and child safety seats—I often discovered the students discussing the importance of car safety with students and staff after our formal presentations.

Changes in behaviors: students involved in the project showed a decrease in disciplinary problems and an increase in teamwork skills as they worked together to achieve their goals and remained on task and managed their time well.

Changes in self-esteem and self-discipline: students who were once withdrawn became more active, more interested and more involved in the project and stepped forward to answer questions during the oral discussion sessions; remained positive and conducted themselves in a professional manner during the project; became more self-motivated; felt a sense of efficacy and pride within themselves as they collected data and presented their findings and designs to parents and community organizations; came to see themselves as leaders in their schools who were trying to make a positive change in the behaviors of their peers; felt more self-confident about their role in the school and the community and were more resourceful; and appeared to discipline themselves to wear a seat belt and to have others buckle up while driving with them.

Changes in interpersonal and leadership skills: students took the initiative to change roles and responsibilities, to articulate concepts to one another, and collaborate as a team when creating the design and doing research for the project and then implementing their project; seemed to have formed a bond to work together while in their leadership group to improve their school and community; appeared to be more patient and respectful toward each other; and developed strong leadership and teamwork skills—they know they are leaders and recognize their leadership ability and are using it to affect change through their interactions during weekly meetings, presentations, and with interactions with other participating students.

Changes in acceptance of responsibility for the community: students increased their awareness of the importance of serving the community and accepted a broader sense of responsibility for communicating the importance of wearing a seat belt to their friends and extended families; realized that they are an important part of their community and can affect change; and assumed a sense of ownership and became receptive to all our service-learning projects.

Changes in desire to make a positive difference in the community: students chose to display the school's seat belt safety slogan on the marquee in front of the building (advertisements exhibited on the school grounds signaled to the community that students support positive change in the safety of their community); established themselves as true leaders in their school and community by setting a good example that others could follow; and assisted with our other community outreach projects (feed the children food drive, blood drive, bone marrow drive, nursing home visits).

Teachers were also asked to reflect on the three most important things they personally learned through their participation in this project.

Responses included: students have an increased sensitivity to and aware-ness of their responsibilities when presented with a problem students can feel empowered through their involvement in this project; were willing to step forward and felt they could make a difference in the lives of others; said it is fun, easy, and very rewarding to work with students; found that there were many more resources available than originally thought; and that there is a need to teach organization and time management, team-work, networking, public speaking, and communication skills to students.

According to their teachers, students had full control over project activ-ities, planning and organizing all project-related activities and presenta-tions and assisting in conducting school parking lot exit surveys. This was corroborated by student comments about their roles in the project. Based on teacher reports, students were involved in planning and designing one or more of the following activities: leading discussions with their peers on seat belt related issues; designing "user-friendly" seat belts; monitoring seat belt use before and after school in the school parking lot; conducting schoolwide slogan contests and campaigns to increase awareness of the importance of seat belt use, working on other media related activities (public service announcements for school, posters); oral and/or written presentations to peers and community groups in small and large forums, pre-prom programs and assemblies emphasizing the importance of seat belt use; sponsoring a "mock crash" scene on school grounds to show what can happen to an auto in a crash; participating in a high school leadership team advocating increased seat belt use; planning large school assemblies with guest speakers, conducting safety programs/activities in individual classrooms and safety programs offered through school clubs or teams or other groups; one-on-one informal contact between program participants and other students; setting up and staffing a booth on seat belt safety at the school's annual spring health fair; and meeting with and/ or speaking with experts on seat belt safety.

THE IMPACT OF PARTICULAR CHARACTERISTICS OF THE SERVICE-LEARNING EXPERIENCE ON STUDENT OUTCOMES

Exhibit 5.2 shows that increased involvement in the design and presenta-tion of materials as part of the service-learning project was positively asso-ciated with personal development outcomes such as self confidence and interpersonal skills. As teachers noted, students enhanced these personal characteristics through teamwork and the success of their projects. A growth in respect for the views of others was associated with both quality of the experience and reflection. Reflection was linked since it involves actively consideration of and exposure to alternative points of view. The

Exhibit 5.2.   Impact of Characteristics of Service-Learning Participation on Personal Development Outcomes—TSLEP (N = 52)

	Self-Confidence	Interpersonal Skill	Communica-tion	Respect for Views	Thinker/Problem Solver
Ethnicity	.023	−.027	−.003	.037	−.008
Quality of service-learning	−.140	−.114	−.177	.268***	−.178
Level of s-l project involvement	.735***	.535***	.678***	−.020	.654***
Reflection	−.029	.178	.065	.679***	.132

Note: Betas from linear regression analysis ***p < .01; **p < .05; *p < .10. Results from single-tail test for all variables except ethnicity; positive beta for ethnicity indicates minority status.

Exhibit 5.3.   Impact of Characteristics of Service-Learning Participation on School and Community Engagement Outcomes

	Efficacy/Making a Difference in the Community	Commitment to Improve the Community	Awareness of Resources in the Community	Involvement in School	Motivation to Learn/Participate in School
Ethnicity	.031	−.010	.265**	.114	.067
Quality of service-learning	.459***	−.203	−.072	.278***	−.210
Level of s-l project involvement	.070	.538***	.360**	.086	.550***
Reflection	.254**	.254**	.038	.449***	.285**

Note: Betas from linear regression analysis ***p < .01; **p < .05; *p < .10. Results from single tail test for all variables except ethnicity; positive beta for ethnicity indicates minority status.

quality dimension includes challenge and interest which are both likely to engage students intellectually and provoke consideration of alternative viewpoints.

Exhibit 5.3 presents relationships between the characteristics of the service-learning experience and outcomes related to preparing students for engaged citizenship.

Efficacy refers to the sense that students feel they have the capacity to make a difference in their community. In addition, there are two measures of commitment or motivation for participating in one's community—one focused on improving the community and the other on learning and participation in school. Students reported a greater involvement in school as a result of participation in the project and increased awareness of community resources.

Reflection was a good predictor of all outcomes except awareness of community resources, which was found to be related to the students' involvement in design and presentation activities during the project. Level of involvement was found to be a strong predictor of both the level of present commitment and future commitment. Quality of the service-learning project, including challenge, interest and contribution, predicted a greater sense of personal effectiveness and school involvement.

The major goal of this project was to change safety knowledge, attitudes and behavior in the area of seat belt usage. While many of the analyses remain to be completed, this chapter provides an initial examination of the impacts of service-learning impacts on the participants. The strongest predictor of positive changes in seat belt safety, knowledge attitudes, and behaviors, was active involvement in the design and presentation of programs in the school and community. Incorporating written and spoken reflection into the service-learning program design also contributed to both knowledge outcomes and to attempts to exert peer influence. Patterns are shown in Exhibit 5.4.

Exhibit 5.4.   Impact of Characteristics of Service-Learning Participation on Automobile Safety Related Outcomes

	Know More About Auto Safety	Tried to Influence Policymakers	Take More Responsibility for Own Safety	Encouraged Others to Use Seat Belts
Ethnicity	.022	.093	.027	.049
Quality of service-learning	−.111	−.020	−.109	.368**
Level of s-l project involvement	−.436***	.676***	.545***	.124
Reflection	.205*	−.200	.080	.200*

Note: Betas from linear regression analysis ***$p < .01$; **$p < .05$; *$p < .10$ Results from single tail test for all variables except ethnicity; positive beta for ethnicity indicates minority status.

Changes in Observed Seat Belt Use Over Course of Projects

Over the course of the study observed seat belt use rose significantly in each participating school and in each subgroup. This pattern held for males and females, drivers and passengers, and African Americans and whites. These results are shown in Exhibits 5.5 and 5.6.

Exhibit 5.6 shows seat belt use by gender of respondents before and after the service-learning interventions for all TSLEP participant high schools combined. Peer interventions resulted in an overall 16% increase in seat belt use among male students, from 63% to 79%, and an 11% increase among female students, from 74% to 85%. Results of this pilot study demonstrate that engaging students in the design of programs to encourage classmates to increase seat belt use has at least a short-term impact on actual seat belt behavior. Follow up observations during the 2006-2007 school year will determine if this change is sustained.

Observation data were also analyzed by ethnicity. These results are shown in Exhibits 5.7 and 5.8.

Exhibit 5.8 shows seat belt use by race of respondents before and after service-learning interventions for all TSLEP participant high schools combined. Among African American students, seat belt use increased by 22%, from 52% to 74%. Among Whites, seat belt use increased by 9%, from 76% to 85%.

While African Americans showed gains, the disparity us usage continued after their exposure to and participation in the service-learning project. There are a number of reasons for this. The first relates to the quality of the service-learning projects. The goal was to engage teachers and their students in high-quality curriculum-based service-learning projects aimed at increasing seat-belt use. However, none of the projects met all of the criteria for quality service-learning. Due to delays in getting IRB approval, no project reached the optimal goal of 70 hours for preparation, planning, implementation and reflection, potentially impacting project outcomes.

Exhibit 5.5.   Observed Seat Belt Use by Gender

	Seat Belt Use		
	Percent Using Seat Belts (Pre)	Percent Using Seat Belts (post)	Total Number of Observations
Student male	63	79	1,118
Student female	74	85	1,071
Adult male	69	78	808
Adult female	75	87	1,379

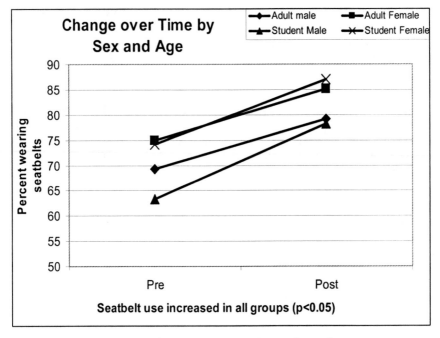

Exhibit 5.6.   Change in seat belt use over time by gender and age group.

Exhibit 5.7.   Observed Seat Belt Use by Ethnicity

	Seat Belt Use (Drivers and Passengers)		
	Percent Using Seat Belts (Pre)	Percent Using Seat Belts (Post)	Total Number of Observations
Students—African American	52	74	523
Students—White	76	85	1,537
Students—other/unknown	62	74	133
Adult—African American	63	80	789
Adult—White	78	86	1,319
Adult—other/unknown	70	88	89

Second, the level of curriculum integration varied significantly—three projects were closely connected to the curriculum, two were loosely connected, and one was only nominally connected. While students involved in the latter three projects provided valuable service to their school and/or community, their projects were connected with school and/or community

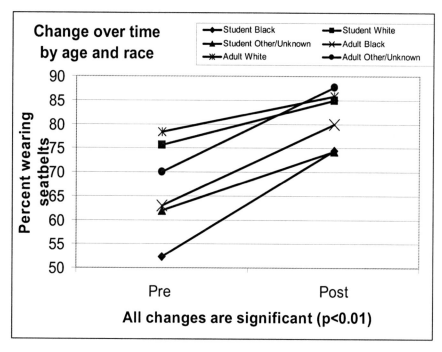

Exhibit 5.8.   Changes in seat belt use by ethnicity and group.

service clubs or organizations, (e.g., cocurricular student organizations such as a high school key clubs or honor societies or other student leadership groups) and are better classified as community service.

A third factor may be the difficulties in changing perceptions about seat belt use among parents, other adults in the community and peer groups (when asked about their reasons for not wearing seat belts consistently, some said things like, "It isn't cool!" or "they're uncomfortable"). These results suggest that long-term changes in seat belt use among African Americans may also need to address the community context in which these projects occur (Juarez et al., 2006).

Exhibits 5.9 and 5.10 reflect the impact of these issues on seat belt use outcomes.

Curriculum-based projects (schools A, C, D) showed the highest increases in seat belt use, especially among drivers. School A showed the most improvement for both drivers and passengers. Schools were projects were only loosely connected to the curriculum (E, F) showed more moderate increases among both drivers and students. While drivers in school B (nominally connected) showed improvement in seat belt use, use by pas-

Exhibit 5.9.   Student Driver Seat Belt Use by School

School	Percent Seat Belt Use (Pre)	Percent Seat Belt Use (Post)	Percent Change
School A—MI	46	86	+ 40
School B—MI	57	65	+ 8
School C—OH	77	91	+ 14
School D—MI	70	85	+ 15
School E—OH	73	82	+ 9
School F—OH	74	82	+ 8
Overall	66	82	+ 16

Exhibit 5.10.   Student Passenger Seat Belt Use by School

School	Percent Seat Belt Use (pre)	Percent Seat Belt Use (post)	Percent Change
School A—MI	51	76	+ 25
School B—MI	72	58	− 14
School C—OH	62	72	+ 10
School D—MI	66	77	+ 11
School E—OH	61	77	+ 16
School F—OH	69	78	+ 9
Overall	64	73	+ 9

sengers declined. This may be due to the fact that, on the day of the post-observations, the school was in lockdown due to gang-related activity in the area. Many students were either released or picked up by parents before our observations were scheduled to begin, significantly decreasing the number of observations.

DISCUSSION

The service-learning activities in this pilot project seemed to have a direct relationship to increased seat belt use among the overall student populations at participating high schools. While females were more likely to use seat belts than males and whites more likely than African Americans, all groups increased their seat belt usage, as measured by parking lot observations.

The data also showed that the involvement of students in the design and presentation of materials as part of the service-learning project was a significant predictor of outcomes in three broad areas:

- **Personal development:** Students who engaged in service-learning showed increases in self-confidence and sense of personal efficacy, improvement in interpersonal and communication skills (public speaking), and increases in critical thinking skills;
- **School and community engagement**: Students who engaged in service-learning showed an increased commitment to improving their communities, increased awareness of available resources, and increased motivation to learn/participate in school; and
- **Seat belt awareness/knowledge**: Students who engaged in service-learning, compared to those who did not, demonstrated an increase in awareness and knowledge about auto safety, particularly the importance of seat belt use, were likely to attempt to influence policymakers, and were more willing to take responsibility for their own safety.

The overall quality of the service-learning experience was also positively related to positive outcomes in the area of seat belt awareness and knowledge. Students who were most actively engaged in the service-learning projects and who reported higher levels of reflection activities related to their service-learning project, were more likely to perceive the projects to be important, challenging and interesting, and show the most positive outcomes.

LIMITATIONS OF THE STUDY

The small size of the data set limits the conclusions that can be drawn from the pilot study. While a model for peer-to-peer service-learning programs addressing seat belt safety issues among African Americans has been successfully piloted, several issues need to be addressed in order to enhance the overall success of future efforts of this type.

The first challenge was difficulty with data collection. Participating teachers were oriented by members of the Meharry-State Farm Alliance staff to ensure that they understand the data collection process and the rationale for adhering to project timelines and using approved surveys. In future efforts, a staff member should be present to assist with survey administration. Second, self-generated student identification codes caused many challenges. To increase the probability of being able to match a higher percentage of pre-/postsurveys, the process used by students to create their personal identification codes has been changed, using a successful model from similar studies done by MMC, A third challenge was posed by the difficulties in obtaining suitable comparison groups: project staff now insisted on a more rigorous method for selecting comparison groups (in most cases, gradewide administration of the pre-/postsurveys in the same content area) and ensuring data collection from these groups.

Researchers also experienced difficulties with the language level and length of the surveys: researchers received some feedback that the language (reading level) of the surveys was too high and that the surveys were too long. This issue was addressed by revising the surveys to include only questions that collect information pertinent to the study and by simplifying the language wherever possible. Difficulties in conducting community-based research also surfaced because the kinds of careful control that researchers would like to have for studies of this type were often difficult within the context of school communities. Factors over which researchers had little control—which may affect observed outcomes—include: the school context and issues occurring in the school and in the school district, issues between and among staff, issues between and among students, issues related to weather and mandated state achievement testing which may affect the timing of planned observations, student interest in the topic, the level of administrative support for service-learning (as evidenced in planning time and/or professional development time), the level of support for the project among colleagues, the level of parental understanding of and support for the project, and the quality of any partnerships formed as part of the project.

Overall, these findings demonstrate that service-learning which engages high school youth in the development and delivery of messages that promote seat belt use among their peers can be an effective strategy. Taken as a whole, these results support the use of service-learning as a potentially important strategy for changing risky teen behaviors. This approach holds promise for the use of peer-to-peer service-learning programs in addressing other risky teen behaviors, such as drinking and driving, speeding, unsafe sex, and drug use. While the small sample size limits the conclusions that can be drawn from this study, the results are encouraging and should inspire further research efforts in this area.

REFERENCES

Benson, P. (1993). *The troubled journey: A portrait of 6th-12th grade youth.* Minneapolis, MN: The Search Institute.

Berkas, T. (1997). *Strategic review of the W. K. Kellogg Foundation's service-learning projects, 1990-1996.* Battle Creek, MI: W. K. Kellogg Foundation.

Benard, B. (2004). *Resiliency: What we have learned.* San Francisco: WestEd.

Billig, S., & Kraft, N. (1997). Resilience. In *Linking improving America's school act and service-learning: A planning, implementation, and evaluation guide.* Denver, CO: RMC Research Corporation.

Billig, S. (2007). Unpacking what works in service-learning: Promising research-based practices to improve student outcomes. In *Growing to greatness 2007* (pp. 18-28). Minneapolis, MN: NYLC.

Bradley, R., & Rodgers, R. (2005). *Using development and learning theory in the design and evaluation of K-16 service-learning programs* (John Glenn Scholars in Service-Learning Paper). Columbus, OH: John Glenn Institute at The Ohio State University.

Bhaerman, R., Cordell, K., & Gomez, B. (1998). *The role of service-learning in educational reform.* Raleigh, NC: National Society for Experiential Education. Needham, MA: Simon and Shuster.

Briggs, N., Schlundt, D., Levine, R., Goldzweig, I., Stinson, N., & Warren, R. (2006). Seat belt law enforcement and racial disparities in seat belt use. *Journal of Preventative Medicine, 31*(2), 135-141.

Bruner, J. (1986). *Actual minds, possible worlds.* Cambridge, MA: Harvard University Press.

Chickering, A., & Reisser, L. (1993). *Education and identity* (2nd ed.). San Francisco: Jossey-Bass.

Conrad, D., & Hedin, D. (1982). Youth participation and experiential education. *Children and Youth Series, 4*(3 & 4). New York: Haworth.

Conrad, D., & Hedin, D. (1987). *Youth service: A guidebook for developing and operating effective programs.* Washington, DC: Independent Sector.

Conrad, D., & Hedin, D. (1989). *High school community service: A review of research and programs.* Madison,: National Center for Effective Schools, University of Wisconsin.

Conrad, D., & Hedin, D. (1991, June). School-based community service: What we know from research and theory. *Phi Delta Kappan,* 743-749.

Duckenfield, M., & Swanson, M. (1992). *Service-learning: Meeting the needs of youth at risk,* Clemson, SC: National Dropout Prevention Center.

Erikson, E. (1963). *Childhood and society* (2nd ed.). New York: Norton.

Erikson, E. (1964). *Insight and responsibility: Lectures on the ethical implications of psychoanalytic insight.* New York: Norton.

Erikson, E. (1968). *Identity: Youth and crisis.* New York: Norton.

Erikson, E. (1982). *The life cycle completed: A review.* New York: Norton.

Eyler, J., & Giles, D. (1999). *Where's the learning in service-learning.* San Francisco: Jossey-Bass.

Fell, J., Baker, T., & McKnight, A. (2005). *Increasing teen safety belt use: A program and literature review.* Washington, DC: National Highway Traffic Safety Administration, U.S. Department of Transportation.

Follman. J. (1998, August). *Florida Learn and Serve: 1996-97 outcomes and correlations with 1994-95 and 1995-96.* Tallahassee: Florida State University, Center for Civic Education and Service.

Gardner, H. (1983). *Frames of mind: The theory of multiple intelligences.* New York: Basic Books.

Gardner, H. (1997). The first seven ... and the eighth. *Educational Leadership, 55*(1), 8-13.

Gilligan, C. (1982). *In a different voice.* Cambridge, MA: Harvard University Press.

Juarez, P., Schlundt. D., Goldzweig, I., & Stinson, N (2006). A conceptual framework for reducing risky teen driving behaviors among minority youth. *Injury Prevention, 12*(Suppl.1), 49-55.

Jung, C. (1971). *Psychological types.* Princeton, NJ: Princeton University Press.

Kolhberg, L. (1981). *The philosophy of moral development.* New York Harper & Row.

Meharry Medical College. (1999). *Achieving a credible health and safety approach to increasing seat belts among African Americans,* Nashville, TN: Author.

Melchior, A. (1999). *Summary report: National evaluation of Learn and Serve America.* Waltham, MA: Center for Human Resources, Brandeis University.

Melchior, A., & Bailis, L. (2002). Impact of service-learning on civic attitudes and behavior of middle and high school youth: Findings from three national evaluations. In A. Furco & S. Billig (Eds.), *Advances in service-learning research: Vol. I. Service-learning: The essence of the pedagogy* (pp. 201-222). Greenwich, CT: Information Age.

Meyer. S., & Billig, S. (2003). *Evaluation of need in deed.* Denver, CO: RMC Research Corporation.

Meyer, S., Billig S., & Hofshire, L. (2004). *Wai'anae High School Hawaiian studies program.* Denver, CO: RMC Research Corporation.

Perry, W. (1970). *The ethical and intellectual development of college students.* New York: Holt, Rinehart, and Winston.

Schaffer, B. (1993). *Service-learning: An academic methodology.* Stanford, CA: Stanford University Department of Education.

Schlundt, D., Easley, S., & Goldzweig, I. (2005). *Racial disparities in seat belt use: An observational study in 4 communities.* Paper presented at the American Public Health Association Conference, Philadelphia, PA.

Vygotsky, L. (1968). *Thought and language.* Cambridge, MA: MIT Press.

Weiler, D., LaGoy, A., Crane, E., & Rovner, A. (1998). *An evaluation of K-12 service-learning in California: Phase II final report.* Emeryville, CA: RPP International with the Search Institute.

Wells, J., & Williams, A. (2002). Seat belt use among African Americans, Hispanics, and Whites. *Accident Analysis & Prevention, 34*(4), 523-529.

CHAPTER 6

SERVICE-LEARNING AS A TRANSFORMATIVE EXPERIENCE

An Analysis of the Impact of Service-Learning on Student Attitudes and Behaviors After Two Years of College

Matthew Bernacki and Frank Bernt

ABSTRACT

This longitudinal study examined the relationship between service-learning (SL) and the attitudes and behaviors of college students during the first 2 years of undergraduate study at a faith-based (Jesuit) university. The study investigated the role SL involvement plays in the timing and depth of students' engagement in campus activities and the attitudinal changes that accompany such activity. Students were surveyed at 3 time points about their social, civic, and religious attitudes and were interviewed each spring about their time use. Freshmen SL students were more likely to attend alternative

From Passion to Objectivity: International and Cross-Disciplinary Perspectives on Service Learning Research, pp. 111–134

spring breaks, and as sophomores were more likely to complete advocacy work and attend retreats. Implications are that freshmen SL experiences seem to promote involvement in activities aimed at formation of students' attitudes and behaviors.

INTRODUCTION

Since the Association of Supervision and Curriculum Development officially endorsed service-learning in 1993, the service-learning initiative has gained credibility as a pedagogy that promotes positive outcomes for students across academic, civic, and personal dimensions (Titlebaum, Williamson, G., Daprano, C., Baer, J., & Brahler, 2004). If its early acceptance relied heavily on anecdotal reports by students and professors, research efforts in the past 10 years have recognized the importance of identifying and of measuring potential positive outcomes of service-learning using quantitative and longitudinal methods (Wilson & Rymph, 2006).

Areas of potential benefit noted in such investigations have included increases in positive social attitudes such as empathy (Wideman, 2005) and commitment to social justice (Roschelle, Turpin, & Elias, 2000); personal growth in areas such as self-understanding (Raman & Pashupati, 2002) and self-confidence (McKenna & Rizzo, 1999); reduction of prejudice (Erickson & O'Connor, 2000); cognitive skill development, such as critical thinking and academic motivation (Bringle, Phillips, & Hudson, 2004; Estanak & Love, 2003-2004; Rosenberger, 2000). Most recently, attention has been paid to service-learning's role as a buffer against alcohol and drug use during college (Weitzman & Chen, 2005).

Although several of these studies have yielded significant modest results, efforts have not consistently demonstrated clear evidence of expected or hoped-for outcomes. The reasons for this are several. In some cases, it is questionable whether the strength of the independent variable (such as intensity, depth, and quality of service-learning experience) is sufficient to influence such change in isolation from other influences. Often, the quality and nature of service involvement differs dramatically from campus to campus and even from course to course (Densmore, 2000). Even in cases where the service-learning experience is sustained, intensive, and relatively homogenous, the use of simple pretest/posttest designs that assess benefits after a single semester or academic year have perhaps hoped for too much too soon.

In response to general difficulties in describing short-term behavioral outcomes, some researchers have conducted studies following students who participated in service-learning several years after graduation

(Roschelle et al., 2000). Though useful, such studies shed little light upon what transpires during the interim that might account for the differences.

Recent reviews of service-learning research have called for the use of longitudinal designs that follow students over several data points. Assessing research on high school service-learning, Furco (2002) states that longitudinal study of service-learning and its impact is valuable in the trajectory of students through the college years and beyond. Volgelgesang, Ikeda, Gilmartin, and Keup (2002) call for research on service-learning outcomes specifically over the first year of college as a vehicle for predicting future outcomes.

In Giles and Eyler's (1998) "A Service-Learning Research Agenda for the Next Five Years," it is indirectly stated that longitudinal data have not been collected on service-learning and its impact on students for more than a semester. The agenda states that "this impact [on students] has been traced over the course of a semester, through cross-sectional data comparing service-learning students with those who did not participate and in qualitative studies" (p. 66). Absent from the literature on service-learning are studies that employ a design that: (1) tracks the same students over a college career; (2) assesses students at multiple measurement points; and (3) employs a single school model in which the definition of service-learning and its requirements are homogenous across a number of courses. At present this experimental design has not been employed. According to Vogelgesang et al. (2002), it is possible that many benefits require more than 1 year of exposure to service-learning to be realized. In the service-learning literature, few (but oft cited) examples exist that track students' service-learning involvement beyond 1 year (Astin & Sax, 1998; Astin, Vogelgesang, Ikeda & Yee, 2000). Fewer still examine the impact of a service-learning curriculum that includes substantial and continuous involvement in service-learning classes.

This study takes an inclusive approach, focusing on the college experience of students and the role service-learning plays in light of other substantial influences such as academic major, peer relations, work and internships, and involvement in campus activity. What follows is a summary of the standard model of longitudinal assessment of service-learning, two large-scale, cross-sectional studies of service-learning outcomes, and the proposed model of a 4-year, five-time-point assessment of service-learning at a single institution.

The Standard Model

Compendia of service-learning research such as Eyler, Giles, Stenson, and Grey (2001) provide evidence that the vast majority of service-learning research involves a quasi-experimental design that encompasses one semester of service-learning involvement. These studies most often employ a pretest and posttest observation and report differences in scores over time. This standard is set by convenience as well as precedent.

The majority of undergraduate curricula that offer service-learning do so on a one-semester basis, with the occasional 1-year commitment, usually offered to incoming freshmen. These courses are self-selected by students, necessitating a quasi-experimental design. They can be easily assessed at the beginning and end of a semester, sometimes within the context of the coursework itself. While this model is often used out of expediency, it has also been proven to be a successful means of contributing significant findings to the study of service-learning.

The quality of the service-learning experience is understood to be dependent upon both the duration of the service experience and intensity of reflection on the experience (Eyler & Giles, 1997). Eyler and Giles assert that service-learning courses that integrate reflection and endure a full year are more likely to have significant impact on students than one-semester service-learning experiences.

If what Eyler and Giles assert is true, a 4-year study of service-learning in which students enroll in a service-learning curriculum of rigorous intensity and sufficient duration should yield even greater gains than a 1-year service-learning experience. While this 4-year model is much more difficult to study, two large-scale studies have been published in the service-learning literature, and each confirms this assertion, as described below.

Four-Year Pretest Posttest Models

In 1998, Astin and Sax published a 4-year study of community service and service-learning titled "How Undergraduates are Affected by Service Participation." Sponsored by Learn & Serve America, this study employed a national survey given to freshmen and seniors at 42 colleges and universities in the United States. Baseline data were collected from the 1990-1994 Cooperative Institutional Research Program (CIRP) Freshman Survey and compared to a sample of the same students using the College Student Survey (CSS) conducted in 1995. Comparing service-learning students to those who took no courses with a service component, Astin and Sax found positive influences of service-learning on nearly three dozen domains, including academic outcomes, civic engagement outcomes, and the development of life skills. Supporting Eyler and Giles' (1997), Astin and Sax report a correlation between the amount of service completed and the degree to which students exhibited gains in the above-mentioned areas. This study focused on the impact of service experience generally—not specifically on service-learning.

Two years later, a study by Astin et al. (2000) was released from the Higher Education Research Institute at UCLA, and reported longitudinal changes in students who completed community service and service-learning coursework. Astin et al. found that service—and particularly service-learning—positively affected students' attitudes about activism, racial understanding and choice of service careers, as well as postgraduate volunteerism. Service-learning students also outscored their peers on grade point average (GPA) and on assessments of critical thinking and of writing skills.

The findings published in these two studies provide generalizable evidence that a service-learning curriculum promotes student development, a belief which in the past could be dismissed as anecdotal and confined to specific academic courses and niches.

Costs and Benefits of Four-Year Longitudinal Designs

These two studies are landmarks in their assessment of service-learning over a longer term. Each study provides a large representative sample and a clear picture of the benefits of service and service-learning. Astin et al. (2000) also performed a qualitative examination of the reasons for gains. In general, the studies provide an accurate picture of how service and service-learning coursework affect students over a 4-year period.

While statistical power and generalizability are tremendous strengths of such a research design, some drawbacks also must be considered. The use of national pretest and posttest measures limits data collections to a two-observation model. Richness is lost when the story of the college experience cannot be told over time. The magnitude of the study also requires the employment of a self-report questionnaire, leaving the measure open to the interpretation of the respondent.

While the benefits of statistical power allow for fine grained analysis of hypotheses, studies of this magnitude raise questions about the consistency of the independent variable. In addition, definitions for service-learning vary widely and cannot be standardized for different courses or institutions. Further, the pretest/posttest model ignores changes that occur throughout the four years of the college experience. A smaller study with a more carefully controlled treatment variable can ensure consistency in definition and practice of service-learning. An additional study with more observations would allow for an examination of the developmental trajectory service-learning students follow while achieving the gains reported by Astin and Sax (1998) and Astin et al. (2000).

THE PROPOSED MODEL

This study aims to evaluate service-learning as a part of the college experience and to demonstrate that when service-learning is included in the freshman year, it can play an important role in the trajectory of college careers. Using a 4-year longitudinal design, the Service-Learning As a Transformative Experience (SLATE) study assesses student attitudes and behavior during orientation to college and each year until graduation. By examining students' beliefs and actions at multiple time points, the study aims to report on the impact service-learning can have on the timing and depth of students' involvement in prosocial activities. The results reported in this study focus on outcomes after 2 years.

Definition and Context of Service-Learning

This study was conducted at a private, Northeastern, Jesuit, Catholic, liberal arts university with an enrollment of 3,500 undergraduate students. Service-learning courses in this study are defined as three-credit courses that require 30 hours of community service paired with academic instruction and participation in personal and group reflection that occurs both inside and outside the classroom. Partnerships with agencies and student service placement and attendance are coordinated by a campus institute and not instructors, though instructors often visit sites and perform some service at one or more of them. Freshmen service-learning students take two consecutive semesters of service-learning and are placed at a site; upperclassmen can select individual one-semester three-credit courses and choose their site from an approved directory. Service-learning occurs here in a faith-justice context, leading evaluators to study domains such as intrinsic religiosity and religious orientation as a correlate of attitude and behavior. Similarly, students' social and civic attitudes are evaluated to determine their general understanding of power issues such as social dominance and their impressions of fairness.

The SL program examined in this study can be described according to language used by Morton (1995) as employing a "charity" paradigm in that direct service to an individual occurs at a community organization. However, this model also includes elements of social analysis and recognition of solidarity with the person being served with an end goal of this relationship-based model developing in the student the ability to advocate for the population he or she serves. These inclusions typify a "social change" paradigm.

Purpose

By studying the impact of service-learning each year over a college career, the aim of this project was to determine if the timing and amount of exposure to service-learning affects attitudes and behaviors of students. Further, this study intended to assess the timing of changes in civic attitudes and the behaviors that correlate with service-learning exposure. The study investigated whether service-learning acted as a protective factor against disengagement. More generally, this study aimed to paint a picture of the organic development of students who enrolled in service-learning courses in relation to their peers who did not pursue such programs. Student development was assessed attitudinally by determining the degree to which students understood issues of fairness and social dominance and their ability to reconcile these through reflection and critical analysis on issues of faith, justice and solidarity. Student activities were assessed to determine translation of these attitudes into practice.

METHOD

Participants

Participants were recruited by mail in June 2004 and during freshman summer orientation sessions in August 2004. Informed consents were collected, enrolling subjects in a 4-year study. Participants were told they would receive monetary reimbursement as an incentive to participate at each interview. At Time 1 (summer 2004), participants were entered into a drawing for money toward textbooks. At Time 2 (spring 2005) and Time 3 (spring 2006), participants received a cash stipend for their participation.

At Time 1, 275 students completed measures and consent forms. Of these students, 233 were eligible to be interviewed at the end of their freshman year (Time 2), the remainder having transferred to other schools or having withdrawn from the study. This sample included 94 males and 139 females. Of this group, 111 students, 38 male and 73 female, were interviewed. At Time 3, 134 of the participants, 53 male and 81 female, were interviewed and completed all written measures. By Time 3, 63 of the original 275 participants recruited had withdrawn or transferred from the university.

Seventy-two students completed all measures at all three time points (25 males and 47 females). These 72 students represented a response rate of 34%. Of the 134 participants from whom data were collected at baseline and at the sophomore year time point, 103 had taken no service-learning coursework. Ten had taken one semester of service-learning coursework. Thirteen had taken two semesters, seven had taken three semesters of SL courses, and one had taken four semesters of SL courses.

Measures

The measures used in this study to assess participants' attitudes are the civic-attitudes test (Mabry, 1995, as cited in Bringle et al, 2004), the Global Belief in a Just World survey (Lipkus, 1991, as cited in Bringle et al, 2004), and the Preference Towards Social Dominance survey (Pratto, Sidanius, Stallworth, & Malle, 1994, as cited in Bringle et al, 2004) as well as the Quest scale (Batson & Schoenrade, 1991) and the Intrinsic Religious Motivation scale (Hoge, 1972).

Civic Attitudes Scale

The Civic Attitudes scale (CA) (Mabry, 1995, as cited in Bringle et al, 2004) is composed of five Likert-scale items which assess civic attitudes and a feeling of responsibility to address social problems. The internal consistency was tested before and after a completion of a service-learning course. Coefficient alphas were .80 (pretest) and .81 (posttest).

Preference for Social Dominance Orientation

The Preference For Social Dominance scale (SDO) was developed by Pratto et al. (1994, as cited in Bringle et al, 2004) and is composed of 16 Likert-scale items which aim to assess the extent of a participant's preference for social dominance of one group over another. Over a 3-month period SDO had a test-retest reliability of .84 and across 13 groups, and the coefficient alphas all exceeded .80.

Global Belief in a Just World Scale

The Global Belief In A Just World scale (GBJW) was developed by Lipkus (1991, as cited in Bringle et al, 2004) and is composed of seven Likert-scale scored items used to assess the respondent's belief that people are deserving of what occurs in their life. Coefficient alpha for the overall scale was reported to be .82.

Intrinsic Religious Motivation Scale

The Intrinsic Religious Motivation (IRM) scale (Hoge, 1972) was used to assess participants' religious commitment; it measures intrinsic religious motivation, as described initially by Allport and Ross (1967). The IRM is a 10-item, 5-point Likert scale that demonstrates high correlations with earlier measures of intrinsic religious motivation (rs range from .85 to .87) and high internal consistency ($\alpha = .90$).

Quest Scale

The revised Quest scale (Batson & Schoenrade, 1991) consists of 12 items measuring three subdimensions of the original (Batson & Ventnis, 1982) quest orientation: complexity, self-criticism and positive doubt, and openness to change. The revised scale aimed to increase the internal consistency of the original 6-item scale (.63); it was successful in doing so, raising the estimate to .78 (Batson & Schoenrade, 1991).

Collegiate Time Use Interview

The time use measure used to assess participant activity was adapted from the After School Time Use Child Interview (2001) used in the Study of Early Child Care (SECC) conducted by the National Institute on Child Health & Human Development (NICHD). The original measure was used to assess the after school activity of children in middle childhood in 15 minute increments from school dismissal until 6 P.M. Interviewers from the NICHD study captured activities completed over a standard time frame and designated these activities into specific categories. The Collegiate Time Use Interview was adapted for the time period assessed (from after school hours to an academic year) and was expanded to include activity codes that reflect academic, extracurricular, and adult social roles.

Similar to the NICHD study, interviewers were trained using a manual, mock interviews and a certification process over a period of 6 weeks. Each interviewer attended six 1-hour training sessions, read the manual, and completed a minimum of 6 mock interviews before becoming certified. All interviewers were certified on both interview technique and coding technique prior to conducting live interviews with participants. A standardized codebook was constructed which assigned specific codes to all activities. Intercoder reliability was addressed during certification in that interviewers were required to successfully obtain and correctly code 90% of data gleaned from a pilot interview. All interviewers were monitored for accuracy after 4 weeks of data collection. All interviewers were retrained and recertified for each data collection period.

Procedures

Data were collected for this study at three time points over the course of the first 2 years of participants' undergraduate career. Time 1 assessment using the attitudinal measures only was completed in the months after participants completed high school and prior to enrollment at the university.

Time 2 data were collected after spring break (beginning the second week of March) of the freshman year. Each participant was contacted via email or phone by investigators and was scheduled for a time use interview which was conducted by an interviewer in a mutually agreed on location and lasted 15-30 minutes. During this time the interviewer obtained information about the activities of the participant during the current academic year. The participant also completed all attitudinal measures after the interview. Time 3 data collection occurred after spring break of the sophomore year using a procedure identical to Time 2.

RESULTS

Attitude Scales—Internal Consistency and Intercorrelations

Internal consistency estimates for each of the six scales were computed for each of the three testing times using the alpha coefficient provided by the SPSS program. Several of the scales yielded alpha coefficients which were problematic.

The five-item Civic Attitudes (CA) scale yielded alpha coefficients between .40 and .52. Given the small set of items in the scale to begin with, elimination of items did not result in a satisfactory internal consistency estimate; accordingly, items were treated as separate dependent variables for the measure.

The seven-item Global Belief in a Just World (GBJW) scale yielded alpha coefficients ranging from .58 to .61; eliminating items 2 and 6 (as listed in Lipkus, 1991, as cited in Bringle et al, 2004) yielded internal consistency estimates ranging from .71 to .76.

Analysis of internal consistency for Intrinsic Religion Motivation (IRM) and Quest (Q) scales yielded satisfactory alpha coefficient values (.80-.84 and .85-.87, respectively). Scale intercorrelations are presented in Exhibit 6.1.

Intergroup Differences—Attitude Scales

A series of 2 (Service-Learning) × 2 (Gender) × 3 (Time) repeated measures analyses of variance were conducted to explore intergroup differences related to these three factors for each of the five attitude scales (and for the five items of the Civic Attitudes scale). Service-Learning represents the group comparison between students who had taken at least one service-learning class (SL) with those who had taken no service learning classes over 2 years (non-SL). Exhibit 6.2 presents F values and significance levels for main effects and interactions.

Exhibit 6.1.   Intercorrelations of Attitude Scales

SDO1	(.87)										
SDO2	.75	(.91)									
SDO3	.63	.80	(.90)								
GBJW1	.26	.16	.23	(.71)							
GBJW2	.37	.36	.36	.52	(.72)						
GBJW3	.38	.38	.36	.47	.46	(.76)					
IRM1	−.20	−.13	−.19	−.17	−.25	−.09	(.85)				
IRM2	−.12	−.12	−.20	−.36	−.19	−.09	.73	(.89)			
IRM3	−.10	−.08	−.21	−.32	−.18	−.13	.73	.87	(.87)		
QST1	−.18	−.28	−.13	−.02	−.25	−.14	−.06	−.10	.07	(.80)	
QST2	−.09	−.26	−.07	−.08	−.19	−.12	−.03	.06	.04	.62	(.84)
QST3	−.20	−.20	−.14	−.11	−.35	−.22	−.03	.06	.08	.60	.56	(.80)
Time	1	2	3	1	2	3	1	2	3	1	2	3
	Social Dominance Orientation (SDO)			Global Belief in a Just World (GBJW)			Intrinsic Religiosity (IRM)			Quest Orientation (QST)		

Note: Internal reliability estimate coefficient alphas are in parentheses.

Exhibit 6.2.   *F* Values From Repeated Measures ANOVA Results for Attitude Scales

	Main Effects			Interactive Effects			
Scale	SL (S)	Gender (G)	Time (T)	$S \times G$	$S \times T$	$G \times T$	$S \times G \times T$
Intrinsic Religous Motivation	<1	2.98* (.04)	<1	<1	3.75** (.09)	<1	<1
Quest	<1	<1	6.80*** (.08)	3.95** (.05)	2.21	1.69	2.21
Global Belief in a Just World	<1	6.85** (.09)	5.21** (.11)	7.97** (.10)	<1	<1	<1
Social Dominace	2.14	2.07	<1	1.05	<1	<1	<1
Civic Attitudes (item 2)	<1	<1	3.44** (.09)	<1	<1	<1	<1

*$p < .10$; **$p < .05$; ***$p < .01$
Note: Numbers in parentheses indicate partial eta-squared values corresponding to significant effects.

Service-Learning and Attitude Scales

A significant Service-Learning × Time interaction was obtained for Intrinsic Religious Motivation ($p = .03$). A test of simple main effects indicated that IRM scores for the SL group did not differ over time, while scores for the non-SL group at Time 3 (end of sophomore year) differed significantly from both Time 1 (baseline) and Time 2 (end of freshman year). The SL group mean was significantly higher than the non-SL mean at Time 3. A comparison of means is presented in Exhibit 6.3. No other interactions involving Service-Learning were significant, nor were any of the main effects for Service-Learning significant. However, a nonsignificant Service-Learning by Time trend for the Quest scale ($p = .12$) is illustrated in Exhibit 6.4 and will be addressed in the Discussion section of this chapter.

Gender and Attitude Scales

A significant main effect was found for Gender on the Global Belief in a Just World scale ($p = .01$) and a nonsignificant trend was obtained for Intrinsic Religious Motivation ($p = .09$). Group means are presented in Exhibit 6.5. Females outscored males on Intrinsic Religious Motivation, while males outscored females on Global Belief in a Just World. A significant interaction between Service-Learning and Gender on the Global

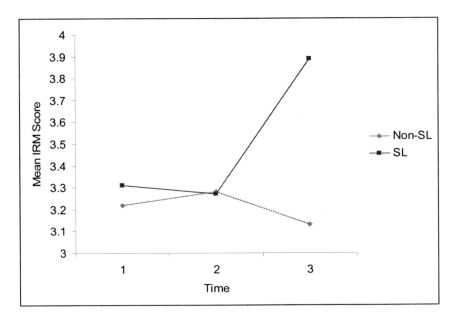

Exhibit 6.3.   Intrinsic Religious Motivation means by SL group.

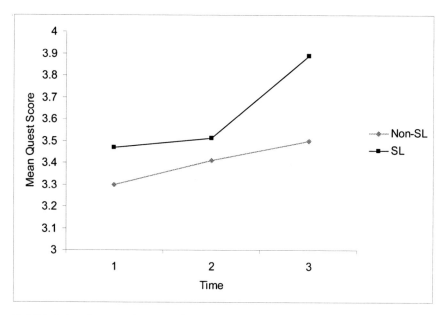

Exhibit 6.4.   Quest scale means by SL group.

**Exhibit 6.5.   Group Means and
Standard Deviations for Attitude Scales**

Quest Scale	Males (n = 31)	Females (n = 49)
SL (n = 18)	3.28	3.80
Non-SL (n = 62)	3.51	3.33
Total (n = 80)	3.50	3.53
GBJW Scale	Males (n = 29)	Females (n = 49)
SL (n = 17)	3.32	2.47
Non-SL (n = 61)	2.91	2.94
Total (n = 78)	3.11	2.70

Belief in a Just World scale (p = .006) warranted a test of simple main effects, which indicated that SL males outscored SL females. No gender differences were found for the non-SL group. Caution for these findings is in order, as the SL male subgroup was inordinately small (n = 6). This subject falls outside the scope of this paper and will be explored more thoroughly in a future text.

Time and Attitude Scales

Significant main effects for Time were obtained for the Quest scale (p = .001) and for the Global Belief in a Just World scale (p = .007). Quest scores increased over time for all groups (overall means were 3.34, 3.43, and 3.58 for Times 1, 2, and 3 respectively); while Global Belief in a Just World scores decreased over time for all groups (overall means were 3.04, 2.84, and 2.76, respectively). There were no significant interactions involving Service-Learning. A trend analysis indicated that both trends were linear rather than quadratic, suggesting a steady change over two years; [$F(1, 76) = 12.64, p = .03$], and [$F(1, 74) = 8.34, p = .02$], for Quest and GBJW scales, respectively. A significant main effect for Time was obtained when item 2 on the Civic Attitudes scales (which asks for agreement with the statement "People, regardless of whether they've been successful or not, ought to help others") was used as the dependent variable; no other effects were significant for any of the Civic Attitudes scale items.

Intergroup Differences—Time Use

A series of 2 (Service-Learning) × 2 (Gender) × 2 (Time) repeated measures analyses of variance were conducted to explore intergroup differences related to these three factors for each of the activity variables. Since the hours reported for certain activities created highly nonnormal frequency distributions (e.g., those participating in a service immersion trip could legitimately report more than a hundred hours, while those not participating would report none), many of the activity variables were dichotomized. Data were subject to three-way repeated measures ANOVA based on evidence provided by Lunney (1970) supporting such statistical treatment (also see D'Agostino (1971)). Exhibit 6.6 presents F values, significance levels, and corresponding eta-squared values for main effects and interactions.

Service-Learning and Time Use

Significant Service-Learning by Time interactions were obtained for Activism-Advocacy (p = .007). Tests of simple main effects indicated that the SL sophomores (25%) were more likely at Time 3 to participate in advocacy-activism than non-SL sophomores (5%); there was a significant increase in participation between the freshman and sophomore years for the SL group (5% to 25%), but not for the non-SL group (0% to 5%). These differences remained significant when data were analyzed using non-parametric alternatives to ANOVA.

A simple main effect of group indicated that SL students were significantly more likely to attend a service immersion trip than non-SL students (F= 4.11, p = .05, eta-squared =.05). This number of participants

Exhibit 6.6.   *F* Values From Repeated Measures ANOVA Results for Activity Measures

	Main Effects			Interactive Effects			
Activity	SL(S)	Gender (G)	Time (T)	S × G	S × T	G × T	S × G × T
Service immersions	4.11** (.05)	<1	7.18*** (.09)	<1	<1	<1	1.48
Activism & Advocacy	7.41** (.09)	<1	13.75*** (.15)	<1	5.99** (.07)	1.35	1.69
Community Service	<1	<1	1.52	<1	<1	<1	3.14* (.04)
Service Events	1.55	5.32** (.07)	1.19	<1	<1	1.59	<1
Religious Activities	<1	<1	<1	<1	<1	<1	4.44** (.06)
Faith-based Retreats	2.43	1.95	8.73*** (.10)	1.22	<1	<1	4.61** (.06)
Academic & Homework	2.42	<1	2.42	<1	<1	<1	<1
Reading	<1	<1	<1	<1	<1	<1	2.18
Campus Events	1.50	2.88* (.04)	1.81	3.01* (.04)	3.42* (.04)	2.17	<1
Parties	3.41* (.04)	<1	<1	<1	<1	<1	<1

*$p < .10$; **$p < .05$; ***$p < .01$.
Note: Numbers in parentheses indicate partial eta-squared values corresponding to significant effects.

per group differed significantly at Time 2 and Time 3. Percentages appear in Exhibit 7.

A significant main effect for Time (see below) indicated that participation in faith-based retreats dropped dramatically between the freshman and sophomore year. In addition, there was a significant Service-Learning by Time by Gender interaction, $p = .04$. A test of simple main effects revealed that the decline occurred for all subgroups except for SL females, which remained steady across both years (14%). In contrast, non-SL females were more likely to participate in their freshman year (22%), but then completely lost interest in their sophomore year (0%). Ignoring gender, participation in faith-based retreats dropped (from 15% to 3%) for the non-SL group between freshman and sophomore years, while it remained relatively more stable (25% to 20%) for the SL group.

**Exhibit 7. Percentages of Students who Participated in
Service Immersion Programs and Activism–Advocacy Activities**

Service Immersions	SL (n = 20)	Non-SL (n = 60)	Total (n = 80)
Time 2	25	7	11
Time 3	45	27	31
Activism-Advocacy	SL	Non-SL	Total
Time 2	5	0	1
Time 3	25	5	10

Gender and Time Use

Significant main effects for Gender for Service Oriented Campus
Events ($p = .02$) and for Nonservice Oriented Campus Events ($p = .09$)
indicated that females were more likely than males to participate in ser-
vice-oriented campus events than males, but less likely to participate in
campus events in general during the first two years of college (48% versus
23% and 6% versus 10%, respectively).

Time and Time Use

A significant three-way interaction for Religious Activities ($p = .04$)
implied a complex dynamic whereby (a) SL females decreased, while SL
males increased, over time; and (b) non-SL females increased, while non-
SL males decreased, over time. Participation in religious activities
decreased significantly between the freshman and sophomore year. This
difference applied to all subgroups. Several three-way (SL × Gender ×
Time) interactions were significant; however, they may be spurious, based
on the small cell size for SL males ($n = 6$). Accordingly, they must be
explored further before speculating about what they mean.

Differences over time and among groups for academic work (coursework and studying), reading and writing, and campus events were not significant. This remained true irrespective of whether activity variables were
treated as interval or as dichotomized data.

DISCUSSION

For college students, early service-learning involvement led to increased
engagement in formative activities such as retreats, service immersion
trips, and advocacy campaigns. The ability of a service-learning experience to affect students' attitudes was mixed. Over 2 years, students' religious attitudes changed to the extent that student beliefs became more

intrinsically religious and their spiritual seeking trended upward. Social and civic attitudes were not significantly affected by SL involvement.

Social Attitudes

The sought-after Service-Learning × Time interaction (which would indicate an impact of service-learning between baseline and posttest measures) was not supported by data analysis for any of the three social attitude scales (Social Dominance Orientation, Global Belief in a Justice World, Civic Attitudes) over a 2-year period. There are several possible explanations for this. It may be that even 2 years was insufficient to have an impact on such attitudes (at least when only 1 year of SL was completed). Or perhaps in a 2-year time frame, too many intervening variables already entered in to allow for a "clean" assessment of the impact of a freshman service-learning experience (i.e., a year was not enough, but a second year without service-learning was not enough either). It also might be that, based on the difficulties encountered with internal consistency, these measures were not sensitive enough to reliably detect change in the sample.

Religious Attitudes

It is of interest that the two religious scales both yielded differences (though only marginally significant in the case of the Quest scale), suggesting an impact of service-learning. In the case of the Intrinsic Religious Motivation scale, there was a clear separation of motivation levels between SL and non-SL groups at the end of the sophomore year. In the case of the Quest scale, a difference appeared at the end of the sophomore year (with the mean for the SL group significantly increasing). These differences were corroborated by differences in student participation in religious activities: the SL group manifests significantly higher levels of activity in service- and faith-based activities at the end of the sophomore year.

Several possible reasons for this impact deserve further exploration. Most obvious is the possibility that the university and program contexts may play a role (the university is Jesuit; the service-learning courses are housed within the Faith-Justice Institute). Although the program neither required nor emphasized a particular faith tradition, consistent emphasis on reflection in coursework, and on the meaning of terms such as service, solidarity, and justice may direct growth in critical thinking toward a deepening of one's own spiritual understanding (whatever that might be) and particularly to a strengthening habit of asking questions and seeking answers (as measured by the Quest scale).

Time Use Measures

Students who enrolled in freshman service-learning courses were significantly more likely to become involved in activities involving advocacy during their sophomore years. It should also be noted that students in service-learning were much more likely to become involved in service immersion trips during their freshman year and that this difference (of 20%) was sustained during the sophomore year, so that nearly twice as many SL as non-SL students participated in such trips. It is very likely that students participating in freshman service-learning experienced the benefits of service (and probably even service-immersion trips) during high school. This study does not conclude that the freshman service-learning experience directly influenced participation in immersion trips; however, the sustained difference is worth noting.

Service-learning seemed to serve as a catalyst for activism-advocacy, increasing participation in the sophomore year for the service-learning group (while no such increase was obtained for its counterpart). This represented a desired effect for this university's particular brand of service-learning, which was rooted in a commitment to social justice demanded by faith, a hallmark which appears in the mission statement of Jesuit universities. This also was an anticipated goal of service-learning programs rooted in the civic engagement model (Watson, 2004). Reflections on solidarity and justice, which were common in all service-learning courses across the curriculum, apparently stimulated an interest in activism and advocacy by the sophomore year. It may be that such an interest will awaken for non-SL members later in their undergraduate careers.

Also worth noting is that students who took part in SL as freshman were significantly more likely to continue participating in faith-based retreats after their freshman year. The impact of service-learning on participation in faith-based retreats seemed to have an insulating effect on the well-established tendency for college students to lose interest in faith-related activities over the course of their four-year experience (Feldman, 1969). It may be that SL students developed a desire for continued structured reflection in their freshman year, which was not readily available in traditional classes, or through much of the undergraduate college experience. Such retreats may represent a means of further exploring issues and realities introduced through their freshman SL experience.

Retreats, such as service immersions and activism-advocacy activities, involve significantly larger commitments of time and energy than church service attendance or one-time service events. It may be that the impact of service-learning somehow ties to a deeper commitment to faith (or spiritual seeking) and to service that is reflected only in measures of more sustained engagement. Differences in academic engagement and other social activities on campus were nonexistent or idiosyncratic, and so will not be further discussed here.

LIMITATIONS OF THE STUDY

Limitations common to service-learning research were considered in the design of this study and attempts were made to minimize their impact on findings. Measures in the study were obtained from seminal sources on service-learning research (Bringle et al., 2004) and based on nationally renowned developmental psychology studies such as the NICHD Study of Early Child Care (2000). By replicating the methods used previously, methodological weaknesses were kept to a minimum with regard to experimenter error in interview technique and coding.

However, some weaknesses remained in the experimental design. Self-selection of students into courses forced the study into employment of a quasi-experimental design. This situation also led to inequalities in cell sizes based on student enrollment.

Another limitation was the self-report nature of participants' attitudes and their involvement in activities. Though a standardized interview is completed to collect data on behavior and hours, participants can make errors and over- or underreport activities. This can be amended in future study for some academic variables by corroborating information with the registrar's office, pending student consent.

Scales and Activity Measures

The Civic Attitudes scale in particular lacked the internal consistency to measure a single domain. Its internal consistency was well below an accepted minimum. Lacking from the remaining attitudinal scales was the sensitivity to document change in students over time.

Mortality Effect and Cell Sizes

Attrition also may have affected the outcomes of this study. Of the 275 participants surveyed at baseline, 42 of them either did not attend the university or transferred prior to spring break. This 15% attrition rate occurred prior to the end-of-freshman-year data collection and may have affected the results of the study based on which participants withdrew. It is possible that, were withdrawn students retained at the university and as participants in this study, their inclusion would have yielded different results. The study also would have been strengthened by increased statistical power that would come with a larger sample size. This attrition rate leveled off slightly over the remainder of the two year period but should be studied specifically to determine if SL has a protective effect on retention rates.

Directions for Future Research

This chapter presents a summary of Phase I findings from a 4-year study. Data represent changes which occurred during the first 2 years of an undergraduate college career. Since students' attitudes and behaviors will continue to vary over time, variables will be analyzed in Phase II at the junior and senior time points using the same method. Additional relevant variables also emerged during the course of Phase I and will be considered during Phase II. These include retention, academic achievement, leadership activity and negative behavior.

Retention. Based on the high attrition rate at baseline, a study of the retention rates of students will be included in future research. By using registrar records, university retention rates can be examined between students who have and have not undertaken service-learning coursework and to determine if participation in service-learning decreases the likelihood that a student will withdraw from the university.

Academic achievement. With the inclusion of a new consent form, participants' academic records, including grade point average and course roster, will be made available to assess the impact of service-learning classes on academic achievement. Also, assessment of the number and timing of students inducted into academic honors societies will be obtained through public university records.

Leadership activities. Beginning in the sophomore year interview (Time 3), data were obtained documenting participants' leadership activities within their work and student groups. Levels of leadership were coded to distinguish between participation as a member, a middle-level leader and an executive-level leader and can be used to track the timing and degree of leadership roles students achieve over time and potentially as a result of service-learning involvement.

Negative behaviors. With the inclusion of an additional consent, participants will have the option to release their residence life and campus security records, allowing for assessment of negative behaviors. These would include alcohol and drug incidents as well as citations by residence life or by campus security.

Additional assessment techniques. The analyses included in this study do not explore the possible role of intervening variables on the outcome variables. The strength of a longitudinal model which includes five measurement points is that it allows for multiple forms of analyses including pre-post and time series methods and the inclusion of mediator or moderator variables. These will be conducted after 4 years of data have been collected. Additionally, regression analyses will be employed to determine the degree to which service-learning alone or in combination with other variables can predict both positive and negative attitudes and behaviors in college students. Finally, growth curve models will be used to construct models which account for variation in academic, attitudinal and behavioral outcomes.

Changes to the sample composition. While the design of this study will stay constant, the cell sizes employed in analyses will constantly evolve. One of the peculiarities of the service-learning program at this university was that there were very few options for service-learning available during the sophomore year. More students will become part of the SL group as they complete courses over their junior and senior years. In addition, the levels of the independent variable will become more sensitive. As students take more SL classes, SL vs. non-SL comparisons will become more balanced and cells containing those completing one, two, three, four and more SL courses will become more populous. Comparisons of students who took one or two SL courses versus those who pursued a concentration in SL will become available, as will comparisons of students who took two semesters of SL as freshmen vs. those who did so as upperclassmen.

CONCLUSION

The implications of the midpoint findings of the SLATE study are two fold. First, empirical evidence supports the belief that including SL in freshman programming promotes positive and significant outcomes (Furco, 2002; Vogelgesang et al., 2002). Second, evidence also supports the notion that a well constructed and implemented SL program can achieve outcomes associated with multiple service paradigms (Morton, 1995). A relationship-based SL program with a focus on social analysis can spur students to engage in additional service in the context of the "charity" paradigm but can simultaneously cue students to pursue the "social change" paradigm. Where Morton argues that SL programs aim to advance from thick to thin versions of a single paradigm, outcomes from the SLATE study suggest that paradigms are not orthogonal; one SL program may contain elements and achieve outcomes of more than one typology.

Two years into the study of Service-Learning as a Transformative Experience (SLATE), significant findings have already begun to emerge regarding students' faith orientations, their commitment to service and justice, and their participation in structured reflection/faith-based retreats. Many nonsignificant trends have also begun to take shape. It remains to be seen whether students will continue to develop along this trajectory, or if these are temporary changes which disappear over a four-year career. With future assessments at two additional time points, the SLATE study intends to provide service-learning professionals with insight as to what outcomes can be expected to emerge immediately, which ones emerge slowly over time and which ones fade as students proceed towards graduation and beyond.

REFERENCES

Astin, A. W., & Sax, L. J. (1998). How Undergraduates are Affected by Service Participation. *Journal of College Student Development, 39*(3), 251-263.

Astin, A., Vogelgesang, L., Ikeda, E., & Yee, J. (2000). *How service-learning affects students.* Los Angeles: University of California, Higher Education Research Institute.

Allport, G. W., & Ross, J. M. (1967). Personal religious orientation and prejudice. *Journal of Personality and Social Psychology, 5*, 432-443.

Batson, C. D., & Schoenrade, P. A. (1991). Measuring religion as question: I. Validity concerns. *Journal for the Scientific Study of Religion, 30*, 416-429.

Batson, C. D., & Ventnis. W. L. (1982). *The religious experience: A social-psychological perspective.* New York: Oxford University Press.

Bringle, R. G., Phillips, M. A., & Hudson, M. (Eds.). (2004). Critical thinking. In *The measure of service-learning; Research scales to assess student experiences* (pp. 201-213). Washington, DC: American Psychological Association.

D'Agostin,o R. B. (1971). A second look at analysis of variance on dichotomous data. *Journal of Educational Measurement, 8*(4), 327-333.

Densmore, K. (2000). Service-learning and multicultural education: Suspect or transformative? In C. R. O'Grady (Ed.), *Integrating service-learning and multicultural education in colleges and universities* (pp. 45-58). Mahwah, NJ: Erlbaum.

Erickson, J. A., & O'Connor, S. E. (2000). Service-learning: Does it promote or reduce prejudice? In C. R. O'Grady (Ed.), *Integrating service-learning and multicultural education in colleges and universities* (pp. 59-70). Mahwah, NJ: Erlbaum.

Estanek, S. M., & Love, P. G. (2003-2004). Critical thinking and seamless learning: A post-modern approach. *Inquiry: Critical Thinking Across the Disciplines, 23*(1-2), 63-68.

Eyler, J,. & Giles, D. E. (1997). The importance of program quality in service-learning. In A. S. Waterman (Ed.), *Service-learning: Applications from the research* (pp. 57-76). Mahwah, NJ: Erlbaum.

Eyler, J., Giles, D. E., Stenson, C. M., & Gray, C. J. (2001). *At a glance: What we know about the effects of service-learning on college students, faculty, institutions and communities, 1993-2000* (3rd ed.). Washington, DC: Corporation for National Service.

Feldman, K. A. (1969). Change and stability of religious orientations during college. *The Review of Religious Research, 11*, 40-60.

Furco, A. (2002). High school service-learning and the preparation of students for college. In E. Zlotkowski (Ed.), *Service-learning and the first year experience: preparing students for personal success and civic responsibility* (pp. 15-26). Columbia: University of South Carolina, National Resource Center for the First-Year Experience and Students in Transition.

Giles, D. E., & Eyler, J. (1998, Spring). A service-learning research agenda for the next five years. *New Directions for Teaching & Learning, 73*, 65-72.

Hoge, D. (1972). A validated intrinsic religious motivation scale. *Journal for the Scientific Study of Religion, 11*, 369-376.

Lipkus, I. (1991). The construction and preliminary validation of a Global Belief in a Just World Scale and the exploratory analysis of the Multidimensional Belief in a Just World Scale. *Personality and Individual Differences, 12*, 1171-1178.

Lunney, G. H. (1970). Using analysis of variance with a dichotomous dependent variable: An empirical study. *Journal of Educational Measurement, 7*(4), 263-269.

Mabry, J. B. (1995). Pedagogical variations in service-learning and student outcomes: How time, contact, and reflection matter. *Michigan Journal of Community Service Learning, 5*, 32-47.

McKenna, M. W., & Rizzo, E. (1999). Student perceptions of the learning in service-learning courses. *Journal of Prevention and Intervention in the Community, 18*(1-2), 111-123.

Morton, K. (1995). The irony of service: Charity, project, and social change in service-learning. *Michigan Journal of Community Service Learning, 2*, 19-32.

Pratto, F., Sidanius, J., Stallworth, L. M., & Malle, B. F. (1994). Social dominance orientation: A personality variable predicting social and political attitudes. *Journal of Personality and Social Psychology, 67*, 741-763.

Raman P., & Pashupati, K. (2002). Turning good citizens into even better ones: The impact of program characteristics and motivations on service-learning outcomes. *Journal of Nonprofit & Public Sector Marketing, 10*(2), 187-206.

Roschelle, A. R., Turpin, J., & Elias, R. (2000). Who learns from service-learning? *American Behavioral Scientist, 43*(5), 839-847.

Rosenberger, C. (2000). Beyond empathy: Developing critical consciousness through service-learning. In C. R. O'Grady (Ed.), *Integrating service-learning and multicultural education in colleges and universities* (pp. 23-43). Mahwah, NJ: Erlbaum.

Study of Early Child Care. (2000). After School Time Use Child Interview. Phase III Manuals (chap. 50). National Institute of Child Health & Human Development. Retrieved October 2, 2004, from http://secc.rti.org/display.cfm?t =m&i=Chapter_50

Titlebaum, P., Williamson, G., Daprano, C., Baer, J., & Brahler, J. (2004). *Annotated history of service-learning, 1862-2002.* Retrieved September 22, 2006, from http://servicelearning.org/filemanager/download/142/ SL%20Comp%20Timeline%203-15-04_rev.pdf

Vogelgesang, L. J., Ikeda, E. K., Gilmartin, S. K., & Keup, J. R. (2002). Service-learning and the first year experience: Outcomes related to learning and persistence. In E. Zlotkowski (Ed.) *Service-learning and the first year experience: preparing students for personal success and civic responsibility* (pp. 15-26). Columbia: University of South Carolina, National Resource Center for the First-Year Experience and Students in Transition.

Watson, J. B. (2004). A justification of the civic engagement model. In B. W. Speck & S. L. Hoppe (Eds), *Service learning: history, theory and issues* (pp. 73-83). Westport, CT: Praeger.

Weitzman, E. R., & Chen, Y. Y. (2005). Risk modifying effect of social capital on measures of heavy alcohol consumption, alcohol abuse, harm, and second-hand effects: National survey finding. *Journal of Epidemiology and Community Health, 59*(4), 303-309.

Wideman, R. E. (2005). Empathy development in undergraduate students through the cross-cultural learning experience. *Dissertation Abstracts International Section A: Humanities and Social Sciences, 66* (2-A), 494.

Wilson, L. B., & Rymph, D. B. (2006). Research issues in civic engagement: Outcomes of a national agenda-setting meeting. In L. B. Wilson & S. P. Simon (Eds.), *Practice perspectives* (pp. 195-210). New York: Hawthorne.

CHAPTER 7

SERVICE-LEARNING AND LITERACY MOTIVATION

Setting a Research Agenda

Steven Hart

ABSTRACT

Literacy achievement is at the core in the current era of accountability in K-12 schools. Literacy achievement is more likely to occur when students are engaged with content and school, and service-learning has been found to be a promising strategy for increasing student engagement. This study explored the ways in which service-learning influenced middle school students to become more engaged in literacy and more motivated to learn. The dynamic interaction between student voice, perceived relevance of the service experience and students' personal funds of knowledge that was prompted by participating in an environmental service-learning project led the students to become more motivated to learn in their regular classrooms. This research suggests multiple ways to advance the research agenda investigating the relationship between service-learning and academic outcomes.

From Passion to Objectivity: International and Cross-Disciplinary Perspectives on Service Learning Research, pp. 135–156
Copyright © 2007 by Information Age Publishing
All rights of reproduction in any form reserved.

INTRODUCTION

Service-learning is broadly defined as a teaching and learning approach that integrates classroom instruction with community service. While studies have shown that service-learning has been implemented in approximately one third of K-12 public schools in the United States, its prevalence has not changed much over the past decade (Berman, 2000; Education Commission of the States, 2001; Kielsmeier, Scales, Roehlkepartain, & Neal, 2004; Skinner & Chapman, 1999). Despite this consistent support for service-learning, these studies illustrate that a majority of students are not provided opportunities to participate in service-learning experiences.

A possible explanation for this limited implementation may be the lack of knowledge of the multiple benefits resulting from service-learning practices. In two comprehensive national studies, the most frequently reported reasons for using service-learning focused on relationships among students, the school, and the community, while student academic achievement was one of the least cited reasons (Kielsmeier et al., 2004; Skinner & Chapman, 1999). These findings suggest that service-learning is most often implemented as a tool to involve youth in the community (Carnegie Corporation & CIRCLE, 2003). If service-learning is to continue to expand in this era of accountability, the field must establish that service-learning is a pedagogical approach that may lead to increased learning.

The purposes of this research are to investigate how various service-learning components and practices impact students' motivation to engage with literacy and to further the examination of service-learning as an approach to literacy education. To gain a deeper understanding of how service-learning contexts impact students' literacy engagement, youth coresearchers assisted with the implementation of this research. Researchers have begun to engage young people, as research partners to better understand youth and the contexts that impact their development (Fredericks, Kaplan, & Zeisler, 2001; Justinianno, Scherer, Johnson, Lewis, Swanson, & Felix, 2001). This study involved youth coresearchers to empower them to validate knowledge about literacy motivation and influence service-learning programs that impact their lives.

First, the literature on the relationship between service-learning and literacy is reviewed. Then the research conducted with a middle school service-learning community is described, and the results are reported through a model of service-learning literacy engagement. The results of this study are then used to provide suggestions for the next steps in the service-learning research agenda addressing academic outcomes.

LITERACY MOTIVATION AND ACHIEVEMENT

Numerous studies have established strong correlations between student achievement and student engagement (National Research Council, 2004; Steinberg, 1996; Stipek, 2002). Since the National Reading Panel report (2000) on literacy development, the roles of motivation and engagement as links between instruction and achievement have been well documented by literacy researchers (Fredricks, Blumenfeld, & Paris, 2004; Guthrie, 2004). Four aspects of instruction have been found to be especially effective in promoting literacy learning: student collaboration, instruction that features real world connections, mastery goal orientation, and student autonomy.

Collaboration

Multiple researchers have found that collaborative literacy events lead to higher student engagement and higher levels of reading achievement (Baker & Wigfield, 1999; Stevens & Slavin, 1995; Sweet, Guthrie, & Ng, 1998; Wigfield & Guthrie, 1997). Collaborative activities allow peers to facilitate understanding of material through discussion and modeling. Working together in groups increases students' sense of belonging, self-efficacy and intrinsic motivation to participate. In turn, students are more motivated to use complex cognitive strategies (Wigfield & Guthrie, 1997).

Real World Connections

In addition, literacy events connected to real world interactions have been shown to lead to better comprehension (Guthrie, Anderson, Alao, & Rinehart, 1999; Moje, Young, Readence, & Moore, 2000). Sensory experiences evoke intrinsically motivated behaviors; students are curious and interested to engage with the content. This active engagement allows students to encounter abstract concepts as concrete experiences and leads to increased understanding (Guthrie et al., 1999).

Mastery Goal Orientation

Research also has indicated that a mastery goal orientation is associated with positive achievement patterns (Anderman, Maehr, & Midgley, 1999; Harackiewicz, Barron, Tauer, Carter, & Elliot, 2000). As contrasted with a performance goal orientation where there is a concern for completing tasks and outperforming others, a mastery goal orientation places value on making meaning and building knowledge. When mastery goals are established students are more engaged and comprehension is increased (Grolnick & Ryan, 1987; Roesser, Midgley, & Urdan, 1996; Wigfield, Eccles, & Rodriguez, 1998).

Student Autonomy

Student autonomy has also been linked to motivation to learn and literacy achievement. Autonomy is the degree to which students perceive control over educational goals and learning experiences. When students feel they have choice and control in the decisions regarding reading tasks and materials, they exhibit higher levels of engagement and increased comprehension (Ryan & Deci, 2000; Skinner, Wellborn, & Connell, 1990; Sweet et al., 1998).

The Promise of Service-Learning

Service-learning represents a promising approach for increasing student motivation to learn and literacy achievement because it encompasses the five components of instruction shown to be linked to literacy motivation and achievement. The promise of service-learning has been documented in several studies. For example, service-learning pedagogy has been shown to motivate students to engage in school practices in general (Loesch-Griffin, Petrides, & Pratt, 1995; Melchior, 1999; Melchior & Bailis, 2002), and with literacy practices in particular (Billig & Klute, 2003; Klute & Billig, 2002). In each of these studies, the researchers reported that the content and the quality of the experiences moderated the impact of service-learning. These and other studies (e.g., Billig, Root & Jesse, 2005) typically specify quality as including collaboration, real world connections, mastery goal orientation, and student autonomy as being among those factors associated with more positive outcomes.

For example, the linkage between academic content and real world application has been closely associated with higher levels of student engagement in many studies (Ammon, Furco, Chi, & Middaugh, 2001; Billig & Klute, 2003; Billig, Meyer, & Hofschire, 2003; Klute & Billig, 2002). Service-learning provides students opportunities to identify and change issues that directly impact their lives and give meaning to academic content. Students are more engaged and motivated to learn when the communities where they live serve as a source of learning and action (Billig et al., 2003).

Service-learning is premised on a bidirectional reciprocal relationship, where students share the decision-making process with teachers and community members (Howard, 1998). These collaborative experiences provide students opportunities to develop their interpersonal skills as they learn from and with peers and other adults (Morgan & Streb, 1999; Weiler, LaGoy, Crane, & Rovner, 1998). Ammon et al. (2001) found that collaborative reflection activities were correlated with higher academic impacts. In addition to supporting learning, collaboration has been found to also serve as a catalyst for engagement (Billig et al., 2003; Loesch-Griffin et al., 1995). As students work with others, the collaborative relationships create a sense of belonging and students are motivated by the value the feel from their peers and other adults.

By definition, service-learning is centered on learning goals (National Commission on Service-Learning, 2002). Students are guided by the goal to master content knowledge in order to provide the services needed in the community. Competition to outperform others is replaced by a commitment to accomplishing a shared goal in the community. This focus on learning goals can be linked to evidence that students engaged in service-learning showed increases in measures of self-efficacy and educational competence (Shaffer, 1993; Switzer, Simmons, Dew, Regalski, & Wang, 1995; Weiler et al., 1998).

Student autonomy and voice is an essential component in planning and implementing service projects and has been found to increase student motivation and achievement (Billig, 2000; Morgan & Streb, 2001). Service-learning transforms the roles of *student* and *teacher*. Students and teachers share in the decision-making process. As students take a more active role in directing their learning process, they experience increases in self-esteem, efficacy, and competence, which increases their levels of engagement (Morgan & Streb, 2001).

This literature review shows that, while there are multiple studies to suggest that service-learning has substantial promise for increasing literacy motivation and achievement, no studies as yet have specifically investigated the separate and combined influence of the four service-learning components of collaboration, real world connection, mastery goal orientation, and student autonomy on literacy motivation and achievement. To examine the extent to which service-learning is an appropriate catalyst for literacy motivation, this research explored the particular ways a middle school service-learning community used, valued, and engaged with various literate practices.

RESEARCH DESIGN

The research questions posed by this study were: (a) What literacy practices do students perform in a service-learning community?; and (b) What factors impact students' levels of engagement with various literacy practices?

Site Description

This study took place at Clara Frye Middle School, located in a working class/poor, racially and ethnically diverse urban neighborhood in the southeastern United States. Approximately 50% of the students attending the school are from the local neighborhood. The rest of the student body is bussed to the school from demographically diverse neighborhoods spread throughout the school district's boundaries. The 1,100 students who attended the school represented almost equal numbers of students from European American, African American, and Latino/a backgrounds, and 62% of the students qualified for the free or reduced price lunch program.

The Environmental Explorers Club was the subject of investigation for this study. As a service-learning organization, the Explorers Club utilized schoolwide science curriculum content to address the environmental issues of their local river. The following sections describe the activities of the club as they relate to service-learning: preparation, service implementation, structured reflection, and celebration or recognition of accomplishments and demonstration of results (Howard, 1998; Morgan & Streb, 2001).

Preparation

First, the students analyzed the ecosystem of the section of the river behind their school. Students conducted tests to gather data on the water quality of the river. Additionally, members digitally photographed the vegetation growing along the banks of the river and used field guides and Internet resources to identify the various plants, flowers, grasses and trees to determine if they were native or invasive. Students concluded that the amount of trash and the large numbers of invasive species could be leading to the poor conditions of the river. During afterschool meetings, members met to analyze the data they had collected and share thoughts about potential projects and activities to address the conditions of the river.

In preparation for their service experiences, the Explorers club visited the state aquarium and a regional state preserve. These trips, organized and supervised by the science teachers, allowed students to connect with experts to support and affirm their data discoveries. These field trips also exposed the Explorers club students to knowledge and first-hand experiences regarding the efforts experts were taking to conserve and preserve natural environments.

Service Implementation

To address these environmental conditions, the students organized a river reclamation project. This project involved several separate activities. First, these students organized a river clean-up as a way to relieve the ecosystem of the trash and waste that polluted the river and its banks. Students created posters to hang around the school, called and wrote letters to the mayor and other city officials, and contacted various news media sources as ways to promote their cause and attract volunteers. In addition to the river clean-up, the students also organized a restoration event. The students worked with a local wildlife conservation institute, peers, and family members to replant native grasses along the banks of the river as a way to restore native vegetation and increase the oxygen levels in the river.

Structured Reflection

During club meetings, the two supervising teachers led discussions about the work the students were doing to preserve the aquatic environment around the school. In addition, students also reflected through peer led discussions about their accomplishments. It was during these reflective discussions that members expressed concern that their efforts alone would not significantly impact the conditions of the river ecosystem, so they decided that teaching younger students about the importance of environmental activism would prompt future generations of concerned youth to continue the work that they were beginning. The groups used their work as a model as they explained their discoveries about the conditions of the river and showed local elementary students how they, too, could help the environment. The Explorers club students created activity packets about aquatic environmentalism and conducted field-based ecotours around the river with local elementary students. During these ecotours, club members taught the elementary students how to conduct water and soil tests. They also constructed a field guide from their digital photographs to use as a scavenger hunt to teach the younger students about the flora and fauna native to the river ecosystem.

Celebration and Demonstration of Results

As a way to reinforce the students' recognition of their efforts and accomplishments, the Explorers club students celebrated their service-learning experiences by sharing their work at regional and state summits with other youth. During the regional summit, students provided a brief oral description of their efforts to address the environmental issues of their local river. Modeling their work with the elementary students, the students led visiting schools on an ecotour of the aquatic areas around the park where the summit was held. At the state summit the Explorers club students constructed a PowerPoint presentation detailing their analysis and restoration of the river and performed a "Scooby-Doo River Pollution Mystery" skit they had written as a way to increase awareness of the importance of river ecosystems. Following their performances, the students went before a panel of environmental scientists to support their findings and their service to the community.

Study Sample

Purposive sampling was used to select eleven students from the larger Explorers community to become case study coresearchers. Involving youth as coresearchers was an important design of the study, allowing for the students to feel empowered in examining the Explorers Club and understanding how the program impacted their development. As described below in the sections on data collection and analysis, the adolescent members of this service-learning community were vital collaborators in this research. The students were the knowledgeable experts regarding specific literacy practices constructed within this service-learning community, and in turn supported the researcher's novice understanding of the motivation for their engagement with particular literacy practices.

After analyzing the field notes, focus group interviews, and visual data from the first two observations of the Explorers Club, the 11 students were selected based on differences they exhibited in their levels of participation in the service-learning contexts, their levels of interactions with peers, and their uses of various literacy practices in the service-learning contexts. The students were also selected to represent the demographics of the entire Explorers club: 6 girls, 5 boys; 1 African America, 1 Asian American, 4 Latino/a, 5 European American; 3 sixth grade, 3 seventh grade, 5 eighth grade.

Data Collection and Analysis

The lead researcher and the youth coresearchers used journals to collect field notes and cameras to collect visual data across a variety of contexts in which the Explorers students worked (e. g., field sites, classrooms, afterschool meetings). In addition, the lead researcher conducted student interviews and focus groups, teacher interviews, and family interviews. All interviews were semistructured (Patton, 2002), audio-recorded, and transcribed.

The field notes and visual data documented the relationships between literacy events and observable levels of engagement. During the interviews, these data sources served as a catalyst for discussion, as the researcher and youth coresearchers collaboratively interrogated each other's observations and interpretations. The sharing of insider/outsider perspectives provided data triangulation and served as a member check to counter the bias of an individual perspective. For example, to corroborate evidence, the coresearchers might have a dialogue like this: "Last time we met we talked about the ways you used digital photography to make the identification booklet and how you all liked that activity. Did I miss anything?" or, " I recorded that you were very into the PowerPoint, but you disagree. Why is that?"

Analytic procedures of event mapping (Tuyay, Floriani, Yeager, Dixon, & Green, 1995) and critical discourse analysis (CDA) (Chouliaraki, & Fairclough, 1999; Gee, 1999) were combined to understand the literacy practices, as well as the values and dispositions driving the practices of the Explorers service-learning community.

Event mapping was conducted in several stages. The initial coding scheme consisted of analyzing data for three domains: the nature of the interaction (who and what roles), the nature of the text (form and use), and the nature of the context (where did the event occur). Once a particular practice was observed, analysis proceeded to move backwards and forwards through the data to identify other contexts in which similar interactions and similar texts were found. This phase of the analysis uncovered patterns of literacy practices that were grouped into larger categories. These broader categories became themes that described the observable textual practices employed within the Explorers service-learning community.

Critical discourse analysis was used to understand the purposes and motivations of these observable literacy practices. Transcripts were examined to determine the patterns of talk and the potential dispositions these languages were attempting to represent. The researcher looked at the patterns across contextual domains that emerged from each individual student and then conducted a cross-case analysis of these patterns across all of the youth coresearchers. This analysis yielded common themes of literate dispositions associated with the service-learning contexts. The combined analysis of discourse construction and event mapping accounted for both the observable literacy practices and the driving ideological motivation for enacting particular practices. Layering the analysis of the observable practices and the values, beliefs, and intentions behind those practices enabled the researcher to locate patterns in students' levels of engagement that correlated with various literacy practices.

Analysis of any group of people of which one is not a member raises concerns, especially regarding representations of young people (Moje et al., 2000). The youth coresearchers played an active role in the analysis of the data throughout the course of this investigation, and they assisted in the final stage of analysis. Initial case study drafts were shared with the respective individual students for their critique and perspective. In addition, teachers and students were provided with the preliminary cross-case analysis to substantiate the interpretations. The following sections focus on the themes that emerged from these analytic procedures.

RESULTS

A variety of literate events were constructed throughout the contexts of the Explorers service-learning community. Members of the club engaged in some of these events and disengaged from others. Tracing the patterns by which students chose to engage or disengage illustrated the dimensions of engagement.

Service Relevance

The dimension of service relevance is the degree to which the students' perceived that the literate events were connected to the service projects. Students engaged more deeply with literacy practices that were perceived to hold strong connections to the service experiences. For example, Veronica [all names are youth-selected pseudonyms] often reported that she detested reading, yet she engaged in reading over the flora identification book for the ecotours many times. She explained the motivation for her engagement in the following way:

> The ecotour book I read so I knew what I was doing at the [summit] thing. You needed to know that for the tours.

For Veronica, reading was not a motivating activity in general. However, the purpose of the reading was directly linked to the service project, and this led to her motivation to read and understand the identification booklets.

Javier reported that he was initially disengaged from the construction of the texts for the ecotours. However, like Veronica, he pursued the construction of the activity packets because he believed they would be valuable learning tools for the younger students.

> The ecotours were fun for me. At first, it was like doing the books, I was like, "Oh man. This is silly. " They took a lot of time to make. But, I figured they would work out well with the kids, though, and they did. They were really into them.

In contrast to the examples above, if the students did not perceive the literacy events to be meaningfully connected to the service-learning projects, they disengaged. An example of this process was demonstrated during a visit to a regional preserve where students conducted water tests at the springs that fed the river in order to draw a comparison to the section of the river at their school site. Students worked in small groups to read directions, conduct water tests, and record data on a worksheet. During this time, the students were actively engaged in reading directions, asking for assistance with technical terms, and supporting data recording on the worksheet. Time constraints caused the students to express concern at not having completed all of the tests. The preserve guide told the students that she had already collected all of the data and would provide it to them. Upon hearing this, all of the students moved away from the activity and expressed boredom with the use of worksheets. Veronica voiced the group's frustration.

> I got to miss worksheets in class, but now we have to do this worksheet out here. Well, if we don't finish it, oh well.

The students were actively engaged in completing the worksheet when the testing held purpose for their service project. The purpose of this new activity structure no longer held relevance to the students' broader service-learning projects. They were just simply completing blanks on a worksheet. Thus, the use of these literacy tools to learn about water testing and water quality for this portion of the river lacked meaning, and the students disengaged from the activity.

Students' Knowledge

The dimension of students' knowledge is the degree to which the students perceived that the literacy event drew upon their personal funds of knowledge. Students engaged more deeply with literate events that built on their personal interests, experiences, and expertise.

The group members were familiar with each other's interests and expertise, and thus they were able to call on certain members to lead certain events. Students' personal interests were represented in both the content and textual forms of literacy practices. Amanda described the ways in which the value placed on expertise guided the daily events of the Explorers club.

> Well, we had a whole lot of things to do, we had people just, like he's [Samuel] really good at science and math, so we gave him the water testing stuff, and he wanted to do it. Then me and her [Joaninha] are writing letters to the mayor because we're just good writers I guess. Then we just kinda split up the work, so that like everybody does the same thing, but one person is in charge of each major section.

Franklin was an avid user of computers in his personal world, and he was often called on to lead events that involved technology, such as Power-Point and video editing. Nikiha was given the task of identifying the flora for the ecotour books because it matched her personal interests with plants. She explained,

> Well, I, this is just my perception. But it's because I'm around a lot of plants a lot because I do, I have woods in my backyard and I go back there and gather herbs and stuff. And I ended up doing the project because Joaninha came up to me and said, "Hey you know a lot about plants, right?" I said, "Yeah, I guess, a fair amount. " Then I was leading that part of it.

The Explorers club literacy practices utilized a variety of textual forms associated with the students' personal lives, such as video, digital photography, skits, books, magazines, and Internet Web pages. In this service-learning context, students' personal literate practices were infused with traditional academic practices to create more engaging events. For example, Tammy viewed the skit for the youth symposium as more engaging from plays she experienced in the classroom.

> You would sometimes do a play in the classes, but most of the stuff didn't involve acting in the classes. The Language Arts one [play] had to do with just reading it. The Scooby-Doo one [symposium skit] had to do with the environment and was more fun.

For Tammy, the skit was more engaging than it would have been in the classroom because it was infused with her personal literacy practices that involved television and cartoon genres.

Similarly, the PowerPoint presentation for the youth symposium was another example of the ways in which combining school literacy practices with personal literacy interests created a unique and engaging literacy event. Veronica explained her engagement with the slide show as such:

> Well, it's not really reading. It's different. It wasn't schoolwork stuff. It was just a little bit of writing to go with the pictures. It wasn't like reading a whole book or anything.

Veronica's level of participation resembled the ways she engaged with similar textual forms in her personal sphere. Veronica was fascinated with visual imagery, drawings, photos, and natural scenery. Most of her engagement with literacy practices outside of school involved some form of textual images.

Student Voice

The dimension of student voice is the degree to which the students perceived they had control over the literacy events. Students' levels of engagement were influenced by their sense of empowerment. The more students believed they were afforded opportunities to be decision makers regarding the literacy events, the more they engaged.

The student-directed nature of the Explorers club provided the conditions for students to feel empowered. Both Amanda and Nikiha reported that the supervising teacher let them run their own meetings. Amanda elaborated:

> We just tell him, "Mr. Vernon, we need you to talk to this person," or, "Did you get this or that?" He kinda supervises. He really doesn't run the meetings. He lets us be independent, which is good.

This sense of empowerment motivated students to take the initiative to adapt the design of literate events for particular service projects. Amanda explained that they constructed certain activities because:

> Everyone knows you don't want to go and listen to someone talk on and on and on about the ecosystem, so we try to make it fun.

Joaninha added:

> We have to make it educational, and make it fun and cool, so they don't go, "Oh my gosh. Water, plants, who cares?"

As a result, the Explorers club students constructed an identification booklet, packets of word puzzles about the environment, and designed physical movement activities about water conservation to match the ages of their different audiences.

However, students disengaged from literate events when they believed that teachers restricted their independence. For example, students were disengaged when supervising teachers led club meetings with lectures or distributed handouts for the students to follow as they were read aloud. Malibu described her lack of engagement with such types of literate practices:

> Sometimes it's cool to learn the stuff, and then sometimes it's just like boring. You just sit there and listen to the teacher talk and talk and talk.

Malibu's comments illustrated how such literate events solely designed by the teacher can lead to disengagement.

Another example of how students disengaged when their autonomy was restricted occurred during the regional youth summit. The students constructed flora and fauna identification booklets to use as field guides during their ecotours. At the summit, a service-learning teacher reorganized the activity, changing the students' initial plans. During the tours, the students were visibly unhappy, walked one group on the tour and then explored the paths on their own. Nikiha explained the group's disengagement:

> We do all of the planning and most of the work putting these ideas together, and then she [Ms. O'Reilly] comes in at the last minute and starts taking over and controlling how things are going to work.

Nikiha's comments provided insight into how the sense of empowerment influenced engagement in the Explorers community. Initially, the students were empowered and engaged in constructing the field guide to lead the ecotours. However, the teacher's changes to the design of the literate event removed students' voices from the shape of the literate practice, and the students disengaged.

In addition to the student-centered structure of the Explorers club, students' shared leadership roles also enabled students to feel empowered. As described in the previous section, individual members of the Explorers club were called on to be in charge of particular tasks. The empowerment gained from these leadership roles was accompanied by the responsibility to be accountable to the entire club and worked to promote student engagement in these literacy practices. For example, Javier gathered information on his own free time after school and during the weekends and reported that his motivation for engaging with the literate practices to this extent was for his friends in the club and to make sure the projects were completed. Likewise, Veronica reported that she spent extra time engaged in working on the PowerPoint project because:

> I took the pictures, so some of the others didn't know what they were of or where I took them. So, I helped match them with the words on the slide to make it right.

Although students were positioned as leaders, the roles of leadership were not always equally shared and led to students' disengagement. Joaninha noted this lack of participation regarding the construction of various literate products for the ecotours.

> I did like half of the work ... I would like give them [other members] stuff. Like I would tell them, "OK, now do this, and I need it by like the next day," and they wouldn't have it.

Joaninha attributed the members' low participation to their lack of desire to be involved. However, Veronica provided a different perspective as she explained her view for the lack of participation.

> I mean mainly it was Joaninha and a few others that did everything. We [the rest of the members] really didn't know what was going on most of the time. They just told us to show up for meetings and we did. They did a lot of the work or just told us what to do.... Everyone should be involved. Like I said, a lot of us didn't know what was going on.

Veronica attributes the lack of participation to not feeling involved. As Veronica noted, the older students made the decisions and then delegated the work to the younger students. This positioning did not include much power to contribute equally to the construction of the literate products or share in the decision-making process.

DISCUSSION

The Service-Learning Model of Literacy Engagement (Exhibit 7.1) illustrates the three dimensions that interacted within the Explorers club: service relevance, students' knowledge, and student voice. The three dimensions are interconnected to emphasize that each did not exist in isolation and was influenced by the others. As the following discussion will demonstrate, each dimension was necessary but not independently sufficient in order for the Explorers members to find the literacy event engaging. Although the dimensions are interdependent, each dimension is presented individually to highlight its unique structure as it contributed to the process of literate engagement in the Explorers service-learning community.

The service-learning literacy engagement model that emerged from this study validates previous research that has shown that factors associated with student engagement are evident in service-learning practice. This model extends the current research to illustrate how these factors can influence student literacy engagement. Understanding these influences may allow practitioners to capitalize on these factors to create a more effective learning environment, increasing the potential to impact student academic achievement.

The dimension of *service relevance* demonstrates how the service project connected students to real-world uses of literacy and served as the purpose for motivation. Student engagement increased when the literacy practices were connected to the real-world service experiences. This link between academics and community can be seen as a key influence in motivating students to increase their cognitive commitment to understanding

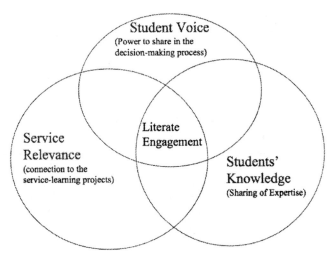

Exhibit 7.1.   Service-learning model of literacy engagement.

content (Billig & Klute, 2003; Billig et al., 2003; Klute & Billig, 2002). Likewise, literacy events connected to real-world experiences have been found to increase students' literacy achievement (Guthrie et al., 1999; Moje et al., 2000).

The dimension of *service relevance* also shows how learning goals increased students' intrinsic motivation to engage with literacy. The Explorers club students' goals focused on understanding the concepts they were studying in order to provide a needed service in the community. Students were more engaged when the literacy practice supported learning that could be applied to the service projects. The perceived connection between academic goals and service activities holds the potential to increase student academic achievement (Ammon et al., 2001; Grolnick & Ryan, 1987).

The dimension of *students' knowledge* demonstrates how the Explorers service-learning club provided a collaborative structure that stimulated literacy motivation. Explorers club students' interests and expertise were called upon to support the group's efforts. This social accountability and interaction increased students' literacy motivation. The inclusion of students' interests provided the conditions that promoted students' sense of competence in their literate abilities. Students believed in their abilities because they were called upon to lead literate tasks or teach their peers. Congruent with previous research, the more the Explorers club students believed their abilities were valued the more they engaged (Weiler et al., 1998; Wigfield et al., 1998).

The dimension of *student voice* demonstrates how the Explorers club was a context where students were afforded control over their literacy practices. This autonomy fostered students' motivation to self-select literacy tools and construct literate products to meet self-selected purposes connected to the service projects. Students' sense of control in the decisions regarding their learning experiences is strongly correlated with higher academic engagement and achievement (Morgan & Streb, 2001; Ryan & Deci, 2000; Sweet et al., 1998).

The key to this model is that these dimensions act dynamically and must all be addressed in order for the students to be engaged in the literate events. Simply building off students' interests but not addressing the dimension of voice leads to disengagement. Although the use of computers and digital photography was interesting to the Explorers students, the lack of shared decision making among peers constructing the project led the students to disconnect from the activity. Positioning students in leadership roles to control literate events but not addressing the dimension of relevance leads to disengagement. Although Explorers students were in control of the collection of water test data, that lack of relevance this literate event held in relation to specific service-learning projects led to the students' active resistance. Connecting literate events directly to the service-learning project but failing to address the dimension of voice leads to disengagement. Although the literate texts in the Explorers club meetings were related to the service-learning projects, students lacked a voice in shaping these particular literate events and actively resisted such activities.

Service-learning is implemented in a variety of forms, and the Explorers club represented one unique way to structure a service-learning context. As such, it is important to recognize how the unique structures of the Explorers club and the investigation of those structures could have created unique findings not comparable to other contexts. As an extracurricular course, the Explorers club was not directly connected to any particular academic course, but rather connected to the broader science curriculum of the school. This structure could have led the students to perceive less stress and pressure in performing at high levels because grades were not attached to the work. Also, the broad scope of the content did not require teachers to adhere to particular textbooks or materials. This allowed for alternative resources to be utilized, which might have facilitated student engagement. Students voluntarily selected to participate in the club. This level of choice as well as the ability to select a club of interest may have led to increased levels of engagement. In light of all of these potential influences, the findings may be even more enlightening to the field. If students who have selected to participate in a club of personal interest, are not bound solely to textbooks and lectures, and not pressured by grades still disengage from particular instructional structures, then it might be highly unlikely for other students to find those same events engaging.

The dimensions of *service relevance, students' knowledge,* and *student voice* are similar to other factors associated with high-quality service-learning (Billig et al., 2005). The model of literacy engagement illustrates that these factors are interrelated. Educators who wish to optimize the impact of service-learning with their students must carefully work to infuse these high-quality factors into their instructional practice.

IMPLICATIONS FOR FUTURE RESEARCH

The model that emerged from this study (Exhibit 7.1) revealed some potential connections between factors of service-learning and literacy motivation and engagement. The Service-Learning Model of Literacy Engagement illustrates how the motivation factors of collaboration, real world connections, student autonomy, and mastery learning goals are located in service-learning practices. This model should be explored across a variety of service-learning contexts to understand how different enactments of service-learning influence student literacy engagement. Studies should analyze and compare voluntary and mandatory service-learning settings at various grade levels; especially since literacy research has shown declines in engagement across grade levels (Guthrie & Davis, 2003; McKenna, Kear, & Ellsworth, 1995).

This study demonstrates that qualitative research can provide thick descriptions of the learning context to determine sources of engagement and how engagement is related to instructional contexts. More qualitative research on this model will be able to detail how engagement changes if conditions are altered. This will allow for deeper understanding of the degree to which the dimensions of student voice, students' knowledge, and service relevance influence each other.

Last, this study illustrates how youth can become engaged as co-researchers to generate useful knowledge about issues that affect their lives. The greatest potential for future research may come from involving struggling readers in researching literacy engagement in service-learning contexts. Although most struggling readers are not presently involved in service-learning experiences, this may be an area for the field to explore (Kielsmeier et al., 2004). Literacy researchers have found that one of the best ways for students and others to increase their understanding of literacy is for them to reflect on their own practices and the everyday practices around them by carrying out their own research on literacy (Barton, 2000; Heath, 1983). By involving the most disengaged students as researchers, those closest to the research issue, the most useful knowledge about service-learning and literacy engagement may be unveiled.

REFERENCES

Ammon, S., Furco, A., Chi, B., & Middaugh, E. (2001). *Service-learning in California: A profile of the CalServe service-learning partnerships, 1997-2000.* Berkeley: University of California, Service-Learning Research and Development Center. Available: http://www.servicelearning.org/article/archive/165

Anderman, E., Machr, M., & Midgley, C. (1999). Declining motivation after the transition to middle school: Schools can make a difference. *Journal of Research and Development in Education, 32,* 131-147.

Baker, L., & Wigfield, A. (1999). Dimensions of children's motivation for reading and their relations to reading activity and reading achievement. *Reading Research Quarterly, 34,* 452-477.

Barton, D. (2000). Researching literacy practices: Learning from activities with teachers and students. In D. Barton, M. Hamilton, & R. Ivanic (Eds.), *Situated literacies: Reading and writing in context* (pp. 167-179). New York: Routledge.

Berman, S. H. (2000). Service as systemic reform. *School Administrator, 57*(7), 20-24.

Billig, S., & Klute, M. (2003, April). *The impact of service-learning on MEAP: A large-scale study of Michigan Learn and Serve grantees.* Presentation at National Service-Learning Conference, Minneapolis, MN.

Billig, S., Meyer, S., & Hofschire, L. (2003). *Evaluation of Center for Research on Education, Diversity, and Excellence demonstration site, the Hawaiian Studies Program at Waianae High School.* Denver, CO: RMC Research.

Billig, S., Root, S., & Jesse, D. (2005). The relationship between quality indicators of service-learning and student outcomes: Testing professional wisdom. In S. Root, J. Callahan, & S. Billig (Eds.), *Advances in service-learning practice: Research on models to enhance impacts* (pp. 97-115). Greenwich, CT: Information Age.

Carnegie Corporation of New York, & CIRCLE. (2003). *The civic mission of schools.* New York: Carnegie Corporation, and College Park, MD: University of Maryland, School of Public Affairs. Available: http://www.civicmissionof schools .org/campaign/documents/ ExecutiveSummary.pdf

Chouliaraki, L., & Fairclough, N. (1999). *Discourse in late modernity: Rethinking critical discourse analysis.* Edinburgh, Scotland: Edinburgh University Press.

Education Commission of the States. (2001). Institutionalized service-learning in the 50 states. Denver, CO: Author. Available: http://www.ecs.org/clearinghouse /23/77/2377.htm

Fredricks, J., Blumenfeld, P., & Paris, A. (2004). School engagement: Potential of the concept, state of the evidence. *Review of Educational Research, 74,* 59-109.

Fredricks, L., Kaplan, E., & Zeisler, J. (2001). *Integrating youth voice in service-learning. Education Commission of the States.* http://www.ecs.org/clearinghouse/ 23/67/2367.pdf

Gee, J. (1999) *An introduction to discourse analysis: Theory and method*. London: Routledge.

Grolnick, W., & Ryan, R. (1987). Autonomy in children's learning: An experimental and individual difference investigation. *Journal of Personality and Social Psychology, 52,* 890-898.

Guthrie, J. (2004). Teaching for literacy engagement. *Journal of Literacy Research, 36*(1), 1-30.

Guthrie, J., Anderson, E., Alao, S., & Rinehart, J. (1999). Influences of concept-oriented reading instruction on strategy use and conceptual learning from text. *Elementary School Journal, 99*(4), 343-366.

Guthrie, J., & Davis, M. (2003). Motivating struggling readers in middle school through an engagement model of classroom practice. *Reading & Writing Quarterly, 19,* 59-85.

Harackiewicz, J. M., Barron, K. E., Tauer, J. M., Carter, S. M., & Elliot, A. J. (2000). Short-term and long-term consequences of achievement goals: Predicting interest and performance over time. *Journal of Educational Psychology, 92,* 316-330.

Heath, S. (1983). *Ways with words: Language, life, and work in communities and classrooms.* New York: Cambridge University Press.

Howard, J. (1998). Academic service learning: A counternormative pedagogy. In R. Rhoads & J. Howard (Eds.), *Academic service learning: A pedagogy of action and reflection* (pp. 21-29). San Francisco, CA: Jossey-Bass.

Justinianno, J., Scherer, C., Johnson, L., Lewis, B., Swanson, R., & Felix, A. (2001). *Youth voice: A guide for engaging young people in leadership and decision-making in service-learning programs.* Points of Light Foundation. Available: http://www.servicelearning.org/filemanager/download/7/YVGuide.pdf

Kielsmeier, J., Scales, P., Roehlkepartain, E., & Neal, M. (2004). Community service and service-learning in public schools. *Reclaiming Children and Youth, 13*(3), 138-143.

Klute, M., & Billig, S. (2002). *The impact of service-learning on MEAP: A large-scale study of Michigan Learn and Serve grantees.* Denver, CO: RMC Research.

Loesch-Griffin, D., Petrides, L., & Pratt, C. (1995). *A comprehensive study of Project YES—Rethinking classrooms and communities: Service-learning as educational reform.* San Francisco, CA: East Bay Conservation Corps.

McKenna, C., Kear, D., & Ellsworth, R. (1995). Children's attitudes toward reading: A national survey. *Reading Research Quarterly, 30,* 934-956.

Melchior, A. (1999). *Summary report: National evaluation of Learn and Serve America.* Waltham, MA: Center for Human Resources, Brandeis University.

Melchior, A., & Bailis, L. N. (2002). Impact of service-learning on civic attitudes and behaviors of middle and high school youth: Findings from three national evaluations. In A. Furco & S. H. Billig (Eds.), *Service-learning: The essence of pedagogy* (pp. 201-222). Greenwich, CT: Information Age.

Moje, E. B., Young, J. P., Readence, J. E., & Moore, D. W. (2000). Reinventing adolescent literacy for new times: Perennial and millennial issues. *Journal of Adolescent & Adult Literacy, 43,* 400-410.

Morgan, W., & Streb, M. (2001). Building citizenship: How student voice in service-learning develops civic values. *Social Science Quarterly, 82,* 154-169.

National Commission on Service-Learning. (2002). *Learning in deed: The power of service-learning for American schools*. Battle Creek, MI: W. K. Kellogg Foundation. Available: http://www.learningindeed.org/slcommission/reportopt.html

National Reading Panel. (2000). *Report of the National Reading Panel: Teaching people to read*. Washington, DC: National Institute of Child Health and Human Development.

National Research Council. (2004). *Engaging schools: Fostering high school students' motivation to learn*. Committee on Increasing High School Students' Engagement and Motivation to Learn. Board on Children, Youth, and Families, Division of Behavioral and Social Sciences and Education. Washington, DC: The National Academies Press.

Patton, M. Q. (2002). *Qualitative research & evaluation methods*. Thousand Oaks, CA: Sage.

Roesser, R., Midgley, C., & Urdan, T. (1996). Perceptions of the school psychological environment and early adolescents' psychological and behavioral functioning in school: The mediating role of goals and belonging. *Journal of Educational Psychology, 88*, 408-422.

Ryan, R., & Deci, E. (2000). Intrinsic and extrinsic motivations: Classic definitions and new directions. *Contemporary Educational Psychology, 25*, 54-67.

Shaffer, B. (1993) *Service-learning: An academic methodology*. Stanford, CA: Stanford University Department of Education.

Skinner, E., Wellborn, J., & Connell, J. (1990). What it takes to do well in school and whether I've got it: A process model of perceived control and children's engagement and achievement in school. *Journal of Educational Psychology, 82*, 22-32.

Skinner, R., & Chapman, C. (1999). *Service-learning and community service in K-12 public schools*. Washington, DC: National Center for Education Statistics.

Steinberg. L. (1996). *Beyond the classroom: Why school reform has failed and what parents need to do*. New York: Simon & Schuster.

Stevens, R., & Slavin, R. (1995). The cooperative elementary school: Effects on students' achievement, attitudes, and social relations. *American Educational Research Journal, 32*, 321-351.

Stipek, D. (2002). Good instruction is motivating. In A. Wigfield & J. Eccles (Eds.), *Development of achievement motivation* (pp. 309-332). San Diego, CA: Academic Press.

Sweet, A., Guthrie, J., & Ng, M. (1998). Teacher perceptions and student reading motivation. *Journal of Educational Psychology, 90*, 210-224.

Switzer, G., Simmons, R., Dew, M., Regalski, J., Wang, C. (1995). The effect of a school-based helper program on adolescent self-image, attitudes, and behavior. *Journal of Early Adolescence, 15*(4), 429-455.

Tuyay, S., Floriani, A., Yeager, B., Dixon, C., & Green, J. (1995). Constructing an integrated, inquiry-oriented approach in classrooms: A cross-case analysis of social, literate, and academic practice. *Journal of Classroom Interaction, 30*(2), 1-15.

Weiler, D., LaGoy, A., Crane, E. & Rovner, A. (1998). *An evaluation of K–12 service-learning in California: Phase II final report*. Emeryville, CA: RPP International.

Wigfield, A., Eccles, J., & Rodriguez, D. (1998). The development of children's motivation in school contexts. *Review of Research in Education, 23*, 73-118.

Wigfield, A., & Guthrie, J. (1997). Relations of children's motivation for reading to the amount and breadth of their reading. *Journal of Educational Psychology, 89*, 420-432.

SECTION III

ENGAGING COMMUNITIES IN
LEARNING AND INSTITUTIONAL CHANGE

CHAPTER 8

ENRICHING SCHOOL CONNECTION AND LEARNING IN AFRICAN AMERICAN URBAN YOUTH

The Impact of a Service-Learning Feasibility Project in Inner-City Philadelphia

Nicole Webster

ABSTRACT

In many communities engagement and civic involvement has been steeped in the traditions and history of the people. In particular, low-income African American communities have a long history of creating grassroots programs to address social and economic conditions. One group within this population which has often times been overlooked has been the youth. Creating opportunities for community involvement and low-income marginalized youth may influence behaviors related to peer and school commitment and civic engagement. This chapter describes the impact of a service-learning

From Passion to Objectivity: International and Cross-Disciplinary Perspectives on Service Learning Research, pp. 159–176

study conducted with African American youth in a low-income marginalized community in Philadelphia. Due to many of the community's rising environmental health issues and concerns about youth awareness of the issue, it was grounded in the principals of Integrated Pest Management (IPM), a stepwise approach to addressing health and environmental issues. Surveys were conducted to evaluate how youth's participation influenced their (1) feeling more committed to their school, (2) greater recognition from their teachers, (3) greater prosocial commitment, and (4) social anxiety. The analysis suggests implications for further service-learning studies with African American youth in marginalized communities. Also, greater attention must be given to creating service-learning programs which promote a sense of group connection and identity.

INTRODUCTION

In recent years, researchers have identified civic engagement as a critical element of positive youth development. Given the increasing rates of health disparities, gaps in educational achievement, poverty, immigration issues and social welfare, particular attention has been given to minority populations in low-income marginalized communities. Some researchers have identified civic involvement and community engagement as a benefit to youth and communities. The benefits derived from engagement and civic involvement for minority youth have been attributed to greater levels of community participation, self-identity, and political affinity (Lopez & Kirby, 2005; Smetana, Campione-Barr, & Metzger, 2006; Torney-Purta, Barber, & Wilkenfeld, in press). Greater involvement in the community will lead to outcomes such as higher self-confidence for individuals and more meaningful connections with positive role models in the community.

Young people are especially vulnerable to factors in their social environments that may serve to disconnect them from the community. An understanding of the causes of this disconnection and potential solutions for greater social involvement will illuminate ways to better assist youth to become more engaged. This is especially important for young minority youth who often times are not part of the social and emotional fabric of their own communities (Atkins & Hart, 2003, Hart & Atkins, 2002; Roach, Yu & Lewis-Charp, 2001; Sanchez-Jawoski, 2002; Stepick & Stepick, 2002). Few studies to date have focused on the connection between their community engagement and positive youth development. It is suggested in this chapter that through experiences of an environmental based service-learning program, these young people may begin to feel a greater connection with peers, school teachers, and community members.

Marginalized African American Communities

There is a plethora of research that documents the relationship between social conditions and wealth in inner-city marginalized African American communities (Jargowsky, 1997; Jencks & Mayer, 1990; Leventhal & Brooks-Gunn, 2000; Park 1926). During the early 1970s, African American communities lost low-skill manufacturing jobs to suburban areas (Kasarda, 1993, 1995), which in turn caused an economic shift in the community from being a highly skilled labor force to becoming largely unemployed. Large concentrations of poor individuals gathered in many U.S. inner cities.

The decline in skilled labor further deepened the political and social upheavals which were happening within many communities. Families began to experience a surge of related misfortunes such as decreased monthly income and the need to work several low-paying jobs to earn a living wage. In addition, economic migration caused stable middle class families to move out to the suburbs. Family-owned businesses which were the cornerstone of the community relocated to the outskirts of the city, making them inaccessible to inner-city residents. All of these issues combined created a new situation for the African American inner-city family, one in which their social and economic well-being was being severely compromised due to geographic and racial segregation.

The new inner city created a number of social problems, such as frequent joblessness, inequitable educational opportunities, dependency on the social system and social restlessness. Although some theorists argued that this situation caused a pattern of deviant social norms and values inherent within the inner-city population (Mead, 1994; Murray, 1984). Others believed that these behaviors were adaptive and necessary to survive within the particular social conditions minorities faced (Coulton & Poudy, 1992). Social exclusion, political bureaucracy, and racial inequality together created a system which helped fuel the behaviors, beliefs, and movements of the urban poor African American individual and community.

Men and women alike had to create a system to keep them connected to the social networks of the greater society. Churches, schools and civic organizations served as essential institutions in this web of resources for the severely marginalized family. They created social programs, opportunities, and informational networks which kept people informed and connected because, "the desolation of social impoverishment compounds the deprivation of economic impoverishment" (Garbarino, 1985, p. 135).

Social capital in the form of strong networks and neighborhood institutions was necessary to provide support to the urban poor resident and to reinforce positive behaviors and norms for the entire community. The lifeline of support helped to establish employment networks, homework help lines, food assistance programs, clothing drives, educational scholarships, and job training. This foundation helped to establish actions and behaviors that many marginalized African American poor have found necessary to survive in the inner-city community. Despite their spatial segregation, many of the urban poor created a network of trust and social obligations useful for their everyday existence. As noted by some researchers, African American families in poverty came from a historical and cultural place that allowed them to create a community both active and able in working to meet its own needs (Robin, 1997).

Resiliency of the African American Community

Community activism and civic leadership have been a constant force in the African American community despite the economic and social welfare of its citizens. Recent research has repeatedly found that African American urban poor youth continue to demonstrate coping mechanisms and strategies to deal with their daily struggles (Annunziata, 2006; Fitzpatrick, Piko, Wright & LaGory, 2005; McGee et al., 2001; Scales, Benson, Leffert & Blyth, 2000). Many of these coping strategies have proven essential for their personal, social, and emotional well-being. Activists such as DuBois believed that through the establishment of community-based institutions, resources, programs, and civic agencies, a cadre of young leaders would emerge who were prepared to change the status quo in America (Franklin, 1990).

Many of the civic experiences occurred in the Black church which served as the pillar for community involvement, family connectedness, and social connection (D'Apolito, 2000; Greenberg, 2000). The Black church served as a place for not only spiritual uplifting and worship, but also as a center for providing social services to advance the race (Mays & Nicholson, 1933). Calhoun-Brown (1996) found that these types of experiences provided a foundation for social integration and civic involvement for many African American youth. Mohamed and Wheeler (2001, p. 4) believe, "particularly for youth who are struggling with issues of identity formation and the differences engendered by race, class, gender, and sexuality, civic activism provides a safe and positive forum in which to work on or through these issues."

Other researchers, though, have found that despite the involvement of ethnic-minority youth, many of the urban poor young people remain disengaged from traditional civic youth development opportunities (Flanagan & Faison, 2001; Finlay, Flanagan, & Black, 2007). In a 2001 article about youth citizenship, for example, Flanagan and Findlay concluded that there were very few accounts about processes by which ethnic minority groups, "develop an affection for the polity and become engaged citizens" (p. 5). Hart and Atkins (2002) and Ginwright and James (2002) considered marginalized youth on the fringes of society, yet engaged within contexts which have developed according to the social and ecological contexts from which they arise. For these marginalized young people, leadership and civic activism can be successfully combined into an effective strategy for achieving youth development outcomes. African American urban youth, especially those from marginalized low-income communities, have an ability to bring distinct vision to social programs and activities (Berjano, 2005; Delgado, 2005; Scales et al., 2005; Mahiri, 2004). It is from this vision that many youth programs are developing within the inner cities. For instance, in Chicago, a youth development civic program was developed using the social norms of the young people such as rap songs, stepping,[1] and spoken word.

African American Youth and Service-Learning

The teaching pedagogy, known as service-learning, is defined as an experiential experience where learning occurs through a cycle of action and reflection in a community. Students apply their knowledge to solve community problems, while simultaneously increasing social and civic skills (Eyler & Giles, 1999). While service-learning holds out promise as a pedagogical approach, the vast majority of studies have analyzed the experience of predominately White, middle-class youth, who reside in suburban areas, thereby limiting generalization to the general population (Sánchez-Jankowski 2002). Scholars and urban education reformists have suggested that service-learning can be used as a way to connect urban students to their community to improve educational achievement and social connectedness (Ginsberg, Shapiro, & Brown, 2004; Lopez & Kirby, 2005; Sirianni & Friedland 2001; Warren, 2005; Watts & Guessous, 2006). Service-learning experiences from an urban youth perspective have the advantage of showing the connections that can be made between urban youth and their own communities. Benefits can also gained by urban youth and communities engaged in service-learning when issues are addressed by individuals who live in and understand the cultural, political, and social nuances within these communities being served (Kahne & Westheimer, 2003; Pickron-Davis, 1999).

Specifically, there is a priori reason to believe that African American urban youth can benefit from the opportunities for empowerment and involvement of service-learning programs. Because service-learning is designed to address needs in communities, youth can build on their existing community knowledge, experience, and contact to feel empowered within and connected to their communities. Indeed, a number of leading theorists and researchers concerned with the social welfare of African American youth are calling for in-depth research relating to the context of marginalized black communities (Blanchett, Mumford, & Beachum, 2005; Brown, 2004; Obiakor & Beachum, 2005; Obidah & Howard, 2005).

Urban Service-Learning

In the few service-learning studies conducted in urban locales, the youth residing there have typically been the recipients and presumed beneficiaries of the projects imported from suburban schools (see, for example, Moore & Sandholtz's 1999 article "Designing Successful Service-learning Projects for Urban Schools"). *Outsiders* are typically brought into urban communities and presented as experts who attempt to *understand* and *fix* the identified community problem. Paradoxically, these "service-learning experts" have often never been to African American communities before and are frequently ill-prepared to deal with the issues, environment, and challenges residing there (Wade, 2000). This approach of bringing outsiders into local communities has been described as an ill-advised and unfortunate side of service-learning (Boyle-Baise, 1999; Butin, 2003; Steinke, Fitch, Johnson & Waldstein, 2002; Wade, 2000). The researchers' contention is that service-learning should be shaped by practitioners and researchers to develop projects that use the experience and knowledge of indigenous African American youth and community stakeholders to address local community issues, needs, and problems of social justice and community development (Wade, 2000). Well designed service-learning in urban schools and communities could provide youth with opportunities for empowerment and involvement that would build on their community knowledge, experience, and contacts to work in a collaborative way on issues relevant to their own community. For example, Youniss, McLellan, Su, and Yates (1999) found that inner-city African American high school youth in Washington, DC demonstrated a number of positive outcomes when learning and service opportunities were strategically combined and grounded within their own communities.

Realizing there is a vital need to create culturally sensitive and engaging academic environments for African American youth, a research project was created in a southwest Philadelphia middle school. The program was designed with a threefold purpose to (a) assist both students and teachers in meeting the immediate needs of their community (e.g., environmental awareness, health awareness, physical safety), (b) to better prepare students to pass state assessment tests and (c) to build an academic setting that would incorporate the unique experiences of the youth and their community.

Environmental Connection to the Community

The Integrated Pest Management (IPM)[2] service-learning program, named by the students, as the *Pest Patrollers*, was the ideal partnership between student civic engagement and addressing real community needs. African American students were given the opportunity to address an important need in their community through a stepwise and interactive approach. More importantly, the IPM methodology allowed the students to work in their own community to address public health issues which directly impacted both they and their families.

Within inner-city Philadelphia, a number of severe environmental issues have plagued the health of children and adolescents. Across several communities, children have been overexposed to high amounts of pesticide and chemical residues, lead paint, drinking water contaminants, landfills and indoor and outdoor pollutants (Environmental Protection Agency, 2003). Exposure to these environmental problems has been the cause of several childhood diseases such as cancer, respiratory ailments (e.g., asthma) and neurological disorders (Farber, Johnson, & Beckerman, 1998; Schettler, 2001). Furthermore, environmental health issues have added an enormous amount of strain to community health budgets. These issues have lead to a number of concerned organizations, governmental agencies and, most importantly, citizens to take steps to address the growing problem. Within this particular community, addressing the degrading environmental issue was not just about creating a quick fix, but rather creating a value-added project to the community that would increase the IPM knowledge base of African American youth, engage them in the solution of a problem and empower them with skills necessary to be environmental stewards of change within their own communities.

The format of the Integrated Pest Management service-learning project was intentionally designed to create a cadre of African American youth who would be able to address a looming public health issue within their own community while gaining valuable social skills and academic knowledge. Activities were designed with the intent of building student voice and helping students to transition into confident and responsible citizens.

Many of the social concerns of urban inner-city youth translate into poor peer relations and negative perceptions of teachers and school. Another purpose of this project was to help these students develop social responsibility in a safe and nurturing environment while building positive relationships with peers and teachers. The academic content in the program would not only prepare them to be informed citizens, but also would better prepare them for the state academic standards on IPM. This new addition to the Pennsylvania state academic standards was a basis for creating a project that combined both civic action and academic content.

Weekly meetings were held during the school day and facilitated by the IPM Philadelphia coordinator.[3] The decision to pull students from classes was made by the school principal. Initial meetings were grounded in learning the basics of IPM and how it fit within the daily lives of the youth. Students worked with the coordinator and a science teacher to understand and identify pest's habits, preventive measures to deal with pests and tactics for better effectiveness in school settings. After 6 months, the students began to plan service projects they wanted to conduct within the school. All of the activities included student participation and, most importantly, their thoughts and ideas of what would work in their urban school environment.

The Pest Patrollers took an interactive and engaging approach to educating fellow peers about environmental health problems in their school community. For example, they created IPM posters which were hung throughout school hallways to remind their peers about the importance of a clean and healthy environment. They also developed morning announcements about keeping a clean school, cleaning up trash from hallways, putting gum in garbage cans and refraining from keeping bagged lunch in lockers. Pest Patrollers also took an active role in informing their surrounding community about the importance of practicing IPM techniques at home by posting signs and flyers on billboards and public spaces. They worked with the IPM coordinator to create a step routine[4] about IPM practices and its importance in their community.

As a result of a lunch room boycott[5] regarding unhealthy lunch room practices and conditions, the students influenced school policy regarding bagged brown lunches. The students also made IPM presentations at Science, Technology, Engineering, and Mathematics night and the National Youth Leadership Conference regarding the importance of their work and the overall environmental health of their school community.

The Study

Sample

The sample for this study consisted of 23 African American middle school students from a Title I resource-poor urban middle school in west Philadelphia. The students resided in the community and 100% of the students were eligible for the free breakfast and lunch program at the school. Four females and 8 males were participants in the IPM service-learning project. Five females and 6 males were in the control group. The average age of the students was 12.5 years.

Measures

The Communities That Care Youth Survey (Arthur, Hawkins, Pollard, Catalano & Baglioni, 2002) is a self-report measure of an array of risk and protective factors (e.g., school, family, peer, individuals) that predict youth health and behavior outcomes. Each of the 31 risk and protective factors scales have demonstrated adequate internal consistency and construct validity for the scores across males and females of various ages, and from ethnic minority groups, including African Americans (Arthur et al., 2002; Glasser, Van Horn, Arthur, Hawkins, & Catalano, 2005).

Three of the scales were used for this study. The commitment to school scale included six items (for example, "How interesting are most of your courses to you?" and "How important do you think the things you are learning in school are going to be for your later life?"). The recognition scale included four items (for example, "My teachers notice when I am doing a good job and let me know about it"). The scale demonstrated adequate internal consistency ($\alpha = .76$). The opportunities for prosocial involvement scale include five items (for example, "Teachers ask me to work on special classroom projects. There are lots of chances of students in my school to talk to teachers one on one"). The scale demonstrated reasonable internal consistency ($\alpha = .76$). Respondents indicated the extent to which they agreed with each statement on a 5-point Likert-type scale.

The Social Anxiety Scale for Children Revised (La Greca & Lopez, 1988) measures children's subjective experience of social anxiety. It contains 18 descriptive self-statements and four filler items reflecting activity references (for example, "I like to read") or social preferences (for example, "I like to play with other kids".) Each item is rated on a 5-point scale according to how much an item is true for the respondent (1 = *not at all*, 5 = *all the time*). Internal consistency and construct validity for the scores have been supported in prior studies (Ginsburg, La Greca, Silverman, 1998; La Greca & Lopez, 1988). In this study, the scale demonstrated adequate internal consistency ($\alpha = .89$).

The Service Attitude Measure (Webster & Worrell, in press) consists of eight items assessing adolescents' global attitudes toward service and learning. Questions assess adolescents' beliefs about (a) helping others in the community, (b) adults engaging in service projects in their communities and in the world, (c) youth and adults working together on service-learning projects, (d) adults helping youth to be more engaged civically, and (e) youth engaging in community service even without adult support. SAM questions are rated on a 5-point Likert scale (1 = *strongly disagree*, 5 = *strongly agree*).

The data were collected as part of the Integrated Pest Management Service-Learning Project funded by the Environmental Protection

Agency's Urban Ecology Initiative Program. The random sample of youth for the service-learning experience and the control group was drawn from a list of 145 students in the 5th, 7th, and 8th grade science cohort by the school principal. The entire sample of students was from classes with an average size of 25. Teachers had previous training in service-learning[6] and focused on environmental science in their classroom instruction. The class lists were separated into males and females to ensure that there was gender balance in each of the groups. A nonresponse of 8 and 9 parental/guardian permission slips resulted in only 12 students participating in the service-learning program and 11 in the control group. A member of the research team administered a series of questionnaires to the students pertaining to school and community connection, prosocial behaviors, and social anxiety. Surveys took about 75 minutes to answer.

The researcher described the study at the beginning of the session and addressed the importance of the participants' confidentiality of their responses. A research team member read aloud the directions, questionnaire items and response choices for each measure of the questionnaire. Participants were instructed not to respond in advance of the oral directions. At the end of the data collection, the researcher thanked the students for their participation in the study and gave the students a pizza party as an incentive to their input.

Challenges of Study

The IPM program provided a basis for a service-learning project which would (a) challenge African American urban youth to address a topic relevant to their community and (c) increase communities with increased knowledge and awareness of and IPM approaches to maintain and solve chronic environmental issues. The study itself provided a unique opportunity to assess a number of social contexts and relationships among youth and their immediate school surroundings.

While the sample consists of youth's representative in other marginalized African American communities, the data were not without limitations. The sample consisted of African American marginalized urban poor youth from one census tract in the west Philadelphia area making the scope of the generalizability limited. The inclusion of African Americans from this background only was warranted because they are the largest majority ethnic group living in urban poor communities (Jarkowsky, 1997). Another limitation of this study was that in contrast to other studies, there was a small sample size limiting the ability to generalize to other urban poor communities and ethnic populations.

RESULTS

Mean scores from the Communities That Care and Social Anxiety scale are presented in Exhibit 8.1. Statistical tests revealed that the groups were basically equivalent in terms of demographics, so a series of independent *t* tests were conducted to test the effects of the program on the sample participants. The tests revealed that none of the group differences were statistically significant. Effect sizes were calculated using Cohen's *d*, and it was determined that the effect sizes were in the medium range for commitment to school ($d = .62$) and social anxiety ($d = .72$). Even if the means between the two groups were not statistically different, a small coefficient of variation for most of the variables for the IPM youth is an indication that, if we increase the sample size, we might find significant difference between the two groups.

The first construct examined was whether youth felt more connected to school as a result of their participation in the IPM service-learning program. The hypothesis was that students who were a part of the service-learning group would feel a closer attachment to their peers and teachers and feel like school was engaging and important. The results indicated that there was not a significant difference ($M = 23.83$, $p = .16$) in school connection between students who engaged in service-learning activities and their nonparticipating peer. While the control group was less inclined to feel connected to school (e.g., sports, clubs) and activities outside the classroom, engagement in service-learning did not seem to impact their attitudes toward their friends, peers, classroom teachers, and administrators. Students also did not perceive any greater recognition from teachers as a result of their participation in the service-learning project.

The hypothesis that the IPM service-learning students' prosocial behavior would increase over time more than their non-participating

Exhibit 8.1.   Mean Scores for IPM Project Youth ($n = 12$) and Matched Controls ($n = 11$)

Variables	IPM Youth			Controls			T-value*	Cohen's d
	M	SD	CV	M	SD	CV		
Commitment to school	23.83	1.59	6.67%	22.40	2.88	12.85%	1.492	.62
Recognition	12.42	2.02	16.62%	12.00	1.63	13.58%	0.456	.23
Prosocial commitment	16.00	1.81	11.31%	15.40	1.89	12.27%	0.778	.33
Social anxiety	55.83	3.67	6.57%	52.90	4.51	8.52%	1.716	.72

Note: At .05 level *t* statistic is = 1.96.

peers was not confirmed. Although the effect of the intervention was not significant the results reflected a trend in the desired direction. Finally, students who were part of the IPM program showed higher rates of social anxiety than those in the comparison group.

DISCUSSION

Overall, findings of the study did not reveal a significant difference between those students who were participants in the IPM service-learning group than those in the control group. The findings are likely related to several factors, including the intervention design and the outcomes studied. Given the nature of the projects the students undertook and the length of the service-learning program it might be expected to see positive results among students. The activities were designed to affect the connection African American students have among peers and their school as well as prosocial behaviors within their school community. Lewis, Sullivan, and Bybee (2006) wrote that intervention projects, especially those designed for the African American student, should have a focus on the identity of the student and include activities which assist in building group identity at the start of the project. Thus, in the future, more attention needs to be given to linking the project to self- and group-identity.

Similarly, the level of prosocial behavior for the intervention group was not consistent with other studies conducted with African American urban middle school youth (Webster & Worrell, in press.). Although students were encouraged to think critically about problems which seriously impacted their health, they did not show greater levels of social involvement and commitment. This may have been due to the environmental subject matter, the types of activities conducted or perhaps the length of time of the project.

The inverse relationship between social anxiety and the service-learning group was expected due to the nature of the project and is consistent with other studies conducted on African American middle school youth and social anxiety. Research on African American youth and anxiety suggests that peer acceptance may manifest itself different among these populations and especially those from inner cities marginalized background (Lambert, Cooley, Campbell, Benoit, & Stansbury, 2004; Lambert, McCreary, et al., 2004). Erath, Flanagan, and Bierman (2007) found that high rates of social anxiety are linked with decreased peer acceptance and peer victimization. The activities of the IPM service-learning participants, such as walking around with clipboards and protective helmets to monitor pest was seen as odd by the other students and the activities in and of themselves may have raised anxiety among the Pest Patrollers. These results are also consistent with the findings of prior research examining the relationship of African American students' and their connection to school and social anxiety when participating in a service-learning program (Crystal & DeBell, 2002). This literature suggests that the more the students engage in service-learning activities, the more they feel connected to their teachers, administrators, and peers, but are also more likely to show signs of social anxiety. Because school connectedness is especially relevant during adolescence (Goodenow, 1993), it is particularly important to help students feel that they belong to the school and believe themselves to be welcomed, respected, and valued by other school members so their motivation to achieve remains high. While the effects were not as strong as desired, the service-learning program did provide a template for creating an integrated work environment in an inner-city school. The subject matter of IPM gave students an avenue to learn a new topic, readily apply the theory and science in their everyday lives and see tangible results. The African American youth were part of a network of individuals who were genuinely concerned about social problems within their own community. Students were engaged in a school-based service-learning program designed to address pressing health and environmental issues which impacted both their school and surrounding community.

CONCLUSION

This study examined the effects of participating in a service-learning pilot project in an urban school in enhancing students' connections to their schools and communities, commitment to civic participation, and social comfort and competence. Results revealed that students in the service-learning sample did not differ from matched comparison groups of non-participating peers on any of the measures, though there were slight gains in scores for three of the four variables. The sample size was quite small and may have accounted for the results. It is also possible that the experiences were not of sufficient duration or intensity and involved a topic that produced rather than inhibited social anxiety.

The findings suggest that more study is needed to determine why service-learning resulted in more social anxiety and what can be done to address this issue. Perhaps future studies could be conducted for a longer duration of time and would include a control group. Far too often service-learning projects have brought exogenous "experts" into marginalized urban African American communities to solve problems and lend a hand to "those in need." This creates a dangerous dynamic where urban African American youth and communities may come to believe they cannot solve their own problems, and outsiders may see the youth and communities as helpless and needy. Therefore, service-learning projects need to be designed where urban youth and communities work together to solve their own problems.

The findings of the study are modest in magnitude, but provide a starting place for service-learning program planners, researchers, and educators interested in African American marginalized youth and civic engagement. In the future, greater attention needs to be paid to studies which include the voice and realities of urban African American youth. Results from a pilot study such as this could help support future service-learning studies and literature related to African American marginalized youth in urban areas. African American marginalized youth have the potential for being empowered to make significant differences within their own communities. Greater understanding of the relationship between inner-city African American youth and civic opportunities may contribute to improving the social and academic and overall well-being of youth in these impoverished areas.

NOTES

1. Stepping is a form of rhythmic dance and communication which originated with African American men working on the railroads. Stepping assisted miners in keeping up morale and esteem to tune out the laborious tasks and dangerous conditions. Step routines continue to be an integral part of the African American fraternity and sorority system and more recently has been incorporated into several forms of dance throughout the United States.
2. In Pennsylvania, Integrated Pest Management (IPM) is one of nine components of the newly adopted Academic Standards in Environment and Ecology and in 2001 the Pennsylvania State Board of Education and the Regulatory Review Commission adopted proposed academic standards in three subject areas (science, technology and environment and ecology) recently, including Integrated Pest Management, or IPM.
3. The IPM coordinator was hired by the entomology at the university to build community partnerships with agencies, schools, federal organizations, and citizens in the area of environmental public health.
4. A step routine is a dance technique that blends rhythmic dance coordinated with hand and foot movement and usually includes social commentary, chants, and/or songs to convey positive and entertaining messages to audiences.
5. Students were not allowed to bring brown bag lunches from home because it was contributing to the roach infestation in the lunch room.
6. Service-learning training was provided by the school district as part of professional development days for teachers in the school district.

REFERENCES

Annunziata, D. (2006). Family functioning and school success in at-risk, inner-city adolescents. *Journal of Youth and Adolescence, 35*(1), 100-108.

Atkins, R., & Hart, D. (2003). Neighborhoods, adults, and the development of civic identity in urban youth. *Applied Developmental Science, 7*(3), 156-164.

Arthur, M. W., Hawkins, J. D., Pollard, J. A., Catalano, R. F., & Baglioni, A. J. (2002). Measuring risk and protective factors for substance use, delinquency and other adolescent problem behaviors: The Communities that Care Youth Survey. *Evaluation Review, 26*(2), 575-601.

Bejarano, C. L. (2005). *Que Onda?: Urban youth culture and border identity.* Tuscon: University of Arizona Press.

Blanchett, W. J., Mumford, V., & Beachum, F. (2005). Urban school failure and disproportionality in a post-Brown era: Benign neglect of the constitutional rights of students of color. *Remedial and Special Education, 26*(2), 70-82.

Brown, D. F. (2004). Urban teacher's professed classroom management strategies: Reflections of culturally responsive teaching. *Urban Education, 5*(39), 266-289.

Boyle-Baise, M. (1999). "As good as it gets?" The impact of philosophical orientations on community-based service learning for multicultural education. *Educational Forum, 63*(4), 310–321.

Butin, D. (2003). Of what use is it? Multiple conceptualizations of service learning within education. *Teachers College Record, 105*(9), 1674-1692.

Calhoun-Brown, A. (1996). African American churches and political mobilization: The psychological impact of organizational resources. *Journal of Politics, 58*(4), 935-953.

Coulton, C. J., & Pandey, S. (1992). Geographic concentration of poverty and risk to children in urban neighborhoods. *American Behavioral Science, 34*, 238–254.

Crystal, D. S., & DeBell, M. (2002). Sources of civic orientation among American youth: Trust, religious valuation, and attributions of responsibility. *Political Psychology, 23*(2), 113-129.

Delgado, M. (2000). *New arenas for community social work practice with urban youth.* New York: Columbia University Press.

D'Apolito, R. (2000). The activist role of the Black church: A theoretical analysis and an empirical investigation of one contemporary activist Black church. *Journal of Black Studies, 31*(1), 96-123.

Environmental Protection Agency. (2003). *America's children and the environment: Measures of containments, body burdens, and illnesses.* Washington, DC: Office of Children's Health Protection. (EPA 240-R-03-001).

Eyler, J., & Giles, J. (1999). *Where's the learning in service-Learning?* San Francisco: Jossey-Bass.

Erath, S. A., Flanagan, K. S., & Bierman, K. L. (2007). Social anxiety and peer relations in early adolescence: Behavioral and cognitive factors. *Journal of Abnormal Child Psychology, 35*, 405-416.

Farber, H. J., Johnson, C., & Beckerman, R. C. (1998). Young inner-city children visiting the emergency room (ER) for asthma: Risk factors and chronic care behaviors. *Journal of Asthma, 35*(7), 547-552.

Finlay, A. K., Flanagan, C., & Black, S. (in press). *Service as a developmental opportunity: Building connections for vulnerable youths.* Saint Paul, MN: National Youth Leadership Council.

Fitzpatrick, K. M., Piko, B., Wright, D., & LaGory, M. (2005). Depressive symptomatology, exposure to violence, and the role of social capital among African-American adolescents. *American Journal of Orthopsychiatry, 75,* 125-137.

Flanagan, C., & Faison, N. (2001). Youth civic development: Implications of research for social policy and programs. *Social Policy Report, 15*(1). Ann Arbor, MI: Society for Research in Child Development.

Franklin, R. M. (1990). *Liberating visions: Human Fulfillment and social justice in African American thought.* Minneapolis, MN: Fortress Press.

Garbarino, J. (1985). Habitats for children: An ecological perspective. In J. F. Wohlwill & W. Van Vliet (Eds.), *Habitats for children: The impacts of density* (pp. 125-143). Hillsdale, NJ: Erlbaum.

Ginsberg, A. E., Shapiro, J. P., & Brown, S. P. (2004). *Gender in urban education: Strategies for student achievement.* Portsmouth, NH: Heinemann.

Ginsburg, G., La Greca, A. M., & Silverman, W. S. (1998). Social anxiety in children with anxiety disorders: Relations with social and emotional functioning. *Journal of Abnormal Child Psychology, 26,* 189-199.

Ginwright, S., & James, T. (2002). From assets to agents of change: Social justice, organizing, and youth development in youth participation: Improving institutions and communities. *New Directions for Youth Leadership, 96,* 27-46.

Glasser, R. R., Van Horn, M. L., Arthur, M. W., Hawkins, J. D., & Catalano, R. F. (2005). Measurement properties of the Communities That Care Youth Survey across demographic groups. *Journal of Quantitative Criminology, 21,* 73-102.

Goodenow, C. (1993). The psychological sense of school membership among adolescents: Scale development and educational correlates. *Psychology in the Schools, 30*(1), 79-90.

Greenberg , A. (2000). The church and the revitalization of politics and community. *Political Science Quarterly, 115*(3), 377-394.

Hart, D. & Atkins, R. (2002). Civic competence in urban youth. *Applied Developmental Science, 6*(4), 227-236.

Jargowsky, P. A. (1997). *Poverty and place: Ghettos, barrios, and the American City.* New York: Sage.

Jencks, C., & Mayer, S. E. (1990). The social consequences of growing up in a poor neighborhood. In L. E. Lynn, Jr. & M. McGreary (Eds.), *Inner-city poverty in the United States* (pp. 118-186). Washington, DC: National Academy Press.

Kahne, J., & Westheimer, J. (2003). Teaching democracy: What schools need to do. *Phi Delta Kappan, 85*(1), 34-40, 57-67.

Kasarda, J. (1993). Inner city concentrated poverty and neighborhood distress: 1970 to 1990. *Housing Policy Debate, 4*(3), 253-302.

Kasarda J., (1985). Urban change and minority opportunities. In P. E. Peterson (Ed.), *The new urban reality* (pp. 33-67). Washington, DC: Brookings Institute.

La Greca, A. M., & Lopez, N. (1998). Social anxiety among adolescents: Linkages with peer relations and friendships. *Journal of Abnormal Child Psychology, 26,* 83-94.

Lambert, S., McCreary, B. T., Preston, J. L., Schidmt, N., Joiner, T. E., & Ialongo, N. S. (2004). Anxiety sensitivity in African-American adolescents: Evidence of symptom specificity of anxiety sensitivity components. *Journal of the American Academy of Child & Adolescent Psychiatry, 43*(7), 887-895.

Lambert, S. F., Cooley, M. R., Campbell, K. D., Benoit, M. Z., & Stansbury, R. (2004). Assessing anxiety sensitivity in inner-city African American children: Psychometric properties of the childhood anxiety sensitivity index. *Journal of Clinical Child & Adolescent Psychology, 33*(2), 248-259.

Leventhal, T., & Brooks-Gunn, J. (2000). The neighborhoods they live in: The effects of neighborhood residence upon child and adolescent outcomes. *Psychological Bulletin, 126,* 309-337.

Lewis, K., Sullivan, C. M., & Bybee, D. (2006). An experimental evaluation of a school-based emancipatory intervention to promote African American well-being and youth leadership. *Journal of Black Psychology, 32*(1), 3-28.

Lopez, M. H., & Kirby, E. (2005). *Electoral engagement among minority youth* (CIRCLE Fact Sheet). College Park, MD: The Center for Information & Research on Civic Learning & Engagement.

Mahiri, J. (2004). *What they don't learn in school: Literacy in the lives of urban youth.* Peter Lang.

Mays, B. E., & Nicholson, J. (1933). *The Negro's church.* New York: Institute of Social and Religious Research.

Mead, L. M. (1994). Poverty: How little we know. *Social Service Review, 68,*322-350.

McGee, Z. T., Davis B. L., Brisbane, T., Collins, N., Nuriddin, T., Irving, S., Mutakkabir, Y., et al. (2001). Urban stress and mental health among African-American youth: Assessing the link between exposure to violence, problem behavior, and coping strategies. *Journal of Cultural Diversity, 8*(3), 94-104.

Mohamed, I. A., & Wheeler, W. (2001). *Broadening the bounds of youth development: Youth as engaged citizens.* New York: The Ford Foundation and Chevy Chase, MD: The Innovation Center for Community and Youth Development.

Moore, K. M., & Sandholtz, J. H. (1999). Designing successful service learning projects for urban schools. *Urban Education, 34*(4), 480-498.

Murray, C. (1984). *Losing ground: American social policy, 1950-1980.* New York: Basic Books.

Obiakor, F. E., & Beachum, F. D. (2005). Developing self-empowerment in African American students using the comprehensive support model. *The Journal of Negro Education, 74*(1), 18-30.

Obidah, J., & Howard, T. C. (2005). Preparing teachers for Monday morning in the urban school classroom: Reflecting on our pedagogies and practices and as effective teacher educators. *Journal of Teacher Education, 56*(3), 248-255.

Park, R. E. (1926). The urban community as a special pattern and moral order. In, E. W. Burgess (Ed.), *The urban community* (pp. 3–18). Chicago: The University of Chicago Press.

Pennsylvania Integrated Pest Management Program. (2001). *IPM for Pennsylvania schools: A how-to manual.* Philadelphia: The Pennsylvania State University.

Pickron-Davis, M. C. (1999). *Black students in community service-learning: Critical reflections about self and identity.* Unpublished doctoral dissertation, University of Pennsylvania.

Roach, C., Yu, H. C., & Lewis-Charp, H. (2001). Race, poverty and youth development. *Poverty & Race, 10*(4), 3-6.

Robin, J. (1995). Growing up poor: The family experience of socially mobile youth in low-income African-American neighborhoods. *Journal of Adolescent Research, 10,* 111-135.

Sánchez-Jankowski, M. (2002). Minority youth and civic engagement: The Impact of group relations. *Applied Developmental Science, 66*(4), 237–245.

Scales, P., Foster, K. C., Mannes, M., Horst, M. A., Pinto, K. C., & Rutherford, A. (2005). School-business partnerships, developmental assets, and positive outcomes among urban high school students: A mixed-methods study. *Urban Education, 40*(3), 144-189.

Scales, P. C., Benson, P. L., Leffert, N., & Blyth, D. A. (2000). Contribution of developmental assets to the prediction of thriving among adolescents. *Applied Developmental Science, 1,* 27-46.

Schettler, T. (2001). Toxic threats to neurologic development of children. *Environmental Health Perspective, 109*(6), 813-6.

Sirianni, C., & Friedland, L. (2001). *Civic innovation in America: Community empowerment, public policy, and the movement for civic renewal.* Berkeley: University of California Press.

Smetana, J. G., Campione-Barr, N., & Metzger, A. (2006). Adolescent development in interpersonal and societal contexts. *Annual Review of Psychology, 57,* 255-284.

Stepick, A., & Stepick, C. (2002). Becoming American, constructing ethnicity: Immigrant youth and civic engagement. *Applied Developmental Science, 6*(4), 246-257.

Steinke, P., Fitch, P., Johnson, C., & Waldstein, F. (2002). An interdisciplinary study of service-learning predictors and outcomes among college students. In S. Billig & A. Furco (Eds.), *Service-learning through a multidisciplinary lens* (pp. 73-102). Greenwich, CT: Information Age.

Torney-Purta, J., Barber, C. H., & Wilenfeld, B. (in press). Latino adolescents' civic development in the United States: Research results from the IEA Civic Education Study. *Journal of Youth and Adolescence.*

Wade, R. C. (2000). Service-Learning for multicultural teaching competency: Insights from the literature for teacher educators. *Equity & Excellence in Education 33*(3), 21-29.

Warren, R. (2005). Communities and schools: A new view of urban education reform. *Harvard Educational Review, 75*(2), 133-175.

Watts, R. J., & Guessous, O. (2006). Sociopolitical development: The missing link in research and policy on adolescents. In S. Ginwright, P. Noguera, & J. Cammarato (Eds.), *Beyond resistance! Youth activism and community change* (pp. 59-80). New York: Routledge.

Webster, N., & Worrell, F. (in press). Academically talented students' attitudes toward service learning. *Gifted Child Quarterly.*

Youniss, J., McLellan, J. A., Su, Y., & Yates, M. (1999). The role of community service in identity development: Normative, unconventional, and deviant orientations. *Journal of Adolescent Research, 14*(2), 248-261.

CHAPTER 9

COMMUNITY ENGAGEMENT'S ROLE IN CREATING INSTITUTIONAL CHANGE WITHIN THE ACADEMY

A Case Study of East Tampa and the University of South Florida

Robin L. Ersing, Judi Jetson, Robin Jones, and Harold Keller

ABSTRACT

Adding a meaningful community-engagement agenda to a major metropolitan university that is singularly focused on becoming a nationally ranked research university is a daunting task, but is made easier for both faculty and community partners by embracing a service-learning approach. The ongoing case study presented here describes a 3-year initiative in 1 urban neighborhood undertaken with faculty leadership, limited financial and structural resources, and a conscious decision to analyze this approach as a pathway toward building the program of community engagement through engaged

From Passion to Objectivity: International and Cross-Disciplinary Perspectives on Service Learning Research, pp. 177–195

scholarship. This chapter discusses the 8 guiding principles that emerged: reciprocal relationships, strengths-based, sustainable, incremental, strategic, enterprising, dissemination-oriented, and creative. The authors discuss specific strategies research-extensive universities can adopt to increase community engagement. Next steps toward institutionalizing the approach are presented.

INTRODUCTION

Vital cities have marvelous innate abilities for understanding, communicating, contriving, and inventing what is required to combat their difficulties ... Lively, diverse, intense cities contain the seeds of their own regeneration, with energy enough to carry over for problems and needs outside themselves.

—Jane Jacobs (1961, p. 448)

The University of South Florida (USF) was created 50 years ago by the Florida State Legislature to serve the growing urban population in the Tampa Bay area. Since then the metropolitan area has grown from half a million to more than 2.5 million. USF has also grown, and now serves 43,250 students, making it the nineth largest university in the United States. As it grew in size, USF was also "climbing" the Carnegie classification ladder, from Comprehensive University and College (1973) to Research University: Very High Research Activity (2006a). In 2004, USF President Judy Genshaft set the goal of becoming one of the top 50 public research universities in the United States within 5 years.

The challenge for the USF faculty who promote university engagement is showing that these two goals—achieving recognition as a major research university and connecting with local, national, and global communities—are not only compatible but are synergistic. Adding community engagement to established research institutions, many of which are 100 years older than USF, is difficult but there are models to follow. The attempt to build engagement into the research agenda for a relatively new university leaves the institution forging its own path.

The case description presented here, USF's East Tampa Initiative, shows how, even with limited financial and structural resources, a faculty-driven effort can provide evidence of the possibility (indeed the necessity, according to one national consultant) of becoming a major research institution through engaged scholarship. During the past 3 years, the East Tampa Initiative has consciously used the service-learning pedagogy to build connections with the community and within the university, enhancing the understanding of how a major metropolitan research university can contribute to the community through its scholarship.

University Infrastructure for Community Engagement

The institutional unit that provided the platform for this initiative is the USF Collaborative for Children, Families, and Communities. In 1996, the University of South Florida faculty created a multidisciplinary Collaborative for Children, Families, and Communities with funding from the provost. Originally intended to coordinate requests from the community, facilitate new research project development, and organize university-community conferences, the collaborative has developed into an important multidisciplinary agent for change within the university and in the community.

The development of the USF collaborative demonstrates the framework of Boyer's (1990) paradigm shift for higher education focused on the forms of scholarship: discovery, integration, application, and teaching. While the discovery of new knowledge rests at the core of USF as a Carnegie-ranked research-extensive institution, the collaborative is instrumental in helping faculty link across disciplines to integrate knowledge in new and innovative ways. The collaborative also excels in forming bridges among faculty, organizations, and the surrounding metropolitan community to apply this knowledge in addressing social issues that have an impact on quality of life. An important vehicle employed by the collaborative to achieve this work is the use of engaged experiential teaching such as service-learning, as a supplement to the more traditional classroom-based pedagogy found at most institutions of higher education. Through engaged scholarship, which represents an overlap of research, teaching and service in conjunction with working community partnerships (Bringle, Games, & Malloy, 1999), the intellectual, technological, and cultural resources of the campus are interwoven with the knowledge and expertise of community members to enhance decision making and ameliorate social problems (Boyer, 1996).

The collaborative is funded by the university, led by a board of faculty and community partners, and governed by a steering committee of deans and community leaders. Over the past 10 years, it has awarded more than $1.5 million in seed grant monies for 120 new engaged research projects which have coprincipal investigators from at least two disciplines and at least one community partner. To date, these grants have yielded at least $6 million in new resources to USF and several million dollars in grants to community groups.

In the summer of 2003, Tampa's newly elected mayor, Pam Iorio, asked USF President Judy Genshaft to join her in a neighborhood revitalization effort in East Tampa. The president asked the USF Collaborative for Children, Families, and Communities to work closely with the mayor's staff and assume a leadership role in mobilizing university involvement. At that time, several neighborhood and civic groups existed in East Tampa, but were not working in harmony. At USF, faculty had occasional involvement, but there was no coordinated university effort or staff infrastructure. Since then, city staff have organized neighborhood groups and nonprofits into the East Tampa Community Revitalization Partnership (ETCRP) and USF has begun its East Tampa Initiative. With the top-down commitments to revitalize the East Tampa neighborhood from both the university and city, collaborative staff and supporting faculty set out to build stronger relationships between USF and the East Tampa community.

The East Tampa Community

The collaborative assembled a multidisciplinary team of faculty to determine how it might have an impact on an urban, underserved neighborhood. East Tampa, Tampa's historical African American enclave, had suffered decades of disinvestment, discrimination, and dislocation, resulting in all the characteristics of a blighted neighborhood. According to data compiled by the City of Tampa (2003, pp. 3-6), of the nearly 30,000 people who live in East Tampa, 70% are African American, 22% White, and 15% Hispanic/Latino. Their poverty rate of 34% is nearly double the city average and 35% of the existing structures are deteriorating. Median household income in East Tampa is $22,468, which is one half of the regional average, and only 15% of East Tampa residents hold professional occupations, compared to 34% citywide. Nearly one quarter of resident households do not have a car, nearly half of the residents 16 years of age and older are not working, and about half of the youth do not complete high school.

Once the collaborative considered these daunting deficits and needs, USF faculty made a conscious decision to adopt an asset-based approach to the East Tampa partnership. Several faculty and staff had previously formed relationships in the neighborhood and advised us about some the assets and resources found within East Tampa—strong indigenous leadership, committed individuals to partner with, more than 100 documented faith-based organizations in the neighborhood, and a mayor and city staff person committed to creating positive change. A member of the collaborative steering committee, who is a leader of the local community development corporation, guided us in learning about neighborhood priorities, and recruited an experienced and retired school social worker and community activist as a volunteer liaison between USF and East Tampa, finding appropriate sites for student placements and reviewing faculty service-learning proposals.

Without the benefit of outside grants, the newly formed Neighbor-hoods and Communities Working Group of the collaborative decided to use an accepted, grassroots community development approach (asset mapping) and an academic technique (service-learning) which would maximize student and faculty involvement at a low cost. The collaborative steering committee embraced the working group strategy as a low-cost opportunity to learn what it takes to mobilize a major urban university to truly make a difference in one community.

Eight Guiding Principles

Over the past 3 years, the collaborative staff, working group, and steer-ing committee discovered important lessons, through active study and reflection of the successes, challenges and experience with the East Tampa Initiative, for changing a university so that it more strongly sup-ports and values community engagement. Eight generalizable principles emerged from these reflections.

In articulating the eight principles, the authors show how each contrib-uted to the attempts to understand and institutionalize engagement at USF. The East Tampa Initiative is described as being based on *reciprocal* relationships and a respect for the community exemplified by a *strength-based* approach. In order for any collaboration to enhance institutional capacity, it must be *sustainable* and recognize the need for *incremental* steps. To enhance faculty involvement a structure must be in place that helps them fit their individual teaching and research agendas into a larger *strategic* plan and shows them how to be *enterprising* in turning their participation into accepted scholarship. A successful collaboration must be *dissemination-oriented*, publicly transferring knowledge, celebrating par-ticipants, and soliciting new recruits. Finally, while the collaborative has

Exhibit 9.1.   Eight Principles for Community Engagement at Metropolitan Research-Extensive Universities

1. Reciprocal relationships
2. Strength-based
3. Sustainable
4. Incremental
5. Strategic
6. Enterprising
7. Dissemination-oriented
8. Creative

built a very successful community partnership by being *creative*, in order for the lessons learned to be "scaled-up," USF's leadership must commit to building an on-going supportive infrastructure.

Principle 1. Reciprocal Relationships

The development of meaningful and reciprocal partnerships between the university and community was critical to the success of this initiative. Ten years earlier, faculty from USF helped residents conduct a comprehensive needs assessment, but since that time other faculty had studied East Tampa and conducted research in its neighborhoods, often with little reciprocity, and no real, lasting partnerships evolved. When a group of faculty met with residents in an East Tampa nonprofit agency to describe the service-learning classes that were to begin in a few months, one resident reminded the group that communities do not operate on university time and semester systems. To accommodate the needs of both the university and the community, the collaborative decided to start small and move slowly, utilizing faculty seasoned in community engagement who would adapt the asset mapping strategy (Kretzman & McKnight, 1993). The USF collaborative seeded four service-learning asset-mapping classes in spring 2004 (taught by faculty from Architecture, Education, Florida Mental Health Institute (FMHI), nursing, and public health) and six service-learning classes in spring 2005 (education, FMHI, nursing, public health, social work, and visual and performing arts). These courses were jointly overseen by representatives of the City of Tampa, USF, and community agencies and organizations.

One class was cotaught by faculty in Education, FMHI, and the East Tampa lifelong resident mentioned above who had volunteered to serve as the USF/East Tampa liaison. The course was cross-listed at the undergraduate and graduate levels as a service-learning/action research class, and was offered every fall, spring, and summer semester for 2 years. The two USF faculty participated in an ETCRP committee on Health, Education, and Social Services, and together faculty, students, and residents framed the action research agenda. A large, ongoing research project was developed to document assets within schools located in East Tampa: (1) services provided to children and families attending those schools, (2) services provided to children and families living in East Tampa but bussed throughout the countywide school district, and (3) services provided to the community and residents even with no school-aged children. Students in the service-learning class, some of whom lived in East Tampa, developed individual projects that, though manageable within a single semester, generated data that fit with integrity into the larger project.

In another class, architecture faculty and students developed design models for a small business corridor through the middle of East Tampa and for beautifying retention ponds in the neighborhoods. They interviewed residents and city staff concerning their visions for the community. The student designs were then presented to the community for additional input. Today, one retention pond is about to begin construction, with funding from the ETCRP.

The reciprocity displayed in these individual courses extends into joint membership in ETCRP, the ETCRP committees, the USF collaborative working group and the USF collaborative steering committee. All four have university as well as community membership.

Principle 2. Strengths-Based

Engaging successfully with historically underserved communities is greatly enhanced by a strengths-based approach (Maton, Schellenbach, Leadbeater, & Solarz, 2004). Meaningful partnerships incorporating reciprocity are not possible when relationships involve unequal status and deficit-based thinking. University faculty and staff and community stakeholders bring complementary and additive strengths to reciprocal partnerships. The USF collaborative engaged in an informal internal scan to determine the university assets that could be brought to bear on this initiative—faculty already knowledgeable about and using the service-learning pedagogy, faculty engaged in the community (particularly in East Tampa) via teaching and research, and the collaborative seed monies that could be allocated toward multidisciplinary and collaborative action research and service-learning in East Tampa. East Tampa is a set of neighborhoods with a rich history in the African American community, and long-standing residents. Representatives from the city and USF collaborative immediately decided to focus on a strengths-based approach in East Tampa, mapping and mobilizing assets through service-learning and action research courses and projects (Kretzman & McKnight, 1993). This approach was implemented from the very beginning. A community representative took each new group of faculty and students on the of East Tampa, introducing them to the assets of the community that were not easily visible to the uninformed.

Principal 3. Sustainable

If the East Tampa Initiative was to become a catalyst for institutional change within USF, it had to produce sustainable partnerships that could generate ongoing initiatives. This was particularly difficult, given the characteristics of the partners. A university, although a formal institution, is highly decentralized with its academic units identifying more with national and international peers than with the local setting. Even more challenging, a community is a social identity and not an organization. In the case of East Tampa, the City of Tampa created the community by

combining nearly a dozen individual neighborhoods to form a new community redevelopment area. In spite of these limitations, both USF and
East Tampa created highly participatory organization. At USF it was the
faculty-based Neighborhoods and Communities Working Group of the
USF collaborative; in East Tampa, it was a coalition of public, private and
nonprofit organizations, ETCRP. Cross-organizational communications
were facilitated when community representatives attended working group
meetings and university representatives participated in ETCRP. As each
partner came to understand the other, the trust needed to establish an
ongoing relationship began to develop. Political scientist Barbara Ferman
(2006) has described the unique role universities can play in enhancing
the social capital of communities: "Because of its vast array of networks
and the legitimacy it wields, the university is particularly well suited to
play the broker role that facilitates connections across networks" (p. 88).

The ongoing dialogue between the university and the community sustained the partnership even when no service-learning theses were being
offered. During those times, the USF collaborative searched within the
university community to expand, as Holland (1999) articulates, "the community involvement beyond early adapters" (p. 69). When members of
the working group discovered faculty, students or staff involved in neigh-
borhood-based community development projects, they were invited to
attend the monthly meetings and explore connections to the East Tampa
Initiative. A new faculty orientation was created to inform new faculty of
the community engagement infrastructure at USF and introduce them to
potential community partners. Volunteer USF and student government
became involved in the East Tampa Initiative through their annual day of
service, Stampede of Service.

Principle 4. Incremental

Taking on the East Tampa Initiative was a bold decision on the part of
the USF collaborative, but the program steps within it have been incremental. When Braybrooke and Lindblom (1970) first introduced the concept of incremental decision making, they dubbed it "muddling through,"
the practice of people adapting to the complexities of real world problem
solving. The collaborative's limited resources necessitated small, gradual
steps, but more often the incrementalism was a conscious decision by the
Neighborhoods and Communities Working Group and steering committee.

The nature of the university/community collaboration dictated that the
East Tampa Initiative support only a small number of projects, that had
strong links to the community. Once a service-learning course proposal
was selected, the faculty member and students were invited to go on a
tour of the neighborhood, led and narrated by the lifelong resident and

activist who was serving as the USF/East Tampa liaison. She chaired a sub-committee of ETCRP which, among other responsibilities, provided the ongoing communication link between the community and the faculty member. She often personalized the role. In one case she informed the faculty member that a particular student was speaking with community members in a "disrespectful manner" and the faculty member counseled the student. More often, she invited the students to her house for lunch and enticed them into continuing their work in East Tampa long after their course was over.

A year into the East Tampa Initiative, a unit within USF approached the City of Tampa for funding to conduct a resident survey in East Tampa. When ETCRP realized that this was not a group participating in the East Tampa Initiative and, more significantly, that they were not going to include residents in the design and implementation of the survey, they told the city not to accept the proposal. Only by slow, incremental project development could sufficient trust be developed that community partners had the confidence to turn down university researchers who were unwilling to work collaboratively.

A second reason for incrementalism is the desire to use the East Tampa Initiative as a catalyst for institutional change within the university. To expand the project, new faculty, students and staff were slowly added to the Neighborhoods and Communities Working Group. To gain institutional legitimacy, the Collaborative Steering Committee, with high level representation from units across the university, was kept informed of the projects. At various points, both the working group and the steering committee discussed the possibility of expanding the initiative to other neighborhoods. Each time, on reflection, a conscious decision was made to continue articulating the East Tampa Initiative. At this stage, the changes USF faculty were able to make within the university to strengthen its identity as an engaged university were incremental and evolutionary, rather than revolutionary. The hope, in the long run, is that this university will follow Tyack and Cuban's (1995) model of educational reform in the public school arena: *Tinkering toward Utopia*.

Principle 5. Strategic

According to university engagement expert Holland (2003), "Perhaps the greatest and unending challenge facing partnerships is the level of time and energy it takes to launch and maintain an effective partnership relationship. Launching a project partnership is fairly easy, but launching a relationship is tricky" (p. 4). For this reason, the thought of infusing community engagement projects into teaching and research can seem daunting to faculty members racing against the tenure and promotion clock. The decision must be made whether time spent courting a potential community partner for service-learning will pay off in the form of peer-reviewed scholarship to support a successful tenure portfolio. In this regard, the USF collaborative devised a successful strategic approach to bridge what otherwise might be viewed by tenure-track faculty as a potential pitfall to engagement.

The USF collaborative was strategic in its thinking to support the work of up and coming academics by drawing them into well established "relationship networks." Using Holland's (2003) notion of partnership relationships, members of the Collaborative and the East Tampa community worked hard to develop a trusting and respectful bond to support the work of junior faculty. During a special new faculty orientation event, the East Tampa Initiative was prominently introduced, emphasizing opportunities for community engagement with eager and enthusiastic neighborhood partners. Faculty learned about the history of the university's relationship with this culturally rich African American community, and heard about the interdisciplinary mix of service-learning research taking place. Newly hired faculty at USF were reassured by the fact that much of the time-intensive work often embedded in community engagement had been successfully accomplished through another arm of the institution, freeing them to focus on developing creative and rigorous service-learning projects with established community partners such as the Corporation to Develop Communities of East Tampa and the East Tampa Community Revitalization Partnership.

Indeed, this strategy to welcome new faculty into established relationship networks also quickened the process for meeting colleagues across disciplines who shared an interest in engaged scholarship related to community development. The collaborative concentrated on weaving together opportunities to engage with East Tampa by offering faculty internal competitive service-learning and faculty research grants. The strategy here was twofold: first, to require that engaged scholarship be conducted primarily within the East Tampa community to further the positive impact for planned change; and second, to partner with a community-based East Tampa organization and, in the case of a faculty research grant, a faculty member from another discipline. This approach served to strengthen ties between new faculty members eager to connect with the community, and to broaden the interdisciplinary ties among colleagues. The strategy of developing relationship networks was also evident to new faculty through the Neighborhoods and Communities Working Group, which continued to meet monthly, and to bring faculty and community members and organizations together to discuss mutual interests for addressing social issues affecting communities in the Tampa Bay region. The end result for junior faculty has been the opportunity to participate in a series of successful service-learning research projects, providing increased knowledge and experiential learning for their students, a growing professional and social relationship with the community and colleagues, and opportunities to showcase engaged scholarship through presentations and publications.

Principle 6. Enterprising

Innovative community development strategies allow for the growth of human and social capital to benefit those working within organizations and the community at large. For faculty members interested in pursuing engaged service-learning to promote community development, the USF collaborative/East Tampa Initiative nurtured their enterprising spirit to produce meaningful scholarship. One aspect of this pursuit is a "cross-pollination" among the work of colleagues from diverse disciplines including social work, anthropology, sociology, communications, public health, geography, and education. The East Tampa Initiative provided a context for integrating disciplinary perspectives to develop innovative approaches for community capacity building.

This same enterprising thinking carried into the classroom as students had an opportunity to participate with peers from other disciplines in a research day conference organized by the collaborative, and gain an understanding of the many paths to achieving the same goal—asset based community development (Kretzman & McKnight, 1993). Together, faculty and students were able to explore the fit between practice and theoretical perspectives from other disciplines. This also provided an opportunity to examine the methods used by other disciplines to evaluate outcomes and impact from engagement activities. The flexible and supportive nature of the USF collaborative led to an enterprising experiment which involved linking practice and research through service-learning.

One cohort of undergraduate students was enrolled in sections of both introduction to social work research and multimethods of social work practice. This unique opportunity created an overlap among teaching, research and service—truly engaged scholarship. Students were able to learn about skills and strategies to work with the assets of communities, examine the effectiveness of this work through empirical methods, and then spend time within the community they were studying to experience the historical, cultural, and political influences between person and place. This inductive approach to research allowed students to use their engagement skills to enter a new community and conduct a quantitative and qualitative contextual assessment, from which hypotheses and research questions could be developed. The experience culminated in students preparing a presentation for community and university members, with implications and recommendations for continued work in building social capital to promote continued planned change within neighborhoods.

For tenure-seeking faculty members, the East Tampa Initiative facilitated an entrepreneurial approach that revealed new outlets for scholarship (e.g., peer-reviewed service-learning journals, service-learning research conferences), additional opportunities for grant funding (e.g., faculty development grants), and new peer relationships to promote success (e.g. coauthorship with project partners, broader venue of journals for submitting interdisciplinary work).

Principle 7. Dissemination-Oriented

For university-community collaborations to have an impact beyond the immediate projects, the knowledge gained must be disseminated within the university, within the community and across the boundaries between the two. Too often, the new knowledge is retained by those participating directly in the project. It is not enough for university students and faculty to gain skills and knowledge, write and deliver papers, or win research grants—they must share the results with the community in a form that is useful to the community. It is not enough for students and faculty to become culturally competent and respect the norms and values of the community—they need to recognize and acknowledge their partners. It is not enough for community partners to integrate the data gathered into revitalization plans—they need to share it as widely as possible within the community. Frequently, measurable changes in the neighborhood take years to achieve, so reports, publications and special events take on a higher level of importance, as they provide both the university and the community with a reminder that the revitalization effort is underway and succeeding.

The USF collaboration has gained a reputation for producing high quality, timely print material, in both hard copy and electronic form (http://usfcollab.usf.edu). Unlike many "slick" productions, the purpose of these materials is community-building and not community relations. Both big and small projects are described in detail and university and community participants are featured. Invitations for newcomers to participate, complete with contact information, are always included and the publications come alive with pictures and quotes.

In the case of the East Tampa Initiative, the collaborative produced and continuously updated the data collected through the service-learning courses. Asset maps were printed and distributed in the community and at the university. Photos of the professors, their contact information, and their class titles were listed as well as illustrations of the assets each discovered. The maps and other East Tampa resource documents have also been posted on the collaborative Web site, with data available in downloadable formats so it can be shared with the community, the city, and other researchers (http://usfcollab.usf.edu/neighborhoodsdetail.cfm?areaID=1).

The collaborative also holds conferences, workshops and networking opportunities that serve to disseminate information and cement relationships. For example, each year the USF collaborative organizes a research day conference where students doing community-based research present their results. This is an important activity aimed at overcoming the university's reputation for studying a community but not sharing the results. Although research day predates the East Tampa Initiative, it has become progressively more focused, reflective and community oriented. In 2004, the student presentations were followed by a panel of university and community representatives reflecting on the lessons learned. In 2005, keynote addresses by a community activist, a former student and the mayor of Tampa were added. In 2006 the event moved off campus, in response to the community members' complaints about parking at the university and their desire to have more residents attend. Even the menu changed from the traditional box lunches to chicken, green beans and pie, prepared by the members of an East Tampa church.

Principle 8. Creative

True to observations of creative city gurus such as Richard Florida and Charles Landry (Florida, 2002; Landry, 2000), researchers discovered that people attracted to the early stages of building partnerships between USF and East Tampa were imaginative problem solvers willing to collaborate in order to reinvigorate and achieve their purpose and goals. Creative people know that, even if the community where they live is not quite what they were hoping for, they enjoy the stimulation, diversity and richness of experience found in urban redevelopment projects (Florida, 2002). Most of the faculty who opted to participate in the East Tampa Initiative had experience in community-based research and were looking for an opportunity to join a multidisciplinary team that was interested in learning from the experience and having a positive impact on the way the University of South Florida carried out its community engagement strategy. When they agreed to participate in community-based teaching, some faculty were not familiar with the term "service-learning" but that did not deter them from agreeing to be part of a team effort between the university and community.

There were no new resources dedicated to the East Tampa Initiative, and that constraint caused administrators, faculty and staff to think creatively about how they could use what they already had in new ways. A small amount of seed money funds moved from the collaborative's established faculty grant program to fund four East Tampa Service-Learning Asset Mapping minigrants of $2,000 each for faculty who agreed to participate in the initiative. Five faculty members applied (two team-taught one class), and each received $1,000 during the Spring 2004 semester for extra expenses associated with the class, and $1,000 later when they had a paper or poster about the experience accepted for presentation at a national conference, which nearly all have done. A sixth faculty member was funded to provide training in asset mapping and to create maps with the data collected in the classes. A seventh faculty member added an East Tampa service-learning component to an existing course without additional funding.

The collaborative's steering committee observed recently, while enumerating the number of new papers, partnerships, classes, grants and contracts now resulting from the East Tampa Initiative, that inadequate funds may have been a blessing in disguise, since creative approaches were chosen by necessity and helped avoid doing too much, too fast. Yet they also agree that faculty cannot remain as "starving artists" if USF is to institutionalize the lessons learned.

Institutionalization Efforts at USF

Within the lifespan of the East Tampa Initiative, several efforts were initiated to dramatically increase the level of institutionalization of engagement at USF. Such efforts had been attempted in the past. While some previous efforts often broke down due to competing views of what community engagement meant, a common vision began to emerge from the universitywide discussions that took place at the Collaborative Neighborhoods and Communities Working Group and steering committee. This visioning process ramped up considerably when one of the members was elected to the presidency of the faculty senate and used this position to place university-community engagement on the leadership agenda. In early 2005, she created the Faculty Senate Ad Hoc Committee on University-Community Engagement and asked faculty and administrators who had been centrally involved in community-based research, service-learning and community partnerships at USF to meet with the explicit purpose of making recommendations for the enhancement of USF's capacity to support effective community collaborations. the ad hoc committee immediately divided into three subcommittees that were charged with developing a strategic plan within each area: (1) research, scholarship, promotion and tenure, (2) curriculum and service-learning, and (3) partnerships and outreach.

Each committee was chaired by an ad hoc committee member who had also been active in the collaborative and the East Tampa Initiative, guaranteeing that the lessons learned through that partnership became part of the strategic plan. However, new university participants were consciously brought into the conversation. The research, scholarship, promotion and tenure subcommittee, in addressing the disparate definitions of scholarship at a major university, included participants from several units and colleges across campus. In addition to faculty who had experience with service-learning, the curriculum and service-learning subcommittee included representatives from student activities, the newly formed center for undergraduate research, and the offices of faculty development and teaching-learning assessment. The partnerships and outreach committee brought together the representatives from several successful outreach centers within the university. Each subcommittee explored the potentials and problems of engagement at USF and surveyed peer universities looking for models of institutionalization.

The Faculty Senate Ad Hoc Committee on University-Community Engagement, with funding from the provost's office, brought two nationally known consultants on community engagement to campus (Barbara Holland and Robert Bringle). Their visits were used as yet another opportunity to bring representatives together from across campus to develop a vision and to receive validation and advice from outside experts. Their visits also provided an opportunity to take the vision of university engagement to university leadership. In one case the consultant was able to present the provost with an informed and honest assessment of the chances of USF achieving its "50 in 5" goal. The consultant argued convincingly that USF's likelihood of becoming one of the top public research universities within 5 years would be substantially enhanced if administrators took full advantage of the metropolitan location and the recently discovered fact that much of the current funded research is conducted within the local community. The consultant was also able to point to peer universities that were successfully implementing the same strategy.

The significance of engagement in university rankings was brought to the attention of USF leadership when the Faculty Senate Ad Hoc Committee on University-Community Engagement convinced President Genshaft to apply for participation in the Carnegie Foundation for the Advancement of Teaching's elective community engagement classification pilot (Carnegie Foundation, 2006a). In her letter of intent the President stated:

> USF is proud of its past and extensive record of community engagement, and we are eager to expand and sustain the partnerships with the local and broader communities we serve while exploring ways to increase faculty involvement and enhance student academic success through such activities. (Genshaft, 2006)

She committed resources to the engagement documentation effort, resulting in an impressive, albeit incomplete, census of engagement partnerships and scholarship. As important as the submission to the Carnegie

Foundation was the message that the documentation effort sent to deans, directors, departmental chairs and faculty—that community engagement is valued at the highest levels of administration. That effort resulted in USF being selected in Carnegie's new Community Engagement classification—one of only 76 U.S. colleges and universities so recognized. USF was the only Florida university to receive the classification, and one of only 10 public research universities accorded this status (Carnegie Foundation, 2006b).

So far, this has not resulted in additional funding for faculty or staff infrastructure to support this work, but the recognition has been incorporated into marketing campaigns, including banners on campus announcing the ranking and a new ad campaign which includes an emphasis on community engagement. Its impact can also be seen in the language and metrics that are part of USF's new strategic plan (University of South Florida Strategic Plan, n.d.).

Leadership support was also sought and received from the USF's Board of Trustees (BOT). The president of the faculty senate, as a member of the BOT, presented the group with the Faculty Senate Ad Hoc Committee on University-Community Engagement recommendations. Prominent in these recommendations was a request for funding to build the infrastructure necessary at an engaged research university. Prior to the East Tampa Initiative many at USF knew that ongoing funding was necessary to support engagement activities, but the "guiding principles" that emerged from the committee's reflections provided clarity about the nature and extent of infrastructure that was necessary. The request was for collaborations among existing faculty-led centers with an increase of $1.5 million in budget. The BOT combined this request with one for the promotion of an entrepreneurship center and sent it as a "legislative budget request" to Tallahassee. It was approved by the statewide board of governors and presented to the Florida legislature in the Spring 2007 session. Although legislative funding was not achieved in 2007, which was overall a bad budget year for Florida, the compatibility of the research and engagement agendas at USF and the funding needs to support the dual goal seem to have been recognized by the president and board of trustees.

CONCLUSIONS AND NEXT STEPS

Just as the mayor's request that USF help the city in its revitalization efforts in East Tampa provided an unanticipated opportunity to explore the compatibility of community engagement and the production of scholarship in a single neighborhood, the near future offers three critical opportunities to further the institutionalization of community engagement at USF.

The first of these is the new strategic plan that has just been adopted at USF. The 2002-2007 Strategic Plan listed the establishment of USF as a "national model for a university fully engaged with its local, national, and global communities" as its ninth (out of 9) strategic goal. But, without the necessary resources, metrics or a common vision, this strategy was overshadowed by the first strategic goal of creating "nationally and internationally distinctive research and graduate programs" (University of South Florida Strategic Plan, n.d.). Community engagement is now more centrally integrated into the new 2007-2012 Strategic Plan, in large part because members of the university community who understand the compatibility of being a major research university and being an engaged university, played an active and central role in the planning process. Community engagement is also listed more prominently in the Strategic Plan, that is, "expanding local and global engagement initiatives to strengthen and sustain healthy communities and to improve the quality of life," and appropriate accompanying metrics have been proposed (University of South Florida Strategic Plan, n.d.). Those metrics, derived from the measures the Carnegie Foundation asked for in the application for ranking, offer a way to benchmark progress over the 5 five years.

Second, a revamping of undergraduate education at USF is currently underway, as outlined in the Quality Enhancement Plan (QEP) approved by the regional accreditation board (SACS). The cognitive and civic competencies that general education and exit courses must develop are precisely those that the literature shows are furthered by well articulated service-learning courses (Eyler & Giles, 2002). The undergraduate research opportunities required by the QEP also lend themselves to service-learning and community-based research pedagogies. Faculty familiar with the potential of the service-learning pedagogy need to promote it with the appropriate USF curricular committees, faculty development personnel and learning assessment experts.

Finally, faculty and administrators must be prepared to educate and advocate with the Florida Legislature as well as other public and private funders for the resources needed to build engagement infrastructure at USF. While advocacy is not a practice which many faculty at the university engage in, the relationships formed in creating the East Tampa Initiative have created partnerships within the community and across the university (including with members of the board of trustees) which can serve us well.

The East Tampa Initiative has taught many lessons, including the knowledge that if an opportunity presents itself, one must take advantage of it before the window of opportunity closes. Adding an engagement agenda to a university that is singularly focused on becoming a nationally ranked research university is a daunting task. Who would have believed that a university that was built in a cow pasture 50 years ago, would have achieved the status that USF possesses today (Greenburg, 2006)?

REFERENCES

Boyer, E. L. (1990). *Scholarship reconsidered: Priorities of the professoriate.* San Francisco: Jossey-Bass.

Boyer, E. L. (1996). The scholarship of engagement. *Journal of Public Service and Outreach, 1,* 11-20

Braybrooke, D., & Lindblom, C. E. (1970). *A strategy of decision: Policy evaluation as a social process.* New York: The Free Press.

Bringle, R. G., Games, R., & Malloy, E. A. (1999). *Colleges and universities as citizens.* Boston: Allyn & Bacon.

Carnegie Foundation for the Advancement of Teaching. (2006a). *Community engagement elective classification.* Retrieved June 22, 2007, from http://www.carnegiefoundation.org/classifications/index.asp?key=1213

Carnegie Foundation for the Advancement of Teaching. (2006b). *Carnegie selects colleges and universities for new elective community engagement classification.* Retrieved June 22, 2007, from http://www.carnegiefoundation.org/news/sub.asp?key=51&subkey=2126

City of Tampa. (2003). *East Tampa: Existing conditions report.* Tampa, FL: Department of Business and Housing Development.

Eyler, J., & Giles, D. E., Jr. (2002). Beyond surveys: Using the problem solving interview to assess the impact of service-learning on understanding and critical thinking. In A. Furco & S.H. Billig (Eds.), *Service-learning: The essence of the pedagogy.* Greenwich, CT: Information Age.

Ferman, B. (2006). Leveraging social capital: The university as educator and broker. In R. Dilworth (Ed.), *Social capital in the city* (pp. 81-100). Philadelphia: Temple University Press.

Florida, R. (2002). *The rise of the creative class.* New York: Basic Books.

Genshaft, J. (2006, May). *Carnegie University-Community Engagement Classification. Letter to the Carnegie Foundation for the advancement of teaching.* Retrieved May 30, 2007, from http://www.ods.usf.edu/Committee/Carnegie/Engagement

Greenburg, M. (2006). *University of South Florida: The first fifty years 1956-2006.* Tampa: University of South Florida.

Holland, B. (1999). From murky to meaningful. In R.G. Bringle, R. Games, & E. A. Malloy (Eds.), *Colleges and universities as citizens* (pp. 48-73). Needham Heights, MA: Allyn & Bacon.

Holland, B. (2003, April). Community-university partnerships: Translating evidence into action. In B. A. Holland, S. Gelmon, L. W. Green, E. Green-Moton, & T. K. Stantonn (Eds.), *National symposium on university-community partnerships: Community-university partnerships: What do we know?* Symposium conducted by the National Community-Campus Partnerships for Health and HUD Office of University Partnerships, San Diego, California.

Jacobs, J. (1961). *The death and life of great American cities.* New York: Random House.

Kretzman, J. P., & McKnight, J. L. (1993). *Building communities from the inside out: A path toward finding and mobilizing a community's assets.* Evanston, IL: Northwestern University Institute for Policy Research.

Landry, C. (2000). *The creative city: A toolkit for urban innovators.* London: United Kingdom: Earthscan Publications.

Maton, K. I. Schellenbach, C. J., Leadbeater, B. J., & Solarz, A. L. (Eds.) (2004). *Investing in children, youth families and communities: Strengths-based research and policy.* Washington, DC: American Psychological Association.

Tyack, D., & Cuban, L. (1995). *Tinkering toward utopia: A century of public school reform.* Boston: Hard University Press.

University of South Florida, Planning, Performance and Accountability. (n.d.). *USF strategic imperatives.* Retrieved May 30, 2007, from http://www.ie.usf.edu/PPA/USFstratimp.asp.

University of South Florida, Strategic Plan. (n.d.). Retrieved May 30, 2007, from http://www.ie.usf.edu/Strategicplan/Strategies.asp

SECTION IV

EXPERIENCES OF SERVICE-LEARNING IN TEACHER EDUCATION

CHAPTER 10

REVERSING THE LENS

Transforming Teacher Education
Through Service-Learning

Margaret Vickers

ABSTRACT

This chapter presents a preliminary study that explores what trainee teachers might learn, especially in relation to working in hard-to-staff schools or with marginalized students, through service-learning activities that place them in alternative educational settings. Trainee teachers' perceptions of what is learned in these settings is contrasted with what is learned through participation in the conventional practicum, where the emphasis is on techniques of classroom management and knowledge of the mandated curriculum documents. At the University of Western Sydney, all secondary teacher-education students undergo an "alternative" practicum, based on the principles of academic service-learning, and all are required to submit written reflections on their experiences at the end of their placements. This chapter provides an analysis of these student reflections, supplemented by data collected from interviews. Service-learning in the UWS teacher education degree is not intended merely to provide extra hours of practicum for

From Passion to Objectivity: International and Cross-Disciplinary Perspectives on Service Learning Research, pp. 199–216
199

preservice teachers but to function as a disruption of students' more regulated classroom-based experiences. The analysis provided here indicates that this disruption can create a space for transformational learning, allowing opportunities for student teachers to develop the capacity to connect with marginalized students and support their learning goals.

INTRODUCTION

This chapter reports a preliminary study that investigates what trainee teachers might learn that would help them to work in hard-to-staff schools or with marginalized students, through service-learning placements that locate them in alternative educational settings, where they relate to students as individuals or in small groups. As an exploratory study, the chapter represents a preliminary part of a larger research program being developed at the University of Western Sydney (UWS). This larger program focuses on examining how teacher educators might prepare beginning teachers to succeed in schools that are hard to staff, that is, schools that constitute exceptionally challenging environments for teaching and learning.

Conventional teacher education programs place a strong emphasis on ensuring that trainee teachers develop techniques of classroom management and the ability to help students acquire the knowledge laid down in mandated curriculum documents. An experiential basis for this knowledge acquisition is customarily provided through the professional field experience or practicum. While it is possible to construct classroom-based "practicum" experiences that might help student teachers establish effective relationships with marginalized students, in many schools this does not happen routinely. Zeichner (1992) drew attention to institutional constraints that tend to restrict what student teachers can learn about young people's lives, the communities in which they live, and the nature of their lives outside of school. Cochran-Smith (1991) argued that when trainee teachers first confront students whose cultural backgrounds are different from their own in classroom settings, their experiences may reinforce their preexisting stereotypes about the "difficulties" of working with these students, rather than leading to a disruption of such stereotypical thinking. Gallego's (2001) research, which contrasted the experiences of trainee teachers in classroom-based practica and community-based small-group settings, examined related issues and has been a valuable tool in framing the approach taken in this study.

As Goodman (1985) found in an early but influential study, the tasks student teachers carry out in their professional experience placements tend to place a strong emphasis on the transmission of information and the management and control of classrooms. Goodman argued that most teacher education programs follow a vocational approach to professional training, which means they privilege a particular way of viewing young people. In effect, young people are often appraised in terms of their ability and willingness to be "good students"—present, prepared, and mentally engaged in scholarly tasks. Viewed through this conventional lens, marginal students are often seen as "troublemakers" who are to be disciplined and brought into line. For many students who have been so positioned, their experience of school is an experience of "being controlled" rather than "being a learner." The idea that marginalised students might be "othered" by teachers in conventional classroom settings, and the possibility of disrupting this "othering" through participation in alternative small-group settings, is an important theme that will be taken up later in the chapter.

Oakes and Lipton (2003, p. 267) asked, "Why is it that children and adolescents—who are by nature eager and voracious learners—become seen as unwilling troublemakers who need to be controlled and manipulated into paying attention at school?" Part of the answer to this question, Oakes and Lipton suggested, comes from the persistence of the idea that children whose families that are poor, or rural, Black or Hispanic, or immigrant, or some combination of the above, are "culturally deprived." Effective and practical critiques of this approach were advanced by educators such as Noddings (1992) and Kohn (1996), and in many schools the focus now has shifted toward the implementation of a more engaging pedagogy and more effective instructional techniques. Yet there are still some schools and some classrooms in which it is assumed that children whose families are poor or who are recent immigrants need strict routines and firm disciplinary policies if they are to be brought up to the standards that White, middle-class children learned at home (Oakes & Lipton, 2003).

In the UWS secondary teacher-education program, a service-learning subject known as Professional Experience 3 (PE3) is a required part of the qualifying degree for beginning teachers. PE3 represents a third practicum alongside the two conventional classroom-based placements that are known as Professional Experience 1 (PE1) and Professional Experience 2 (PE2). The conventional PE1 and PE2 are block-placement practicums where most of the students' effort is focused on the preparaton and delivery of classroom lessons in the disciplnes in which the student is aiming to qualify (for example, mathematics, science, English). PE3 has a different focus. It provides a series of contexts through which trainee teachers can become aware of the broader professional responsibilites that are carried out in public schools across the Western Sydney region, and can provide needed services to targetted groups of students within schools, as well as to students who may be on their way out, or alternatively, may be seeking re-entry to school.

PE3 placements meet the principles of academic service-learning that are used within the context of community-engaged teaching and learning at UWS. In service-learning programs at UWS, it is expected that (1) students will be engaged in service-related activities that link academic learning with community agencies, (2) student placements are designed so as to meet community-defined needs, and their activities are mutually arranged and agreed on by agency personnel and teaching staff, (3) students' experiences provide a basis for guided reflection, which may take the form of written assignments given to students by faculty, but may also involve reflective discussions facilitated by agency staff, and (4) agency placements are based on partnerships among students, teaching staff and agency personnel.[1] Within this context, the usual teacher-education block practicum does not meet the criteria of academic service-learning. A basic definition of academic service-learning adopted by UWS is that "service-learning links academic learning with community service guided by reflection" (McCarthy, Damrongmanee, Pushpalatha, Chithra, & Yamamoto, 2005).

This chapter is largely based on an examination of the written reflections produced by student teachers who completed PE3 in 2005 and 2006. In addition to these documents, interviews with PE3 students were conducted by Morrow (2006), and further reports and analyses of the PE3 experience were provided by Roots (see Gannon & Roots, 2006). The intention here is to use these reflections and supplemenary materials to explore and identify the multiple forms of learning that may emerge as trainee teachers interact with marginlaized students, individually or in small groups, in alternative settings. While these data are limited, the purpose of this preliminary study was to make a useful contribution to a larger UWS study which is now under way. In the larger study, samples of beginning teachers will be interviewed during their training as well as during their first and second years in the teaching service. Intensive interviewing will be used, together with short surveys. The preliminary study reported here provides useful guidance for the larger research project by identifying issues that need to be explored in greater depth, as the researchers seek to understand the potential contributions PE3 might make in preparing teachers for hard-to-staff schools.

TEACHER EDUCATION IN WESTERN SYDNEY

The University of Western Sydney prepares teachers for schools that predominantly serve students of low socioeconomic status (Vickers, Muckerjee, Dowson, & Livermore, 2000). The family circumstances of many of these students are complex and difficult. In the outer suburbs of Western and South-Western Sydney, it is not uncommon to find high-school-aged students who are responsible for the care of younger siblings, who may be victims of physical and emotional abuse, or whose living arangements may be "mobile," in that they sleep at different family locactions each night with no fixed place to call home (Lamb, Teese, Walstab, Vickers, & Rumberger, 2004; Thomson, 2002). When UWS student teachers graduate, they are mostly employed by the New South Wales Department of Education, and assigned to schools that are populated by young people whose chances of success are jeopardized by family poverty, low levels of parental education, and family mobility.

In addition, Western Sydney is the first destination of the majority of immigrants and refugees arriving in Australia. Over time, this has shaped the demography of the region. For example, 62% of school students in South-Western Sydney come from families in which one or both parents regularly speak a language other than English (Vinson, 2002). To take another example, 82% of all African born humanitarian refugees arriving in New South Wales between 2001 and 2006 became residents of Western Sydney (Report of the Community Relations Commission for a Multicultural NSW, 2006).

Students attending schools in Sydney's Western suburbs often need professional support that goes beyond the routine requirements of the teacher's role. These responsibilities may include intensive English language instruction for recent immigrants, providing a safe and supportive place for homework centers, additional support for students with disabilities and special needs, liaison with student welfare officers, and interviews with parents. Within the New South Wales (NSW) system, schools that carry these additional responsibilities are often hard to staff. As teachers gain experience and seniority they are able to transfer away from "tough" Western Sydney schools to "easier" schools in the middle-class suburbs. It follows that the hard-to-staff schools of Sydney's West tend to receive a disproportionate number of beginning teachers.

A recent report on public education in NSW indicates that beginning teachers typically comprise between 10 and 20% of the teaching staff in the hard-to-staff schools of this state (NSW Public Education Council, Report, 2005). Since this pattern is repeated year after year, the schools of Sydney's West and Southwest often have only a small minority of teachers who have more than 5 years of experience and very few who have remained in the same school consistently over a longer period of time. Yet conventional professional experience programs, with their emphasis on prepared lesson plans, set classroom performance expectations, and the attachment of the trainee teacher to a single supervisor often fails to introduce beginning teachers to the full scope of their professional responsibilities (Cochran-Smith, 1991). Recent studies suggest that beginning and early career teachers will only remain in hard-to-staff schools if their initial preparation is better matched to the complexities of the contexts they enter, if they have sufficient knowledge and skills to help all students learn, and if expert teachers are available to serve as leaders and mentors (Glennie, Coble & Allen, 2004; Moore-Johnson, 2004).

The service-learning subject discussed above, known as PE3, represents one strategy through which the UWS secondary teacher-education faculty seeks to better prepare student teachers for hard-to-staff schools. Over 300 secondary teacher education students complete PE3 each year. The university organizes a smorgasbord of placement options and students may choose among these, working individually or in groups in a range of settings. These placement options include working in afterschool homework centres, travelling to remote rural areas to support students and schools through the "Beyond the Line" program, providing small-group literacy tutoring support for recent refugees and immigrants, engaging in youth mentoring, or working with out-of-school youth in community learning programs. Every PE3 student is required to complete a total of sixty hours in their community placement activity. In most placement options, staff who operate the community agencies hold reflection sesions with the teacher education students, encouraging them to examine the effects of mentoring and immersion in alternative educational environments on the young people participating in the programs. All students submit written reflections on their experiences at the end of their placements. Examinaton of these written records allows for a comparison of student-teacher responses to these different kinds of placements.

In this chapter, attention is focused on student-teacher responses to two particular placement options, known as *Plan-it-Youth* and *Next Generation*. These two placement options are of special interest because they focus on young people who may have dropped out of school prematurely, or been suspended, or expressed a desire to leave school, or who are doing poorly in terms of their school's standard academic and behavioural requirements. In addition, some of these students are juvenile offenders who have been assigned to alternative learning programs. In the context of the ubiquitous and taken-for-granted power relations of high schools, these young people are often defined as marginal and as failures whose removal may in fact benefit this school. Some of these young people have lost heart, beleiving they have lost their entitlement to the level of support and continuing commitment that might enable them to complete high school qualifications (Vickers, Harris & McCarthy, 2004). The Plan-it-Youth and Next Generation placements create situations in which student teachers develop personal relationships with these young people and work with them as mentors on alternative learning programs over a 10- to 12-week period.

Through the Plan-it-Youth and Next Generation placement options, student teachers form personal relationships with an individual young person or a small group of young people. These two programs have transformational possibilities, in at least two senses. First, they offer the possibility that these young people might be reclaimed from the margins, and might move back and reengage with the education system. Second, by participating in these service-learning options, teacher-education students who have already moved well along the process of becoming teachers are provoked into examining how the schooling practices into which they are becoming inculcated have failed the young people they meet, and are in need of reform (Gannon, 2005). As students examine the assumptions underlying conventional practices dedicated to the management and control of student behavior, they consruct new ways of thinking about marginalised students, and in many cases, develop a broader view of what it means to be an effective teacher.

SERVICE-LEARNING IN TEACHER EDUCATION

Service-learning has become increasingly popular among educational institutions over the past two decades, and is now emerging in teacher education in Australia (Butcher, Howard, McMeniman, & Thom, 2003; Vickers et al., 2004). A number of studies suggested that service-learning can foster pre-service teachers' engagement with the profession, enhance their self-esteem and leadership, develop their mentoring ability, and increase their respect for and understanding of diverse communities (Henderson & Brookhart, 1997; Shimmons-Torres, Drew-Cates, Johnson & Overbeek, 2002). Service-learning may also provide a broadening context that has the potential to transform teacher learning, leading to new understandings of ways that teachers (and teacher trainees) might connect with students at the margins (Dudderar & Stover, 2003; Gallego, 2001; Gannon, 2005; King, 2004).

King (2004) provided a useful discussion of the potentially transformative effects of service-learning. To be transformative, service-learning must involve students in a critical examination of their own preconceived opinions. It should lead them to reexamine taken-for-granted assumptions about the way things are. As King (2004) described it, this process of critical reflection contains an element of defamiliarization, in which "what was strange becomes familiar, and what was familiar becomes strange again … doubt and hesitancy are introduced into situations with which we are comfortable and secure, while those previously considered alien or incomprehensible are rendered more widely recognisable" (2004, p. 125).

King (2004) followed Brunner (1994) in defining transformation as a process that "ruptures the codes of conventional thinking" (p. 34). In the context of this study of PE3 at UWS, the question being asked is whether, or to what extent, the experience of working with marginalized students in small groups in alternative settings leads to a disruption of trainee teachers' preexisting ideas about these students. What is desirable here is the opening of new opportunities to interact with marginalized students, not as disruptive elements that need to be controlled, but as learners who have a genuine desire for knowledge. Noddings (1992) suggested that this is most likely to occur when the partners in a service-learning program. The trainee teacher and the student form a personal relationship. When one human being comes to care for another, Noddings wrote, they are drawn out of their own narrow perspectives and come to really hear and feel what the "other" conveys.

Earlier studies suggested that service-learning in teacher education may indeed achieve such transformational outcomes. In one example from a teacher education institution in Maryland, Dudderar and Stover (2003) described a program in which teacher education students were involved in a number or alternative learning settings. They tutored and mentored "at-risk" middle school students, worked in Graduate Equivalency Diploma programs, helped deliver environmental education units, or taught after-school enrichment classes at local schools. Dudderar and Stover (2003) contrasted the narrow kinds of learning that occur in the traditional "practicum" with the learning that occurs when student teachers are able to work directly with young people in more "natural" community settings. As Dudderar and Stover (2003) argued, these alternative settings differ from schools, in the sense that they allow individual students to speak about their own needs and negotiate learning activities that help them to achieve goals they value, rather than expecting them to perform according to conventional criteria laid down in the formal curriculum.

In exploring how student teachers might learn from the experience of service-learning, Gallego (2001) structured a program in which teacher education trainees participated concurrently in both a traditional classroom-based practicum in elementary schools, and an alternative learning program in a community-based setting. The trainees were then explicitly asked to reflect on the contrasts across these two distinctly different field-based experiences. Whereas the traditional practicum entails an implicit endorsement of standard classroom procedures, so that these procedures become "familiar" and "naturalized," what Gallego found was that when student teachers participated in community-based service-learning as a parallel practicum experience, they developed the ability to stand aside from the "naturalized" practices of schools, critiquing them and contrasting them with the kinds of learning environments they encountered in alternative out-of-school settings.

From her study, Gallego (2001) concluded that there are three conditions that facilitate transformational learning among student teachers who work in community-based settings. These conditions are expressed in terms of recommendations for structuring community-based field experience. First, Gallego says, it should operate in a physically distinct environment, apart from schools and classrooms. Second, a genuine learning activity tied to the content of the teacher education program needs to be integrated into the academic content of the alternative learning program. Unless this is done, there is a danger that the activity will be "service rich and learning poor" (p. 324). Third, student teachers need consistent opportunities to reflect on their experiences and examine the implications for reforming classroom practice and school policy. As the next section indicates, these conditions are met in the strands of PE3 at UWS that form the focus of this study.

EFFECTS OF STUDENT-TEACHER
PARTICIPATION IN SERVICE-LEARNING

The two service-learning options examined here are known within UWS as Plan-it-Youth and Next Generation. A brief description of the nature of these placements is provided to indicate what kind of work the community-based agencies aim to carry out with young people, and what kinds of learning opportunities occus in these alternative settings.

Plan it Youth is a state-funded youth program that recuits and trains community volunteers, links them with high school students who are seeking mentoring, and supports the mentors through weekly debriefing sessions. Each year, through a special arrangement with this program, approximately 15 teacher education students complete an accredited mentor training course. They then are matched with students who are grappling with academic, social or personal problems, and are often considering leaving school. Teacher education students mentor these young people over a period of 10 weeks and also engage in weekly reflective sessions in which they debrief with other mentors, and refine their understandings of what is happening in the lives of their mentees. When they have completed their Plan it Youth placements, the student teachers prepare a brief summary of their reflections which is submitted as a course requirement.

The other program—Next Generation—is sponsored by the Dusseldorp Skills Forum, a philanthropic organization that carries out youth
advocacy and provides a range of support programs for out-of-school
youth. Next Generation places student teachers in community youth support programs outside of the school system. Most of the young people in
these programs have progressed beyond the "at risk of failure" category.
In many cases they have been suspended or fully excluded by schools, and
they have often themselves rejected schooling. Supported by the New
South Wales state government, alternative learning programs for these
young people are provided by a range of local community organizations,
adult education centers, community colleges, and local councils. UWS
teacher-education students who choose the Next Generation option begin
by browsing the Web site where and finding out about programs that are
linked with UWS through Next Generation. They make contact with the
project coordinator responsible for one of these programs, put forward a
project idea, visit the program, and if there is a "match," their project can
begin.

Examples of student-teacher initiatives that have been carried out in
collaboration with these different youth organizations include a project in
which student teachers work with young people as they construct model
dragsters, and then race them; developing magazines or comic books and
publishing them; and working with young people in a youth café, teaching basic food skills and food handling. In each project, student teachers
develop an evaluation for the youth participants to complete. Student
teachers also upload their own reflections on the Next Generation Web
site (www.dsf.org.au/learningchoices/nextgeneration). Excerpts from these
online reflections are presented and analyzed below, together with quota-
tions from Morrow's (2006) evaluative interviews, and citations from a
work by a recent UWS graduate who presented at the 2006 Australian
College of Educators conference (Gannon & Roots, 2006).

Reframing Who They Are: Respect as a Basis for Learning

Of the many observations that emerge from these student reflections,
three themes can be identified. First, several of the UWS teacher education students found that when in-school and out-of-school contexts are
compared, there are significant differences between the discourses that
frame who marginalized young people "are" and what can be expected of
them:

On my previous practicum I had noticed that it was common to hear students referred to in terms that related to their behavioral, academic or wel-

fare status. In [the community program I chose] the students were introduced to me as people, not in terms of their "problems." The students were given a clean slate, hence leaving me with an open mind, able to form my own perceptions and relationships with the students. This practice of explicitly treating the students as people set up an environment of respect and equality, the teacher student dynamic was changed—for the better. (Roots, cited in Gannon & Roots, 2006, p. 4)

In a similar vein, one student teacher wrote, in relation to the community setting:

It was good seeing troubled students treated with respect.

Another student teacher found that, although these young people may act bored and resistant in school, they really do want to learn, and this becomes evident in the flexible out-of-school setting:

The kids I worked with were eager to learn, not necessarily about maths, science, English, etc., but more about life, about what it takes to do certain things, why we choose the careers we do, and where we come from. My students were as interested in me as I was in them; they wanted to know who I really was, and why I really wanted to teach.

UWS teacher education students described the community settings as places where young people enjoyed "an environment of respect and equality." They contrasted these contexts with some of the formal school settings they had observed, where some students were apparently defined mainly in terms of their problems. Implicit in this contrast is the suggestion that marginalized students are sometimes relegated to the category of "the other," that they are not like "good students" because they are not seen as routinely present and mentally engaged in scholarly tasks.

If these "other" young people have little in common with "good students" it is a short step to assume that they cannot learn or are not interested in learning. While in formal school settings one may find marginal students framed as nonlearners, new ways of seeing these students emerged when student teachers worked in community settings:

I am glad that I got to experience this part of teaching. Often the teachers in schools do not get to see these students as anything other than "bad kids." I probably would have been like that too had I not seen students that have been suspended so many times and who have very little respect for teachers [who nevertheless] completed our project [in the community setting].

Another student wrote:

As a practice teacher with 30 students, much of my focus and energy went to using the planning techniques I had studied to control my classes and control students with "behavior problems"... [Next Generation] allowed me to meet amazing students with amazing talents on a level I probably wouldn't have found in the classroom. It opened my eyes to the fact that many of the students who felt they don't "fit" in class are just the type of students that I want: ones who see things differently, are creative, energetic, passionate and challenge me to give their learning purpose, and this illustrated to me just how important it is that my students feel they belong. (A 2004 Next Generation student, cited in Gannon & Roots, 2006, p. 1)

Students who are defined as the "other" may reciprocate by defining teachers as the "other." In this next example we find a student who considers that teachers (as a category) are not seen as a source of learning. The implicit suggestion is that teachers are people who uphold and enforce the authority of the system, rather than supporting opportunities for learning.

One conversation that remains in my mind is one I shared with one of the boys. He asked me if I was a teacher, and when I said "yes," he looked confused. Then the boy said "you can't be" and when I asked him why he thought this he said "because I learned something." At that moment I realized how alienated these students had become from learning in a classroom environment due to behavioral or learning problems. (Teacher education student Paige Roots, cited in Gannon & Roots, 2006, p. 4)

This extraordinary exchange illustrates how a marginalized student's taken-for-granted view of "what a teacher is" was disrupted through his mutual engagement in a service-learning program. In this case, the student saw for the first time that a teacher can be someone a student learns from, not just someone who tries to control young people. The idea that service-learning might have transformational potential for marginalized students as well as for teachers is one that has gained scant attention in the literature to date. Although based in this case on one interview, it is an idea that needs to be carried forward into larger systematic studies.

Becoming Confident in Working With Marginalized Students

A second theme emerging from student teachers' reflections related to the transformation of their ideas about being a teacher, and a newfound confidence in working with marginalized students. As the Next Generation Web site indicates, the target populations for these programs include "students who are disengaged from mainstream education," who may be juvenile offenders, or may have been suspended from school. They are "often victims of abuse, bullying, neglect, and unstable home lives." They also include recent refugees who have completed a period in intensive English language centers but have not integrated into mainstream high schools. These groups tend to provoke a reaction of fear among beginning teachers. However, having worked with them in community settings, UWS student teachers wrote:

> I no longer have any fear about getting a tough school. (Morrow, 2006, p. 11)

> I became confident about communicating with, and motivating, kids who choose whether or not they are going to participate. (Morrow, 2006, p. 11)

UWS students who have participated in Next Generation see these students as "creative, energetic, and passionate," and interested in learning provided they can "see the purpose." Following their experiences in community settings they develop the ability to engage marginal students in successful learning, and a confidence that they will be able to continue these effective practices when they are appointed to mainstream high schools:

In the future with my teaching I will try new strategies in the classroom which worked while undertaking this project. I will also try to make myself aware of what other influences may be acting on a student's inability or reluctance to meet their outcomes.

One student described the experience as "an apprenticeship for teaching" (Morrow, 2006, p. 11) and another claimed: "I'll be a different sort of a teacher because of this" (Gannon, 2005, p. 2). Believing in young people and helping them believe in themselves was seen as an essential insight that emerged from this experience:

> When I go into a school, I'm going to ensure that every kid knows their potential, no matter what others tell them. I'm going to inspire them! (Morrow, 2006, p. 11).

For student teachers, participation in community learning settings through Next Generation proved to be transformational. Instead of framing marginal students as the "other," participants in Next Generation learned to view the more oppressive practices of formal schooling as "othering" the teacher. This "othering" occurs when a marginalized student views his teacher as a source of control and authority, as having no belief in him as a learner, and therefore no capacity to help him learn.

Developing Young People's Sense of Agency,
Not Taking Control

A third theme emerges from the reflective comments of UWS students who participated in the Plan-it-Youth placement option. In this option the goal is to establish a supportive relationship with a student and, over a 10-week period, help that student sort through issues that they feel are disrupting their lives. The theme that emerged here related to the mentor's growing understanding that if an individual is going to help someone, then he or she must allow them to fix things up. If adults continue to try and control the situation, young people will not develop their own sense of agency.

One participant wrote, Plan-it-Youth "gave us hands-on experience interacting with some of the more challenging students in the high school. These students are, without exception, delightful young people who mostly need nothing more than someone to talk to who is REALLY listening" (Sam, a 2005 Plan-it-Youth student). Sam's comment here reiterates a theme already identified by other student teachers, that if a teacher reverses the lens on marginalized young people, they prove to be "delightful" and interested in learning. She also introduces the idea of "really listening" which is taken further in the next reflection:

> I believed that by being a parent, a qualified Rehabilitation Counselor, having worked in the mental health field, and currently training as a teacher, I had a set of skills, experience and knowledge that would be helpful and useful in being a mentor (maybe even make me a good mentor). What I discovered … is that each week I have had to grapple with not being "the counselor," "the parent," "the vocational counselor," or "the teacher.… My greatest challenge has been to avoid trying to "fix" things and instead be there for my mentee to support, encourage and empower him to achieve his goals. It has been amazing to see outcomes from our mentoring sessions. These outcomes have ranged from increased eye contact when talking [about] completing assignments by their due date to the mentee reporting that he was making choices about his behavior in his classes based on thinking about how it would ultimately impact on achieving his medium term goals. (Plan-it-Youth teacher education student, Kath, 2005).

The importance of listening, simply and nonjudgmentally, is further emphasised in this reflection:

> I have learned that people really respond well when someone just listens without judging them and that often this is what people really need—just someone to listen to them. (Plan-it-Youth teacher education student, Heidi, 2005).

These statements (especially Kath's) draw attention to the ways in which professional training in fields such as counseling and social work tend to inculcate a particular frame of reference, one that focuses on intervention and "fixing things up." The transformative experience gained by participants in Plan-it-Youth was to find that through respectful and nonjudgmental listening mentors were able to help young people define and meet their own goals.

CONCLUSIONS AND IMPLICATIONS

A number of possibilities for transformational learning have been identified in this chapter. As has been demonstrated, marginalized students views about "school" and what they would like to acheive often stand in sharp juxtaposition to the low aspirations some teachers attribute to them. Through their parallel participation as teachers in formal school settings and their roles as "learning supports" in alternative community settings, student teachers enrolled in the service-learning program (PE3) became aware of these contrasting perspectives. Experience itself does not automatically lead to these insights, but rather, as Gallego (2001) suggests, systematic reflection is an essential catalyst for such learning.

The recognition by student teachers of the legitimacy of the marginal students perspectives about "school" is described here as a "reversal of the lens." It corresponds to the kind of transformation that Noddings (1992) described, in which student teachers go beyond their previous perceptions and take up the perspectives of the marginalized as their own. It also reflects King's (2004) emphasis on defamiliarization, and the disruption of conventional thinking. Participation in the Next Generation and Plan-it-Youth options in PE3 created the possibility for such transformations, though it should be noted that such participation does not automatically lead to transformation. Several of the teacher trainees who had this experience developed the ability to see marginalized students as kids who really wanted to learn, and "school" as a place that was not responding adequately to their needs. All of them became acutely aware of the ways in which the family problems many young people have to grapple with may make it difficult for them to attend school on a regular basis, and even more difficult to focus their minds on academic problems. They committed themselves to being vigilant in their relationships with students, and aware of situations in which personal support might be required, where solving life's problems might have a higher priority than solving math problems or doing assignments.

The reflections recorded and analyzed in this chapter indicate that through their participation in service-learning, student teachers gained a new confidence in working with marginalised students. By engaging them in challenging projects in out-of-school settings, they discovered that these young people did want to learn and were prepared to work hard. In many cases they became advocates for these students, finding them to be really delightful young people, who had, in many cases, become negative and rebellious because they felt teachers were mainly interested in controlling them, and were not helping them to learn.

It is important to note that the learning opportunities provided through Plan-it-Youth and Next Generation met the conditions that Gallego (2001) proposed for effective service-learning in a teacher education context. Both took place in a physically distinct environment, apart from regular classrooms. Each entailed a genuine learning activity tied to the content of the teacher education program. In each of these placements, student teachers had consistent opportunities to reflect on their experiences and examine the implications in terms of how one might make a difference for students who are at the margins.

Service-learning in the UWS teacher education degree is not intended merely to provide extra hours of practicum for pre-service teachers but to function as a disruption of students' more linear and regulated classroom-based experiences. There are lessons here for other fields of higher education which also have a vocational focus, such as nursing, social work, or law. As in teacher education, professional training in these fields tends to inculcate a particular frame of reference on the participants. An important issue for future investigation is to explore how these perspectives might be disrupted through service-learning placements that challenge the usual ways that these professions frame their patients, clients, and pupils.

NOTE

1.   These principles are elaborated in the UWS College of Arts guidelines for grants that support academic service-learning activities.

REFERENCES

Brunner, D. (1994). *Inquiry and reflection: Engaging narrative practice in education.* Albany: State University of New York.

Butcher, J., Howard, P., McMeniman, M., & Thom, G. (2003). *Engaging community-service or learning? Benchmarking community service in teacher education.* Canberra, Australia: Department of Education, Science and Training.

Cochran-Smith, M. (1991). Reinventing student teaching. *Journal of Teacher Education, 42* (2) 104-119

Dudderar, D., & Stover, L. T. (2003) Putting service-learning experiences at the heart of a teacher education curriculum. *Educational Research Quarterly, 27*(2), 18-32.

Gallego, M. (2001). Is experience the best teacher? *Journal of Teacher Education, 52*(4), 313-325.

Gannon, S. (2005, December). *"I'll be a different sort of a teacher because of this": Creating the Next Generation.* Paper presented at the Australian Association for Research in Education Conference, Parramatta, NSW.

Gannon, S., & Roots, P. (2006, May). *Transforming teaching for the Next Generation: Learning Choices and the UWS-DSF practicum partnership.* Paper presented at the Australian College of Educators Conference, Adelaide.

Glennie, E., Coble, C., & Allen, M. (2004). *Teacher perceptions of the work environment in hard-to-staff schools.* Washington, DC: US Education Commission of the States.

Goodman, J. (1985). What students learn from early field experiences: A case study and critical analysis. *Journal of Teacher Education, 36*(6), 42-48.

Henderson, J. E., & Brookhart, S. M. (1997, March). *Service-learning for aspiring school leaders: An exploratory study.* Paper presented at the Annual Meeting of the American Educational Research Association, Chicago.

King, J. T. (2004). Service-learning as a critical site for pedagogy: A case of collaboration, caring, and defamiliarization across borders. *Journal of Experiential Education, 26*(3), 121-137.

Kohn, A. (1996). *Beyond discipline: From compliance to community.* Alexandria, VA: Association for Supervision and Curriculum Development.

Lamb, S., Teese, R., Walstab, A., Vickers, M., & Rumberger, R. (2004). *Staying on at school: Improving school retention in Australia.* Brisbane, Australia: Queensland Department of Education.

McCarthy, M., Damrongmanee, Y., Pushpalatha, M., Chithra, J., & Yamamoto, K. (2005). Practices and possibilities of service-learning among colleges and universities in Asia. *Asia-Pacific Journal of Teacher Education, 32*(2), 59-70.

Moore-Johnson, S. M. (2004). *Finders and keepers: Helping new teachers survive and thrive in our schools.* San Francisco: Jossey Bass.

Morrow, A. (2006). *"It's like an apprenticeship for teaching" Critical friend review of 'Next Generation': Final report.* Sydney, Australia: Dusseldorp Skills Forum.

Noddings, N. (1992). *The challenge to care in schools: An alternative approach to education.* New York: Teachers College Press.

NSW Public Education Council Report. (2005). *Building on strong foundations.* Sydney, Australia: NSW Department of Education and Training.

Oakes, J., & Lipton, M. (1999) *Teaching to change the world.* New York: McGraw Hill.

Report of the Community Relations Commission for a Multicultural NSW. (2006). *Investigation into African humanitarian settlement in NSW.* Sydney, Australia: Community Relations Commission.

Shimmons-Torres, C., Drew-Cates, J., Johnson, J., & Overbeek, D. (2002). Community-driven partnership: A Unique RN-to-BSN clinical experience. *Journal of Nursing Education, 41*(12), 544-561.

Thomson, P. (2002). *Schooling the rust belt kids.* Sydney, Australia: Allen & Unwin.

Vickers, M., Harris, C., & McCarthy, F. E. (2004) University-community engagement: Exploring service-learning options within the practicum. *Asia-Pacific Journal of Teacher Education, 32*(2), 129-141.

Vickers, M., Muckerjee, D., Dowson, M., & Livermore, R. (2000). *Learning from early school leavers.* Sydney, Australia: New South Wales Department of Education and Training. Research Report prepared for the Campbelltown Full Service Schools Project.

Vinson, T. (2002). *Inquiry into the provision of public education in NSW.* Sydney: Pluto Press and NSW Teachers Federation.

Zeichner, K. (1992). Conceptions of reflective teaching in contemporary US teacher education programs. In L. Valli (Ed.), *Reflective teacher education: Cases and critiques* (pp. 161-173). Albany, NY: State University of New York Press.

CHAPTER 11

MAKING "MYTHICAL CREATURES" REAL

Developing an Awareness of Adolscent Needs Through Service-Learning

Angela M. Harwood, Lauren G. McClanahan, and Trula Nicholas

ABSTRACT

There is widespread and growing support for the adoption of service-learning practices in colleges of education. While several research studies have shown that service-learning can be a powerful experience that enhances important competencies for preservice teachers, there is much to learn about the impact of these experiences. This chapter presents a triangulated analysis of a first-quarter service-learning immersion approach in a master's in teaching certification program. Using questionnaires, focus group data, and reflective essays, the authors analyze the ways in which the service-learning experiences helped preservice teachers make sense of abstract concepts and develop reflective practitioner skills. Results indicated that service-learning helped preservice teachers examine concepts related to adolescent development, teaching, theory-practice connections, self, and general schooling issues.

From Passion to Objectivity: International and Cross-Disciplinary Perspectives on Service Learning Research, pp. 217–237
Copyright © 2007 by Information Age Publishing

INTRODUCTION

There is widespread and growing support for the adoption of service-learning practices in colleges of education. While several researchers reported that service-learning can be a worthwhile and powerful experience that enhanced participants' self-esteem, self-efficacy, positive views of diverse others, an ethic of caring, and additional important competencies for preservice teachers (e.g., Anderson & Guest, 1993; L. Boyle-Baise, 1997; Donahue, Bowyer, & Rosenberg, 2003; Freeman & Swick, 2001; Middleton, 2003; Root, Callahan, & Sepanski, 2002a; Root & Furco, 2001; Tellez, Hlebowitsh, Cohen, & Norwood, 1995; Wade & Yarbrough, 1997). The aspects of service-learning that contribute to preservice teachers' development however, have not been fully explored. This chapter provides information to help fill this gap in the research by addressing two central questions: (1) How do service-learning experiences help preservice teachers to make sense of the abstract concepts addressed within teacher education programs? and (2) How does an early service-learning field experience contribute to the development of reflective practitioner skills?

Service-Learning and Reflective Practice in Teacher Education

Increased interest in service-learning in the field of teacher education coincides with growing interest in the pedagogy in K-20 settings. Ball (2003) argued that for service-learning to be effective in teacher education, it should be fully incorporated throughout the program, with introductory activities beginning the first quarter and continuing through a capstone experience in which preservice teachers design and implement service-learning projects during their student teaching. Multiple researchers found that preservice teachers who participated in service-learning were more likely to incorporate service-learning in their future classrooms or to have positive attitudes about the pedagogy (Ball, 2003; Donahue, 2000; Flottemesch, Heide, Pedras, & Karp, 2001; Root, Callahan, & Sepanski, 2002b; Wade et al., 1999; Wade & Yarbrough, 1997). Researchers also reported that service-learning experiences helped preservice teachers better understand the contents of adolescent psychology courses (Shastri, 1999), and gain increased awareness of the needs of students from diverse backgrounds (Barton, 2000; Bolye-Baise, 1998; Brown & Howard, 2005; Donahue et al, 2003; LaMaster, 2001; Tellez et al., 1994; Spencer, Cox-Petersen, & Crawford, 2005; Swick & Rowls, 2000).

A concurrently developing trend in teacher education is a focus on reflective practice wherein preservice teachers develop the habits and skills of carefully observing the impact of their teaching and adjusting their strategies accordingly. Since Schön's (1983, 1987) influential publications, the focus on reflection as a key element of teacher preparation programs continued to grow, resulting in its inclusion in major teacher education professional standards, notably those developed by the Interstate New Teacher Assessment and Support Consortium (INTASC) and the National Council for the Accreditation of Teacher Education (NCATE) (Interstate New Teacher Assessment and Support Consortium, 1992; National Council for the Accreditation of Teacher Education, 2002). INTASC standard principle #9 is "The teacher is a reflective practitioner who continually evaluates the effects of his/her choices and actions on others and who actively seeks out opportunities to grow professionally," including valuing critical thinking and self-directed learning, and possessing a commitment to reflection, assessment, and learning as an ongoing process (INTASC, 1992, section Supporting Explanations, para. 5). NCATE guidelines assert that teachers should be able to "reflect on and continually evaluate the effects of choices and actions on others and actively seek out opportunities to grow professionally" (NCATE, 2002, p. 15). But how exactly is the definition of "reflection," and in what form is reflective practice best manifested?

Historically, Dewey (1933) is acknowledged as the originator of concept of reflective practice in teacher education. He conceived of reflection as a particular form of problem solving, resolving an issue based on information gathered through a process, believing that any form of knowledge or belief deserved careful consideration (Hatton & Smith, 1995). Dewey believed that thinking was natural, but that reflective thinking was something that must be learned (Spalding & Wilson, 2002). Dewey also thought that reflection benefited individuals by giving them more control over their experiences, thereby increasing the value of those experiences.

Researchers also discovered that when preservice teachers make clear in writing the meanings they ascribe to the material and theory being taught in class, "they reveal the extent of their learning" (Knowles & Holt-Reynolds, 1991, p. 106). Their writing is a means by which to measure the relevancy and effectiveness of instruction and programs in teacher education.

Reflection is a central tenet of virtually every definition of service-learning and is steeped in the theories of both Dewey's model of reflective learning of and Kolb's cycle of experiential education (Eyler, Giles, & Schmiede, 1996). Connecting these traditions to both service-learning and standards-based teacher education, Callahan, Diez, and Ryan (2001) asserted that service-learning can help to develop reflective teachers who learn from and engage in reflection to better their practice. Brown and Howard (2005) also reported that novice teachers who had participated in service-learning during their education programs reviewed and revised their teaching approaches to fit learners' needs, a result which suggested that service-learning may aid in the development of preservice teachers' reflective skills.

It was against this backdrop of research on how service-learning in teacher education might contribute to preservice teachers' understanding of adolescents and the development of preservice teachers' reflective practice that the authors conducted the following evaluation of their first quarter service-learning immersion pilot program.

Program Description

The data reported in this chapter were collected to assist faculty in evaluating a pilot integration of service-learning in a secondary education master's in teaching (MIT) program at a northwest regional comprehensive university. Through this program, students earn both a master's degree and initial state teaching certification. In the first quarter block, preservice teachers enroll in three core courses: an introduction to adolescent development, a literacy course, and an educational research methods course.

In an effort to the make the program more field-based and to provide a greater variety of field placements, in the fall of 2005 designers piloted three school-based service-learning projects. Students were required to participate in their choice of one of these three placements, and assignments in both the adolescent development and literacy courses were tied to their field experiences. In addition, the students participated in a community-based action research project, paralleling learning in the educational research methods course. The three school-based service-learning experiences were designed to help expose students to emergent curriculum programming and "big picture" schooling issues in local middle and high schools.

The first placement option was working with a partner middle school, assisting in the implementation of "Project Connect," a service-learning curriculum approach in which eighth graders learn about community issues by engaging in service-learning activities at sites throughout our community. The MIT. students who selected this placement option participated in an average of 16 field hours, serving as learning facilitators that traveled from the school to community sites with eighth graders, worked at the sites and then responded to eighth graders' written reflection journals.

In the second placement option, MIT. students worked an average of 9 hours in a "Community Connections" course for ninth graders at a partner high school. The Community Connections course, offered for the first time, was designed for ninth graders who are identified as "not yet at standard" due to failing state-mandated tests or core courses in middle school. The MIT students who worked in this class provided homework and skill-building assistance. Some of them also had the opportunity to accompany ninth graders as they worked in the community.

The final placement option consisted of working with 12th-grade students who were writing scholarly papers as part of the graduation requirements for their culminating project. MIT. students in this placement assisted 12th graders with Internet literature searches and other aspects of the writing process.

METHODOLOGY

The sample for this study was comprised of the 21 MIT students enrolled in the secondary education program during fall quarter of 2005. This cohort reflected a typical range of content areas, with 8 students pursing social studies endorsements, 6 science, 5 English, 3 math, 3 middle school humanities, 2 visual arts, and 1 world language. Several students in this cohort will receive multiple endorsements. Of the 21 participants, 5 selected to work in the middle school service-learning project, 6 with the "not yet at standard" study skills class, and 10 with the high school culminating project class.

Procedures

This study evaluation was conducted by three professors in the Department of Secondary Education and a fourth from the Department of Human Services. To provide a full range of information for our evaluation of this pilot, researchers triangulated data by employing questionnaires, focus groups, and student reflective essays written for the adolescent development and literacy courses. Researchers developed a triangulated approach to enable them to cross-check the accuracy of the data and to correct biases that might emerge from a single data collection method (Denzin, 1989; Goetz & LeCompte, 1984; Janesick, 1994). The evaluation team created the questionnaire, which was administered during the ninth week of our 11-week quarter.

Based on responses from the questionnaire, the team then developed a focus group protocol, and conducted focus groups for each school-based placement group the following week. Reflective essay questions were developed for each course prior to the start of the quarter and were distributed on the first day of class. The final reflective essays were turned in the 2 days after the focus groups were conducted. The study team used an analytic induction approach in the analysis of each data set (Bogden & Bicklen, 1992; Glasser & Strauss, 1999; Patton, 1990). The approach began with open coding, letting themes emerge from the data. As themes emerged, formalized coding schemas for each data set were developed and applied. Details about each type of instrumentation and the analysis procedures are presented in the following sections.

Questionnaires. The questionnaire contained 31 items that addressed both the community- and school-based projects, along with some basic demographic information. Six of the open-ended questions that related to the school-based project are reported in this chapter. Researchers asked respondents which course concepts they learned the most about during their field placement, the most important things they learned about schools, middle school or high school students, and themselves, and then finally how they thought their school-based experience contributed to their development as a teacher and what big questions about schooling it generated.

Questionnaires were distributed to students during one of their regular class sessions. Students were allowed as much time as they needed to complete the questionnaire. Descriptive statistics were generated and themes were identified and coded.

Focus Group. The evaluation team designed a standardized focus group protocol which was administered during a regularly scheduled class session. Students were grouped for the focus groups according to the school-based project in which they worked. This chapter presents an analysis of the responses to the school-based projects gathered through five open-ended questions: (1) What was the most important thing you learned from the school-based experience? (2) What did you learn about yourself as a result of the school-based experience? (3) What did you learn about teaching as a result of your school-based experience? (4) What did you learn about adolescents as a result of the school-based experience? and (5) Is there anything else you'd like to share about the impact of the school-based experience?

Each focus group was audio-taped and the tapes were then transcribed by one member of the evaluation team. During the transcription process researchers discovered that responses for the Project Connect middle-school site group had not been recorded due to a glitch with the taping equipment; so that focus group was subsequently rerun 5 weeks into the winter 2006 quarter. Transcripts of each interview were printed for each member of the evaluation team; that met to create a coding schema which was applied separately and then compared to determine a consensus coding for each transcript passage. The transcript codes were entered into a data set in the QSR NVivo (1999) qualitative research analysis program, which was used to run analyses.

Reflective Essays. Students enrolled in the literacy and adolescent development courses were asked to write three reflective essays in each class during the quarter, responding to prompts designed to help them focus their thinking on what they observed in the field, and how those observations might transfer to broader issues in education. Because the courses addressed different concepts, prompts were designed separately for each class, and only the third, culminating essay for each class was coded for this study.

Students in the literacy class were provided prompts that helped them to focus on the literacy practices of high school and middle school students. The content of this course was reading, writing, and learning skills and strategies, and techniques for assessing texts and student literacy levels. In a series three reflective essays written over the course of the quarter, preservice teachers were asked to observe reading, writing and speaking events, relate them to concepts discussed in class, and come up with questions they would like to answer during their field time. In their final reflective essay, students were instructed to answer the questions they raised, providing evidence from their experiences, and illuminating their thinking about what they learned about teaching and learning, action research and education in general.

The adolescent development course addressed the biological, psychological, and sociological development of adolescents, with the goal of helping preservice teachers link the developmental stages of their students to curriculum, instruction and management. In a series of three essays similar to that used in the literacy class, students were asked to focus their observations of adolescent development, generate a question to explore, and answer that question in their final reflective essay. Preservice teachers were specifically asked to think about theories of development, connect them with student behavior, and contemplate what they were curious about regarding student behavior, relationships, cognitive skills, and development.

To analyze the reflective essays, the research team began initial coding by selecting eight essays. The team coded these essays collectively, discussing and recording emerging patterns. Once the coding schema was established, the remaining essays were coded twice—once individually, and once collectively, by consensus. Each passage was ultimately coded using the final coding scheme. Based on our consensus coding, a data set of reflective essays was created in the QSR NVivo (1999) qualitative research analysis program, which was used for analyses.

Exhibit 11.1.   Triangulated Data Results

| | Number of Coded Passages from Each Data Source | | | |
Theme	Questionnaires (N = 284)	Reflective Essays (N = 622)	Focus Groups (N = 162)	Total (N = 1,068)
Adolescents/adolescent development	45	272	32	349
Examining teaching	66	139	56	261
Theory-practice connections	92	37	13	142
Understanding of self	27	62	41	130
Schooling issues	15	28	0	43
Project recommendations	39	84	20	143

RESULTS

A total of 21 questionnaires were returned, and included 284 passages of coded data. The transcriptions of the three focus groups yielded 162 total passages of coded text, and the 37 reflective essays provided 622 coded passages. After coding each data set and then considering them as a whole, six prevalent and consistent themes emerged: (1) learning about adolescents/adolescent development; (2) examining teaching; (3) theory – practice connections; (4) understanding of self; (5) considering general schooling issues; and (6) recommending improvements for the field experience. The number of coded passages for each theme from each element of our data set is presented in Exhibit 11.1.

Each of these themes and the most prevalent subthemes within them is summarized in the following sections.

Adolescents/Adolescent Development

Across the three data sets, the preservice teachers indicated that during the school-based service-learning experience, they gained insight about the students with whom they will work in the future. Overall, 349 passages were coded in this thematic category. The subthemes that emerged under this broad category included student motivation, development (specifically social), and abilities.

The most frequently cited subtheme related to learning about students was student motivation ($n = 111$). In questionnaire responses preservice teachers asked questions such as "Are all students essentially unmotivated?", and "How can students be motivated to use class time wisely?" During the focus group sessions, the preservice teachers particularly noted the ways in which listening to students and expressing interest in what they were doing impacted student motivation:

> I really thought about how much it matters to them when you are interested in what they are doing.... There was a huge change that comes over them when they realize that you were really interested. It was like it really, really matters.

Another focus group member recalled that one student generally sat and did nothing, but when engaged in conversation with the preservice teacher about the culmination project "He like opened up, and talked me all about, you know, AIDS." Others pondered how they would handle students who did not want to work, or to be helped in their future classroom.

In both the reflective essays and the questionnaire, preservice teachers closely connected motivation with relevancy of the topic being studied. A preservice teacher working with high school students on their culminating projects said:

> Two of the students admitted to me that they just wrote the paper the night before and did not care about what they had written. Hence, I felt as if the students were just 'jumping through hoops' to accomplish just enough of what was required of them.

Another preservice teacher agreed, stating

> Even though [student name] started the paper the year before, he still had some revising to do. So what does that say about his attitude towards the writing process in general and revising his work in particular?

Relevancy and motivation were linked in questionnaire responses such as "[I noticed] their resentment toward anything they find—'irrelevant' to their lives," and "[I wondered] what are the connections being drawn between projects and outside life?"

Not all of the students, however, were unmotivated to do their class work. A preservice teacher working with the middle school students said: "The students worked well together and were marvelously self-motivated!" Another similarly noted, "The kids were engaged and enthusiastic all day at the wildlife sanctuary, and were telling me about what they were doing and what they were learning." However, a majority of the preservice teachers across the three data sets reported a strong sense of student apathy, and were concerned about how to handle, or avoid, such apathy in their own classrooms.

Results from the three data sets showed that student social development was the second most frequently cited sub-theme ($n = 68$). Questionnaire responses such as "Socialization is a *major* component of school culture," "These kids do not enjoy school, yet they really like the social scene," and "They have a hard time focusing on school; they like to be *social*" give a flavor of the types of comments that were made. The focus group data also demonstrated that preservice teachers observed a lot about the social aspects of the adolescents with whom they worked, including the ways in which peer influences and adult interactions affected them. Some preservice teachers noted the dynamics they observed between different groups, while others discussed the roles adolescents adopted around one another—"but they're so conscious of making their image, you know, 'This is me, this is me,' you know, even though it probably isn't really them." Preservice teachers expressed surprise at the personality, depth and intensity of adolescents, as the following quote demonstrates:

> They think about really intense things, and they have intense lives, and they're just like whole people. . .They aren't just a part of a person and then they'll like graduate and turn into a whole person, but that they are a whole person and they just need these certain conditions to be able to you know express it.

Others echoed this sentiment, noting "I think adolescents have a lot to say," "I mean they're much more extensive," and "They're a lot more interested than when I was in middle school … they were totally interested and ready to get started to do stuff."

This theme also emerged in the reflective essays. One MIT. student involved with the culminating projects wrote:

> It was very interesting to observe the students' social interactions while I circled the library/computer lab…. Social interactions in the classroom have a considerable impact on the learning environment. The students in this class spent a lot of class-time chatting with one another about social topics, wasting their in-class opportunity to work on their research papers.

Another preservice teacher who worked with the culminating project went so far as to conduct a small survey, and found that "5 out of the 6 students listed 'seeing friends' as a reason for liking high school."

In discussing students' writing abilities, preservice teachers mentioned the frequency of Internet plagiarism. An MIT student working with the culminating projects wrote:

The first thing that sparked my interest about this project was that in our review of student works cited pages for their "scholarly papers," we noticed that most students only used electronic/Internet resources.

Comments like these were made repeatedly, prompting the preservice teachers to consider how they will handle research papers in their own classrooms, something many of them had not considered previously. In response to a survey question, one preservice teacher was amazed at the "incredible diversity of ... cognitive abilities," while another was concerned that "high schoolers need help developing fundamental skills—developing a research question, how to narrow a search."

An additional 117 comments about students comprised 13 other subthemes about students. Overall, the data indicated that preservice teachers learned a lot about student motivation, social development, and abilities through their service-learning placements.

Examining Teaching

Switching from the role of student to that of teacher represented a shift in thinking for many of the preservice teachers. This shift was evident in the number of times observations about teaching were made across all three data sets ($n = 261$). Combined responses from the questionnaires, focus groups and reflective essays, yielded four central themes related to teaching: pedagogy, teacher-student relationships, classroom management, and curricular issues.

Many of the MIT students came to realize that the key to effective student learning outcomes was a well developed and executed pedagogical plan ($n = 56$). Responses indicated that students were closely observing the "nuts and bolts" of effective teaching techniques. One MIT student working with the culminating projects commented in a reflective essay on the structure of the class that was observed:

I think that this atmosphere could have been changed if the teacher had attempted to structure the class time in some manner, instead of giving them two hours to structure the time as they wished. The teacher rarely circulated around the students to check up on them and aid them in their research.

However, not all observations of pedagogy were critical. One student working with Project Connect stated:

The presentations that [the students] will create have been sufficiently scaffolded to create clear, visible goals that will build into a fairly large reflection of the experience.

This student went on to praise the teacher for helping students generate topic ideas and for helping to steer them in the right direction to locate research materials for their final papers.

One MIT student involved with Project Connect wrestled with synthesizing what he/she had learned about peer relationships, pedagogy, and student self-efficacy. In this comment, the student made connections between relationships, pedagogy and student learning, and posed an important question about how these intersect with the curriculum:

> If the creation of peer relationships increases a student's sense of belonging, and increases achievement and efficacy, what are the professional implications to educators? Shouldn't part of our priorities in building multi-modal curriculum be to incorporate lots of opportunities for students to create bonds and relationships with one another? The next step is to sift through these questions and to think of ways to apply what I've learned about the importance of relationship building to my own curriculum. What would this look like?

The MIT students discovered the importance of developing relationships with students ($n = 51$). As one student put it during a focus-group:

> The quality of the conversations I had with the kids was really contingent on the amount of time and energy I put into it, I mean, it really depended on relationships.

As they worked throughout the quarter to get to know the students, the preservice teachers realized that those relationships gave them greater ability to assist students with both their social and academic needs. As a student noted in a reflective essay:

> What I've learned about relationship building, students will struggle to communicate openly to adults who they have not yet established a relationship with.... This illustrates the importance of relationship building, and creating an ethic of care in the classroom.

Perhaps more than any other issue, classroom management was paramount in preservice teachers' minds, and that was reflected in the number of mentions this topic received ($n = 37$). Throughout this field-based experience, MIT. students commented on the link between pedagogy and classroom management. They noted the importance of constant monitoring and using humor as a motivator, and pondered how to make non-English speaking students feel included. During the focus group one student commented:

There is definitely that testing thing. When you're a teacher it's like automatically—you got to know where to draw the line. You got to know before they do because (laughter) if you're not sure, then it will be their choice!

Several students commented on a connection between behavioral management issues and teacher expectations in the classroom, which links back to pedagogy. An MIT student working with the Community Connections class wrote in a reflective essay:

The teachers did not appear to have strict rules or enforce the expectations of the classroom. There were many instances when I felt angry at the lack of respect that students demonstrated towards each other and their teachers … I have gained insight about the importance of classroom management in creating an effective learning environment, and I hope that my future practice has been influenced by this experience.

Many of the preservice teachers wished to see more structure in the programs that they had observed, commenting that a lack of structure, while preferable for some students, was distracting for others.

Finally, once the students had been placed in their various field assignments, they began to question both the structure and the content of the curricula they were observing ($n = 38$). These observations ranged from noting how the curriculum progressed throughout their time there, to the acknowledged challenges of adopting new projects mandated by the state. As one student during the focus group framed the issue:

What would be more effective…to help [the secondary students] succeed in other classes, help them meet their progress on the [state standardized test], you know … [and have a] better attitude towards school?"

Others noted that the students with whom they were working did not always seem to understand the purpose of the curriculum.

I wonder if there was a sort of a disconnect between what the goals are and what is happening to achieve those goals.

Responses on the survey were similar, with students stating, "Does the culmination project impact the students?" and "Is this [service-learning] model an effective model for improving academic achievement?"

Across data sets, students demonstrated understanding that strong teacher-student relationships were the cornerstone of classrooms where pedagogy, management, and the curriculum came together in the name of effective student learning outcomes. In addition to the subthemes presented here, 79 other outcomes comprising 12 subthemes were also coded in the examining teaching category.

Theory-Practice Connections

The third major theme that emerged from the data was preservice teachers' linking of educational theory to practice they observed in the field ($n = 142$). When asked which course concepts they learned most about during their field-based experience, questionnaire respondents identified 15 different concepts from the literacy course and 16 from the adolescent development course. The ability to link theory to practice also emerged frequently in reflective essays and in the focus groups. In an essay for the adolescent development course, a student who participated in the culminating project wrote:

> It was interesting to have Dr. [professor's name] discuss the idea of transference in class today because it directly relates to the issues the seniors were having with writing their scholarly paper. Most likely, the seniors felt comfortable writing an acceptable scholarly paper for a similar type of class where they learned this skill. However, most of the seniors had difficulty making the leap and transferring what they already know to a vague graduation requirement they have never seen before.

Another MIT student involved with the Project Connect class found similar benefits to connecting theory with real-world observations:

> It has been helpful to investigate concepts of adolescent development learned in class out in the field. It makes the ideas more "real" than listening to lectures and discussing kids as mythical creatures in far off places.

In these and many other examples from across the three data sets, preservice teachers specified course concepts about which they had read, and specifically connected them to the students and educational practices there were observing in field placements.

Understanding of Self

In each of the three elements of the data set, preservice teachers articulated things they had learned about themselves as a result of their school-based experience ($n = 130$). Preservice teachers identified ways that the school-based experience helped them to understand their own skills as future teachers, including their ability to relate to students, to move from the student to instructor role, and to develop their management skills. Subthemes also included confirmation of their decision to teach, and noting the differences they were making in their field placements.

The ways individuals developed themselves as teachers were noted in reflective essays. One student wrote "I really enjoyed working with the students and having the opportunity to observe them from a more teacher-y point of view," and another stated:

> Being in the schools this first quarter and actually being a part of what is going on was helpful in my understanding of adolescent and teacher roles.

One student noted a shift in his/her conceptualization of schooling, the ways in which personal experiences color the lens through which one sees teachers and the curriculum:

> In terms of my thoughts on teaching and learning, I was a bit surprised at the critical perspectives I have developed since I last worked in the public school system. Soon after completing my bachelor's degree, I spent two years working as a family support worker at two elementary schools. I spent some time in the classroom, but most of my time was spent out in the community, doing home visits, etc. As I focused upon helping to stabilize the external environment where students spent their time outside of school, I did not think much about the influence that teachers and curriculum were having upon the students with whom I worked.... In preparation for becoming a high school teacher ... I do feel that it is healthy for me to be aware of how my own experiences may influence my views of curriculum, course design, and instruction.

For many of the MIT students, involvement in the field so early in their educational experience served to reinforce their desire to become teachers. One student stated:

> The adjustment from being out of school for the last seven years to being back as a graduate student was a big one for me, and having the chance to work with students immediately was a very grounding experience, reminding me of why I came back to school.

Another student showed similar enthusiasm to return to the classroom as a teacher by stating:

> I have learned that I can easily establish some rapport with students and am eager to see what kind of potential that kind of rapport can have [in my classroom].

Schooling Issues

Participation in the school-based service-learning projects also gave the preservice teachers an opportunity to think about the bigger issues of schooling (n = 43). Specifically asked about this in the questionnaire, respondents primarily commented on the organization of schools and the new requirements for graduation they were observing. Those comments were echoed in the focus groups and reflective essays. For example, this preservice teacher questioned the high-stakes nature of the culminating projects as a requirement for high school graduation:

> I question the motivation for Washington State to make this project a state requirement. I have witnessed how it puts a lot of pressure on the teachers to have their students complete the project so they can graduate.

Another student observed how difficult implementing such a large project can be, and how stressful it can be for both students and teachers. "The teachers and students appeared to feel strained in completing the project."

One MIT student, involved with the Community Connections program, questioned the different set of expectations that seemed to be established for college-prep students and at-risk students:

> As I was working with the students at [the high school] this quarter, I found myself particularly sensitive to what I perceived as different sets of expectations for certain students in the class, and for the class as a whole. Why was it acceptable for the only African American in the class to be the only student allowed to listen to his Ipod during class? By not hearing instruction from the teacher, what message was he receiving about how much his learning, input, and education were valued? What did this tell the other students in the class about the importance of his contribution to discussions and projects? ... Shouldn't these kids, who are already at the highest risk for dropping out (low-performing freshmen), be receiving the best instruction, from the best teachers? Won't the A.P. students do well no matter who is teaching them?

DISCUSSION

Results from the combined data sets indicate that preservice teachers learned many valuable things as a result of their early service-learning field experience. Gaining this exposure to adolescents, teachers, and schools early on in a preservice teacher education program, and writing about the experience reflective essays, helped these preservice teachers to link adolescent development and curriculum theories to practice. Connecting classroom discussions and reflective writing to what students are observing in the field, may give preservice teachers the opportunity to make those connections much more quickly than if they were simply read-ing about them (Knowles & Holt-Reynolds, 1991).

The ideals of educational theory taught at the university often morph into something quite different in the halls of schools. By placing students in challenging field experiences early on, we can help them to develop what Schön (1983) identified as "knowledge-in-action" an essential bridge between the "swampy lowland" world of professional practice and the research-based theories they read about in their classes. Participation in the service-learning experiences helped preservice teachers make sense of what can be very complex, theoretical issues. To see the connections between students, pedagogy, teachers, school and self come to life in a "real-world" context possibly helped these MIT students gain a perspec-tive on education that many teachers do not understand until they are well into the first years of their careers.

In addition, the results of this study indicate that the early service-learning field experience may help students to develop into reflective practitioners. Zeichner and Liston (1996) identify examining, framing and attempting to solve the dilemmas of classroom practice, and attend-ing to the institutional and cultural contexts of teaching as two key fea-tures of reflective practice. The data suggest that participation in the school-based service-learning projects helped preservice teachers to begin to develop these aspects of reflective practice. In addition, teachers who were developing new curriculum designed to address identified needs of students were exposed to another feature identified by Zeichner and Lis-ton: taking part in curriculum development and involvement in school change efforts. The exposure that preservice teachers gained to reflective practice during their first quarter can potentially help them to establish a reflective habit of mind that will carry through the rest of their program and into their professional lives.

The data analysis also suggests some important issues related both to evaluative practice and program development, raising issues for both fur-ther research and improved teaching practice. This project reinforced the importance of triangulating data sets since doing so allowed the research-ers to identify most important themes by analyzing the consistency across data sets. Given the data collection strategies and the specific prompts in each of them, reliance on only one or even two of the approaches may have led to misinterpretation of the results. Further, by working as an interdisciplinary evaluation team, the researchers found that assumptions made given the various background and experiences of the team were challenged in a healthy way through lively discussions. The dynamic cod-ing sessions enabled the team to carefully examine one another's inter-pretive framework and expose underlying assumptions. The result of the triangulation of both data sets and evaluator backgrounds was a more strongly grounded interpretation of the results.

The analysis also led to suggestions for program improvement. Although logistical challenges related to time are likely to remain an issue, program designers are working on restructuring the scheduling of classes and the incorporation of field time in a way to better facilitate preservice teachers' participation.

In addition, in reading the data from this project, the power and importance of carefully constructed reflection prompts became obvious. Reflections were a good vehicle for guiding preservice teachers' thinking as they connected their field work with more specific course concepts.

This project raised additional questions to explore. Although these results indicated that students were beginning to develop reflective skills, whether or not they continued to develop and later apply those skills to their own teaching remained to be seen. In addition, longitudinal research is needed to see if their early recognition of issues of motivation, curriculum, pedagogy, and the importance of developing good relationships with students are acted upon during their student teaching and early years in the classroom. Further, studies should be developed to determine whether this early field experience will encourage any of our students to adopt service-learning pedagogy in their future classrooms. Finally, researchers should explore how service-learning experiences may help preservice teachers develop the other skills, knowledge, and dispositions indicated in professional standards.

REFERENCES

Anderson, J., & Guest, K. (1993, April). *Linking campus and community: Seattle University's community service internship for pre-service teachers.* Paper presented at the National Service-Learning Conference, Minneapolis, MN.

Ball, D. (2003). Teacher education service-learning: Assessment. In *Learning to serve, serving to learn: View for higher education* (pp. 67-89). Salisbury, MD: Salisbury University.

Barton, A. C. (2000). Crafting multicultural science education with preservice teachers through service-learning. *Journal of Curriculum Studies, 32*(6), 797-820.

Bogden, R., & Bicklen, S. (1992). *Qualitative research for education: An introduction to theory and* methods. Boston: Allyn & Bacon.

Boyle-Baise, M. (1998). Community service-learning for multicultural education: An exploratory study with preservice teachers. *Equity and Excellence in Education, 31*(2), 52-60.

Boyle-Baise, L. (1997, November). *Community service-learning for multicultural education: An exploratory study with pre-service teachers.* Paper presented at the College and University Faculty Assembly of the National Council for the Social Studies, Cincinnati, OH.

Brown, E. L., & Howard, B. R., II. (2005). Becoming culturally responsive teachers through service-learning: A case study of five novice classroom teachers. *Multicultural Education*, *12*(4). Retrieved September 10, 2006, from http://proquest.umi.com/pqdweb?index=4&did=867275621&SrchMode=3&sid=1 & Fmt=4&VInst=PROD&VType=PQD&RQT=309&

Callahan, J. P., Diez, M. E., & Ryan, L. (2001). Service-Learning and standards-based teacher education. In J. B. Anderson, K. J. Swick, & J. Yff (Eds.), *Service-learning in teacher education: Enhancing the growth of new teachers, their students, and communities* (pp. 53-68). Washington, DC: American Association of Colleges of Teacher Education.

Denzin, N. (1989). *Interpretive interactionism*. Newbury Park, CA: Sage.

Dewey, J. (1933). *How we think*. New York: Heath.

Donahue, D. M. (2000). Charity basket or revolution: Beliefs, experiences and context in pre-service teachers' service-learning. *Curriculum Inquiry, 30*(4), 429-450.

Donahue, D. M., Bowyer, J., & Rosenberg, D. (2003). Learning with and learning from: Reciprocity in service-learning teacher education. *Equity & Excellence in Education, 36*(1), 15-27.

Eyler, J., Giles, D. W., & Schmiede, A. (1996). *A practitioner's guide to reflection in service-learning: Student voices & reflections*. Nashville, TN: Vanderbilt University.

Flottemesch, K., Heide, T., Pedras, M., & Karp, G. G. (2001). Initial service-learning experience through the lenses of pre-service teachers. In J. B. Anderson, K. J. Swick, & J. Yff (Eds.), *Service-learning in teacher education: Enhancing the growth of new teachers, their students, and communities* (pp. 126-133). Washington, DC: American Association of Colleges of Teacher Education.

Freeman, N. K., & Swick, K. (2001). Early childhood teacher education students strengthen their caring and competence through service-learning. In J. A. Anderson, K. J. Swick, & J. Yff (Eds.), *Service-learning in teacher education: Enhancing the growth of new teachers, their students, and communities* (pp. 134-140). Washington, DC: American Association of Colleges of Teacher Education.

Glasser, B. G., & Strauss, A. L. (1999). *The discovery of grounded theory: Strategies for qualitative research*. New York: Aldine de Gruyter.

Goetz, J. P., & LeCompte, M. D. (1984). *Ethnography and qualitative design in educational research*. San Diego, CA: Academic Press.

Hatton, N., & Smith, D. (1995). Reflection in teacher education; Towards definition and implementation. *Teaching and Teacher Education, 11*(1), 33-49.

Interstate New Teacher Assessment and Support Consortium. (1992). Model *standards for beginning teacher licensing, assessment and development: A resource for state dialogue*. Retrieved March 16, 2005, from http://www.ccsso.org/contentpdfs/corestrd.pdf.

Janesick, V. (1994). The dance of qualitative research design. In N. Denzin & Y. Lincoln (Eds.), *Handbook of qualitative research* (pp. 209-219). Thousand Oaks, CA: Sage.

Knowles, J., & Holt-Reynolds, D. (1991). Shaping pedagogies through personal histories in preservice teacher education. *Teachers College Record, 93*(1), 87-111.

LaMaster, K. J. (2001). Enhancing preservice teachers field experiences through the addition of a service-learning component. *Journal of Experiential Education, 24*(1), 27-33.

Middleton, V. A. (2003). A diversity-based, service-learning PDS partnership. *Equity & Excellence in Education, 36*(3), 231-237.

National Council for the Accreditation of Teacher Education. (2002). *NCATE Unit Standards, 2002 Edition.* Retrieved March 23, 2006 from http://www.ncate.org/public/unitStandardsRubrics.asp?ch=4#1

Patton, M. Q. (1990). *Qualitative evaluation and research methods.* Newbury Park, CA: Sage.

Qualitative Solutions and Research Pty. (1999). QSR NUD*IST Vivo (Version 1.0). [Computer Software]. Melbourne, Australia: Qualitative Solutions and Research Pty. Ltd.

Root, S., Callahan, J., & Sepanski, J. (2002a). Service-learning in teacher education. In A. Furco & S. H. Billig (Eds.), *Service-learning: The essence of the pedagogy* (pp. 223-243). Greenwich, CT: Information Age.

Root, S., Callahan, J., & Sepanski, J. (2002b). Building teaching dispositions and service-learning practice: a multi-site study. *Michigan Journal of Community Service-learning, 9*(1), 50-60.

Root, S., & Furco, A. (2001). A review of research on service-learning in pre-service teacher education. In J. A. Anderson, K. J. Swick, & J. Yff (Eds.), *Service-learning in teacher education: Enhancing the growth of new teachers, their students, and communities* (pp. 86-101). Washington, DC: American Association of Colleges of Teacher Education.

Schön, D. (1983). *The reflective practitioner.* New York: Basic Books.

Schön, D. (1987). *Educating the reflective practitioner: Toward a new design for teaching and learning in the professions.* San Francisco: Jossey-Bass.

Shastri, A. (1999, April). *Investigating content knowledge gains in academic service-learning: A quasi-experimental study in an educational psychology course.* Paper presented at the annual meeting of the American Educational Research Association, Montreal, PQ.

Spalding, E., & Wilson, A. (2002). Demystifying reflection: A study of pedagogical strategies that encourage reflective journal writing. *Teachers College Record, 104*(7), 1393-1421.

Spencer, B. H., Cox-Petersen, A. M., & Crawford. T. (2005). Assessing the impact of service-learning on preservice teachers in an after-school program. *Teacher Education Quarterly, 32*(4), 119-135. Retrieved September 10, 2006, from http://proquest.umi.com/pqdweb?index=3&did=923929661&SrchMode=3&sid=1&Fmt=4VInst=PROD&VType= PQD&RQT=309&

Swick, K. H,. & Rowls, M. (2000). The "voices" of preservice teachers on the meaning and value of their service-learning. *Education, 120*(3), 461-468. Retrieved March 23, 2006, from http://proquest.umi.com/pqdweb?index=30did=52137371&SrchMode=3&sid=2&Fmt=3&VInst=PROD&VType=PQD&RQT=309&

Tellez, K., Hlebowitsh, P. S., Cohen, M., & Norwood, P. (1995). Social service field experiences and teacher education. In J. M. Larkin & C. E. Sleeter (Eds.), *Developing multicultural teacher education curricula* (pp. 65-78). Albany: State University of New York Press.

Wade, R., Anderson, J., Yarbrough, D., Pickeral, T., Erickson, J., & Kromer, T. (1999). Novice teachers' experiences of community service-learning. *Teaching and Teacher Education, 15*, 668-684.

Wade, R. C., & Yarbrough, D. B. (1997). Community service-learning in student teaching: toward the development of an active citizenry, *Michigan Journal of Community Service-learning, 4*, 42-55.

Zeichner, K. M., & Liston, D. P. (1996). *Reflective teaching: An introduction*. Mahwah, NJ: Erlbaum.

SECTION V

BUILDING UNDERSTANDING OF ENGAGED SCHOLARSHIP

CHAPTER 12

ENGAGED SCHOLARSHIP

Current Context and Future Directions

Sherril B. Gelmon

ABSTRACT

This chapter sets out some broad definitions of engaged scholarship, providing the context of models of practice, discussion of faculty recognition and rewards, and challenges for faculty and institutions in embracing this work. The chapter ends with a description of some promising practices and resources that may be useful for individuals and/or institutions interested in making institutional changes to recognize and reward engaged scholarship.

The chapters in this volume are all examples of new work that is engaged scholarship—scholarship that documents various aspects of faculty, staff and graduate student work with and in multiple communities. This chapter sets out some broad definitions of engaged scholarship, providing context of models of practice, discussion of faculty recognition and rewards, and challenges for faculty and institutions in embracing this work. The chapter ends with a description of some promising practices

From Passion to Objectivity: International and Cross-Disciplinary Perspectives on Service Learning Research, pp. 241–254
Copyright © 2007 by Information Age Publishing

that may be useful for individuals and/or institutions interested in making institutional changes to recognize and reward engaged scholarship.

DEFINING ENGAGEMENT

As students and faculty become involved in "engagement" activities, they frequently encounter questions as to what exactly is meant by this term. Robert Putnam, in *Bowling Alone* (2000), described engagement as a response to the question, "How can I participate effectively in the public life of my community?" Campus Compact, a national organization in the United States that advocates university and community college involvement in and with communities, called for universities and colleges to become engaged in communities by "committing ourselves to helping catalyze and lead a national movement to reinvigorate the public purposes and civic mission of higher education" (Campus Compact, 1999, p. 4). A scan of definitions of engagement on multiple institutions of higher education Web sites reveals language related to community-university partnerships, programmatic emphases within academic curriculum development, commitments to community development and public involvement as part of institutional strategy, and special opportunities for research collaborations.

For well over a decade, the language used by groups such as Campus Compact, funders, and other academics, has referred to a specific kind of engagement: civic engagement. This term has many meanings, depending on institutional and disciplinary context. Battistoni (2002) identified many of these, including civic professionalism, social responsibility, social justice, connected knowing, public leadership, public work, and engaged or public scholarship. The term "civic engagement," which has its roots in political science, is often linked to good citizenship. This connection, however, may be misleading to some, especially those who work with large populations of immigrants or other dispossessed population groups who have varying perceptions of what being a "citizen" is. In part to address this concern, some institutions have placed an emphasis on the partnership dimension of civic engagement (see, for example, many of the projects of Community-Campus Partnerships for Health as found at www.ccph.info). "Community involvement" may not offer a strong enough descriptor to reflect the depth of commitment and participation that is seen in many community-university partnerships. As a result, the term "community engagement" has become increasingly widely used, especially in circles outside of the United States where the concept of "civics" may not be well understood or in general use. As an example, the relatively new higher education organization in Australia has been called the

Australian Universities Community Engagement Alliance (www.aucea
.net.au), giving emphasis to its mission as an alliance addressing community engagement.

Similarly, there is much debate about the use of the term "service-
learning" as an overarching term to describe strategies related to learning
in the community. Some institutions and initiatives, such as Portland State
University in the United States and many of the institutions that comprise
the Community Higher Education Service Partnership project in South
Africa, are adopting the term "community-based learning." The term
"community service-learning" was adopted by the Canadian Association
for Community Service-Learning. The primary reason for the change in
terminology derives from the notion that there are multiple community-
based teaching and learning strategies such as cooperative placements,
field experiences, internships, practice teaching, student community-
based research, that may help students to gain awareness of community
needs and assets, and use many of the principles of traditional service-
learning, such as mutuality, reciprocity, and reflection. Nonetheless, in
some aspects of the education spectrum and particularly in K-12 education, service-learning remains the dominant term for student and teacher
engagement with communities, and is a useful and replicable pedagogy
for students in all levels of education for engaging with communities.

COMMUNITY-ENGAGED SCHOLARSHIP

In 2005, the Commission on Community-Engaged Scholarship in the
Health Professions, funded by the W.K. Kellogg Foundation, issued its
report which, although focused on the health professions, included key
definitions that can be applied across the entire educational spectrum
(Commission on Community-Engaged Scholarship in the Health Professions, 2005). It defined community engagement as:

> applying institutional resources (e.g., knowledge and expertise of students,
> faculty and staff, political position, buildings and land) to address and solve
> challenges facing communities through collaboration with these communi-
> ties. The methods for community engagement of academic institutions
> include community service, service-learning, community-based participa-
> tory research, training and technical assistance, capacity-building and eco-
> nomic development. (p. 12)

The commission went on to define community-engaged scholarship as:

> teaching, discovery, integration, application and engagement that involves
> the faculty member in a mutually beneficial partnership with the commu-

nity and has the following characteristics: clear goals, adequate preparation, appropriate methods, significant results, effective presentation, reflective critique, rigor and peer-review. (p. 12)

Where, then, is the scholarship in community engagement? Community engagement in and of itself may not necessarily be scholarly. It may be evident in traditional disciplinary scholarship such as might be found in teacher education, in public health, or in anthropology. Similarly, using a community-based pedagogy such as service-learning may not necessarily be scholarly. The scholarship of service-learning may be evident through the study of the scholarship of teaching using this pedagogy, documenting investigation of new or enhanced methods of teaching and learning that take traditional disciplinary content and facilitate learning in community-based settings with nonacademic partners (Huber, Hutchings & Shulman, 2005). Finally, providing capacity-building or economic development through technical assistance or training also is not scholarly by itself, but presents considerable opportunities for scholarly inquiry and dissemination of lessons learned.

Another term is also used to capture the same concept: the scholarship of outreach or engagement—inquiry into activities relevant to community(ies). This is the reframed notion of scholarship contributed by Boyer in his landmark work *Scholarship Reconsidered* (Boyer, 1990). Boyer described multiple interrelated dimensions of scholarship that included the scholarship of teaching, discovery, integration, application, and engagement. His approach offered a rich, deep, broad, and unified approach to scholarship; it has since served as the philosophical framework for revised tenure and promotion criteria at some institutions (see, for example, Portland State University, 1996).

No matter what nomenclature is used, it is important to remember that to be scholarly requires the typical methods of inquiry that characterize any kind of scholarship (community-based or not)—speculation on a topic, development of a focused question, methods for data collection, analysis, synthesis, and reporting. As revealed in anecdotal information at conferences and in personal communications with the author, there have been some unfortunate events in some academic settings in recent years where faculty became confused by the zeal with which service-learning advocates proselytized the value of this pedagogy without illuminating how scholarship could be developed from this teaching strategy. Service-learning and other community-based pedagogies offer incredible opportunities for teaching and learning, but the practice of the pedagogy itself is not scholarly. Faculty development and training is necessary to help faculty understand how to conduct scholarly analyses of these pedagogies and create scholarly products that will contribute to the knowledge base and become part of their scholarly dossier.

What terminology best describes this scholarship? Many have used the term "the scholarship of engagement" reflecting Boyer's elaboration of scholarship (Boyer, 1996). However, community members may resent this term as it puts the emphasis on scholarship as the first word, and may feel alienated by this emphasis that focuses on the academy rather than the community. The term "community-engaged scholarship" may be more acceptable, as community comes first, scholarship is placed last, and engagement is given prominence as the link between the two. Community-engaged scholarship enables scholars to apply their own disciplinary knowledge and methods to collaborative community problem identification and solutions, resulting in synthesis and integration that can be shared through various forms of dissemination.

EVALUATING COMMUNITY-ENGAGED SCHOLARSHIP

Community-engaged scholarship presents challenges for faculty documentation and evaluation since it is often a collaboration of multiple stakeholders, and may be driven not only by a faculty member's scholarly agenda but also by community agendas and priorities. Faculty must be able to show their contribution to the work clearly, and this may be particularly challenging when all products are authored as collaborations and reviewers may be seeking to identify the contribution of one individual faculty member. The way in which faculty document and describe their scholarship will thus have a great impact on the outcome of their review.

Similarly, the audience for the products and outcomes of community-engaged scholarship may include many groups outside of academia, and faculty may be challenged to demonstrate the importance and significance of dissemination outlets that go beyond the traditional peer-reviewed scholarly journals and the disciplinary societies. Their work may ultimately have many spheres of influence, resulting in the need to provide documentation of community-engaged scholarship in the form of evidence of influence and impact that substantiates the importance and contribution of the work.

The need to clarify assessment of engaged scholarship was recognized soon after Boyer's 1990 work. In 1997, Glassick, Huber, and Maeroff (1997) published *Scholarship Assessed*, which set out criteria by which to evaluate scholarly work. These criteria were adapted by the National Review Board on the Scholarship of Engagement (www.scholarshipofengagement.org, 2000) and promoted as a sound framework on which to assess engaged scholarship.

More recently, there has been further elaboration of these criteria by the Community-Engaged Scholarship for Health Collaborative (2006) into a set of characteristics of community-engaged scholarship that can be used both as a framework for faculty development programs and for the actual evaluation of faculty scholarship. The collaborative has recommended the use of eight characteristics as criteria for evaluation of community-engaged scholarship:

1. clear goals;
2. adequate preparation;
3. use of appropriate methods meeting the standards of scientific rigor and appropriate for community engagement;
4. demonstration of significant results/impact;
5. effective presentation/dissemination;
6. use of reflective critique;
7. individual leadership and personal contribution; and
8. demonstration of consistently ethical behavior.

More detailed elaboration of these characteristics is available at www.ccph.info. The Collaborative's Working Group on Peer Review is currently refining supporting materials to assist faculty in developing documentation of their scholarly work. These materials may also be found at the collaborative pages on the CCPH Web site.

ISSUES AND CHALLENGES IN COMMUNITY-ENGAGED SCHOLARSHIP

A number of issues and challenges emerge in attempting to create professional and institutional support for community-engaged scholarship. These issues can be categorized in terms of the role of disciplines, the role of the academic department, the role and activities of faculty and institutional challenges.

Role of the Disciplines

For many faculty, the most important personal recognition comes from one's own discipline, both within one's own home institution but more importantly, at the national and international levels. Given the grounding many scholars have in their disciplines and the important role disciplinary journals and meetings have as a venue for dissemination of scholarly work that has been peer reviewed, the national and international disciplinary associations have been viewed as a fertile opportunity for seeding engagement agendas and promoting related activities to a broad constituency. Campus Compact's "Engaged Disciplines" project (2002-2004) promoted activities such as targeted conference sessions or themes, faculty development initiatives, faculty fellows programs, development of resources such as syllabi collections and Web sites, and special journal articles and issues devoted to engagement as seen through the respective disciplinary lens. With the involvement of the disciplinary association, such work was validated by peers at respected institutions, and in some cases provided leverage for funding and new scholarly work. Examples of associations that have seeded new engagement activities and strategies include the National Communications Association, the Academy of Management, the American Dental Education Association, and the Association of University Programs in Health Administration (see, for example, Applegate & Morreale, 2001, or Zlotkowski, 2000).

Role of the Department

The department or other relevant academic unit may be one of the most important organizational factors in facilitating or creating barriers to engaged scholarship. For most faculty, one's home department consists of the disciplinary colleagues with interests closest to one's own. It is the academic home where peers will conduct the initial reviews for faculty evaluation for tenure, promotion or other recognition. Departments typically have shared cultures, responsibilities, and goals, and thus the "engaged" department may be the highest leverage point for promoting an agenda on community engagement as well as community-engaged scholarship (Battistoni et al., 2003).

Academic departments may be viewed as a "collective" that engages in, and embraces, collaborative work in teaching, scholarship, and outreach in partnership with communities. This may occur through multiple teaching and learning pedagogies, field work, community-based research, or volunteer service activities. Yet the reality is that many academic departments are more accurately described as a loose collection of individuals who pursue independent agendas with some common purpose, but resist any collaboration or cohesion other than a name (Battistoni et al., 2003). As a result, the department can be a major facilitator of community-engaged research, but departmental culture may also be a substantial barrier. Colleagues may question whether community-engaged scholarship is really substantive academic work (Calleson, Jordan, & Seifer, 2005). Nonetheless, early efforts to document the role of "engaged departments" demonstrate the potential of the department to promote community-engaged scholarship (Kecskes, 2006).

Roles and Activities of Faculty

Faculty encounter new roles and responsibilities in community-based scholarship, and their previous scholarly experiences may not have adequately prepared them for some of the related challenges. A disciplinary tradition of teaching and learning may put the emphasis on the faculty as expert, but experiences working with community partners quickly reveal the wealth of expertise offered by community leaders who may lack traditional academic credentials. For some faculty, this may challenge their confidence and create uncertainty about community needs, assets, and priorities. Faculty have the disciplinary base of knowledge, but may need to develop new strategies for responding to the shifting needs of community work and usually need to learn to share power and control over the research enterprise.

Given the nature of the academic department, faculty may encounter mixed messages regarding the value given to community-based scholarship in the disciplinary context, and may be unsure of the approval of senior faculty of such work. Finding peers and mentors within the academic department, let alone within one's discipline, may be a challenge—and thus require additional effort on the part of the individual faculty. Related to this is the need to be somewhat self-sufficient and creative in identifying relevant faculty development opportunities. All of this may be occurring in the midst of changing organizational culture, as departments, disciplinary associations, and institutions make changes in their strategies, policies, and operational activities in order to be more supportive of community-engaged scholarship.

While facing these challenges, faculty need to persevere in order to do what they believe is right without making compromises in their scholarly agendas. If a faculty member is committed to developing community-based scholarship, yet a chair or dean recommends pursuit of more traditional scholarship because of greater security of external funding, the faculty member must decide the best direction to pursue, and be confident that they are not redirecting their scholarly interests only because of funding opportunities. Several mechanisms to support faculty are necessary at all levels of the institution throughout the faculty's journey toward tenure, promotion or other recognition: clarity of expectations for faculty recognition and promotion, specification of the nature of documentation required for faculty evaluation, availability of sample dossiers/portfolios, training of review committees, and development opportunities to understand procedural guidelines and implications (Gelmon & Agre-Kippen-han, 2003).

Scholarship that does not follow traditional disciplinary norms may require new forms of documentation. Faculty may need to write a narrative for their evaluation portfolio that clearly demonstrates the importance of community-engaged scholarship and that links this scholarship to mission, strategy, and academic core purposes. In many cases, faculty have indicated that to be convincing as a community-engaged scholar, one cannot be simply adequate but must be exemplary (Gelmon & Agre-Kippenhan, 2003). Faculty may be aided by the resources that have been developed by CCPH, including the *Community-Engaged Scholarship Toolkit* (Community-Campus Partnerships for Health, 2005).

Institutional Challenges

There are many reasons why faculty might pursue community-engaged scholarship, including social responsibility, relation to institutional mission, funding opportunities, and related reasons, but the experiences of many faculty have shown that this form of scholarship will not be a high priority unless their academic institutions recognize and reward community-engaged scholarship. However, in its review of the higher education landscape in the United States, the Commission on Community-Engaged Scholarship in the Health Professions (2005) found that there are institutions both within and outside of the health professions that support and recognize community-engaged scholarship, and faculty are being specifically recruited, recognized and retained because of their community engagement activities and scholarly work. Increasingly, institutions are adding recognition criteria that value interdisciplinary and team-based scholarship, giving greater attention to a variety of sources of funding as indicators of excellence, and placing value on multiple mechanisms for dissemination of products and outcomes. In some institutions, community partners are being invited to sit as full members of faculty review committees, giving greater recognition to the important role played by these community members in faculty work.

Portland State University is often recognized as one of the first U.S. higher education institutions to adopt revised promotion and tenure criteria that are based on Boyer's description of scholarship (Portland State University, 1996). At Portland State, scholarly accomplishments can be demonstrated through research, teaching, and community engagement, with scholarship expressed through discovery, integration, interpretation, and/or analysis. The Portland State policies give strong emphasis to the developmental use of an individual scholarly agenda to articulate scholarly effort and to guide faculty development through the early years of a faculty member's career.

These policies serve as a good role model for other institutions because of the explicit use of language for assessment of scholarship such as the following (Portland State University, 1996, pp. 10-11):

- "Demonstrate significance of results;"
- "Make a difference in communities;"
- "Define/resolve relevant social problems and/or issues;"
- "Improve existing practices or programs;"
- "Make substantive contributions to public policy;" and
- "Widely disseminate knowledge gained."

While the faculty member is not expected to show that their work necessarily accomplishes all of these things, these kinds of descriptors are both relevant and liberating for community-engaged faculty, as they see that the institution values and supports work that reflects these descriptors.

If institutions are going to attempt to make change to become supportive of community-engaged scholars, they must identify champions and leaders of organizational change. A commitment to a new or enhanced strategy around community engagement must not in any way compromise institutional prestige—either perceived or that expressed through various university rankings (such as those of *US News & World Report* in the United States or *Macleans* in Canada) or categorizations (such as the Carnegie classification in the United States or those used in Australia to cluster similar kinds of institutions based on mission). Institutions may find it difficult to commit new resources or reallocate existing resources to a community engagement agenda in times of budget constraints.

Leaders also need to be able to separate fads from long-term trends that will shape the future of higher education. Ultimately, just as faculty cannot compromise their beliefs or careers, institutions must be true both to their institutional mission and values *and* to the communities with whom they collaborate. The institutional self-assessment developed by the Community-Engaged Scholarship for Health Collaborative (Gelmon, Seifer, Kauper-Brown & Mikkelsen, 2005) is a useful metric for institutions to use for assessing current practices and planning future strategies, and builds upon previous institutional self-assessments (such as Furco, 2003 and Holland, 1997) to incorporate an additional emphasis on community-engaged scholarship.

PROMISING PRACTICES

As interest in community engagement increases, it is becoming clear that there needs to be institutional change in order to support this work. Faculty may be motivated to engage with communities for a variety of reasons, but their work will only be sustained if they are recognized and rewarded for community-engaged scholarship in a manner identical to that of more traditional, disciplinary-based scholarship. One of the fundamental changes needed in institutional policies is to reframe guidelines for faculty evaluation and recognition to respect scholarly work related to engagement, recognizing that the work must still be scholarly (as described previously) but clearly articulating that community engaged scholarship is valued. In some institutions, faculty are made aware of such faculty evaluation guidelines during the search and hiring processes, establishing from the very beginning of a faculty member's career that this is, indeed, a valued form of scholarship (Gelmon & Agre-Kippenhan, 2003). Nonetheless, administrators and evaluation committees need to be better informed about new strategies within guidelines, especially the changes that have occurred since the time when these senior faculty were themselves evaluated for tenure and promotion.

One of the most important strategies is to ensure that institutional philosophies are clearly communicated, and that messages regarding the valuing of community-engaged scholarship are consistent. In a study of the first five years of experience with revised guidelines at Portland State University, Gelmon and Agre-Kippenhan (2003) found that a lack of clarity in communication by department chairs, deans, and/or senior academic officials resulted in confusion among junior faculty about the true value of community-engaged scholarship. This confusion may have had an impact on choices junior faculty made about scholarly directions. Five years later, preliminary results of a follow-up study at Portland State University revealed that greater clarity in communicating the strategy of support of community-engaged scholarship helped to guide faculty in selecting to focus on such scholarly work (Gelmon, Koch, Norvell & Stoering, in press). It still remains important that all levels of faculty and administrative committees reviewing individual cases for tenure, promotion, or other recognition are clear on the content and emphasis of evaluation guidelines.

Early work on institutional change to support community-engaged scholarship, as demonstrated by the Community Engaged Scholarship for Health Collaborative (Seifer, Gelmon, & Wong, in press), shows the value of the use of John Kotter's model of change (Kotter, 1995) as a framework for guiding change. Eight health professions schools,representing a variety of disciplines participated in a 3-year national collaborative in the

United States with the explicit goal of making change in policies for faculty recognition and rewards to encourage community-engaged scholarship. By the end of the 3 years, several schools had identified both facilitators of and barriers to change that reflected key elements of the Kotter model. These elements included establishing a sense of urgency, forming a powerful guiding coalition, creating and communicating a vision, empowering others to act on the vision, planning for and creating short-term wins, consolidating improvements, and institutionalizing new approaches through the approval of policies and practices that promote community-engaged scholarship (Gelmon, Lederer, Seifer, Wong, & Grignon, 2007).

The final important set of promising practices relate to mentoring and faculty development. Faculty that had experiences with community-engaged scholarship in their graduate education may be prepared for the scholarly work, but may need guidance in managing this scholarship as part of their overall academic portfolio. Faculty who do not have the background in community engagement will benefit from support to see how they can (a) engage with communities and (b) build this into their scholarly profile. Once a career path of community-engaged scholarship is established, there will be a continuing need for faculty development to prepare for various levels of evaluation and review for tenure/promotion, which includes recommending external reviewers who reflect the domains of one's scholarship (Gelmon & Agre-Kippenhan, 2003). Resources such as the National Review Board on the Scholarship of Engagement (www.scholarshipofengagement.org) can be very valuable in helping to identify such reviewers.

CONCLUSION

Community-engaged scholarship is becoming increasingly well-developed as a recognizable and respected form of scholarship, but there is still much work to do to support continuing changes in the organizational cultures of universities and colleges, disciplinary associations, and faculty scholars themselves in order to further clarify what is community-engaged scholarship and how it can be recognized and rewarded. Much progress has been made, and the new International Association for Research on Service-Learning and Community Engagement (see chapter 13) will help to seed continuing efforts to further validate the importance of such scholarship and to prepare researchers to contribute to communities both through their work and through their scholarly pursuits. In order to validate community-engaged scholarship as a viable academic pursuit, institutions need to modify reward and recognition systems and provide sufficient faculty development resources; departments and disciplines need to reconsider how their respective cultures embrace and can foster community engagement and related scholarship; faculty need to be given opportunities to explore community-engaged scholarship in the context of their expertise; and community members need to be invited by faculty and institutions to collaborate on scholarly programs that will ultimately enhance communities and contribute to the accomplishment of institutional missions related to community development and outreach.

REFERENCES

Applegate, J. L., & Morreale, S. P. (2001). Creating engaged disciplines. *AAHE Bulletin, 53*(9), 7-9.

Battistoni, R. M. (2002). *Civic engagement across the curriculum.* Providence, RI: Campus Compact.

Battistoni, R. M., Gelmon, S. B., Saltmarsh, J. A., Wergin, J. F., & Zlotkowski, E. (2003). *The engaged department toolkit.* Providence, RI: Campus Compact.

Boyer, E. (1990). *Scholarship reconsidered: Priorities of the professoriate.* Princeton, NJ: The Carnegie Foundation for the Advancement of Teaching.

Boyer, E. L. (1996). The scholarship of engagement. *Journal of Public Service and Outreach, 1*(1), 11-20.

Calleson, D. C., Jordan, C., & Seifer, S. D. (2005). Community-engaged scholarship: Is faculty work in communities a true academic enterprise? *Academic Medicine, 80*(4), 317-321.

Campus Compact. (1999). *Presidents' declaration on the civic responsibility of higher education.* Providence, RI: Author.

Commission on Community-Engaged Scholarship in the Health Professions. (2005). *Linking scholarship and communities: Report of the Commission on Community-Engaged Scholarship in the Health Professions.* Seattle, WA: Community-Campus Partnerships for Health.

Community-Engaged Scholarship for Health Collaborative. (2006). *Collaborative project documentation.* Seattle, WA: Community-Campus Partnerships for Health. Available: http://depts.washington.edu/ccph/healthcollab.html

Community-Campus Partnerships for Health. (2005). *Community-engaged scholarship toolkit.* Seattle, WA: Community-Campus Partnerships for Health. Availablet: http://depts.washington.edu/ccph/toolkit.html

Furco, A. (2003). *Self-assessment rubric for the institutionalization of service-learning in higher education.* Providence, RI: Campus Compact.

Gelmon, S. B., Koch, R., Norvell, K., & Stoering, J. (in press). *Faculty experience with the promotion and tenure process.* Portland, OR: Portland State University.

Gelmon, S. B., Lederer, M., Seifer, S. D., Wong, K., & Grignon, J. (2007, April). *Progress in new models of faculty recognition and rewards.* Presented at the Community-Campus Partnerships for Health Annual Conference, Toronto, Ontario, Canada. Available: www.ccph.info

Gelmon, S. B., Seifer, S. D., Kauper-Brown, J., & Mikkelsen, M. (2005). *Building capacity for community engagement: Institutional self-assessment.* Seattle, WA: Community-Campus Partnerships for Health. Available: www.ccph.info

Glassick, C., Huber, M., & Maeroff, G. (1997). *Scholarship assessed: Evaluation of the professoriate.* San Francisco: Jossey-Bass.

Holland, B. (1997). Analyzing institutional commitment to service: A model of key organizational factors. *Michigan Journal of Community Service Learning, 4,* 30-41.

Huber, M. T., Hutchings, P., & Shulman, L. S. (2005). The scholarship of teaching and learning today. In K. O'Meara & R. E. Rice (Eds.), *Faculty priorities reconsidered: Rewarding multiple forms of scholarship* (pp. 34-42). San Francisco: Jossey-Bass.

Kecskes, K. (Ed.). (2006). *Engaging departments: Moving faculty culture from private to public, individual to collective focus for the common good.* Boston: Anker.

Kotter, J. P. (1995, March-April). Leading change: Why transformation efforts fail. *Harvard Business Review,* 59-67.

Portland State University. (1996). *Policies and procedures for the evaluation of faculty for tenure, promotion, and merit increases.* Portland, OR: Portland State University. Available: www.oaa.pdx.edu

Putnam, R. D. (2000). *Bowling alone: The collapse and revival of American community.* New York: Simon and Schuster.

Seifer, S., Gelmon, S., & Wong, K. (Eds.). (in press). The community engaged scholarship for health collaborative. *Metropolitan Universities.*

Zlotkowski, E. (2000). Civic engagement in the disciplines. In T. Ehrlich (Ed.), *Civic responsibility and higher education* (pp. 309-322). Phoenix, AZ: Oryx Press.

CHAPTER 13

THE INTERNATIONAL ASSOCIATION FOR RESEARCH ON SERVICE-LEARNING AND COMMUNITY ENGAGEMENT

Sherril B. Gelmon

In 2005, Shelley Billig issued a "Call to Action" for a new international research association (Billig, 2005). This was acted upon at the 2005 International Service-Learning Research Conference, and steps were initiated to create a professional association for the service-learning and community engagement research community. The International Association for Research on Service-Learning and Community Engagement (IARSLCE) has now been incorporated as a nonprofit organization, and a founding board of directors has been elected. Bylaws and other founding documents have been created, and the association is moving forward with strategy development and conceptualization of relevant programs and services to meet the needs of the members. The association's Web site is www.ResearchSLCE.org.

The mission of IARSLCE is "To promote the development and dissemination of research on service-learning and community engagement internationally and across all levels of the education system" (IARSLCE, 2007).

From Passion to Objectivity: International and Cross-Disciplinary Perspectives on Service Learning Research, pp. 255–257
Copyright © 2007 by Information Age Publishing
255

The association's objectives are to advance the fields of service-learning and community engagement research across the educational spectrum (primary, secondary, postsecondary, and further education) by:

- promoting the exchange of ideas, experiences, data, and research among its members;
- disseminating knowledge and research on service-learning and community engagement both within the membership and beyond the members to other communities of scholars and practitioners;
- encouraging the continual improvement of the quality and rigor of research in these fields;
- providing a forum for the presentation of research findings, ideas, methods, and opinions across educational systems;
- facilitating the exchange of information and creation of collaborations among scholars and practitioners around the world;
- supporting and facilitating the development of new scholars entering the fields of research on service-learning and community engagement; and
- creating venues for ongoing learning and communication among the members.

Initially, the primary activities of the association will be to sponsor the annual International Research Conference on Service-Learning and Community Engagement, produce the annual peer-reviewed volume of papers arising from the conference, and manage a Web site to facilitate information exchange among members and other interested individuals. Over time, it is anticipated that other activities may be developed in response to requests from the members.

This association is an important step in the continuing evolution of research on community engagement, service-learning and related strategies. It provides a focal point for communication and information exchange to further advance knowledge about service-learning and community engagement research, and is the only forum internationally that focuses exclusively on the *research*—knowledge of results, methods used, associated training and development needs, and dissemination opportunities. While the association is based in the United States, the board membership requires international representation, and extensive efforts are underway to identify relevant opportunities for collaborations with existing sister associations in other countries (such as the Australian Universities Community Engagement Alliance and the Canadian Association for Community Service-Learning) or with other international networks that are concerned with advancing community engagement and service-learning research.

Through both the conference and the annual volume, the association will encourage the dissemination of research and stimulate development of new scholars, with particular attention given offering venues for presentation and publication for emerging scholars and graduate students. The association will also collaborate with other interested associations to jointly promote and/or support events that can help to further advance the fields of service-learning and community engagement research.

All attendees at the 2006 International Service-Learning Research Conference were given initial membership in the association. Membership is included as part of the registration for the 2007 International Research Conference on Service-Learning and Community Engagement, and individuals may also join independently. We encourage visits to our Web site at www.ResearchSLCE.org for more information, and welcome participation in the association through its committees.

REFERENCES

Billig, S. H. (2005). The International K-H Service-Learning Research Association. In S. Root, J. Callahan, & S. H. Billig (Eds). *Improving service-learning practice: Research on models to enhance impacts* (pp. 215-224). Greenwich, CT: Information Age.

International Association for Research on Service-learning and Community Engagement. (2007). *Bylaws*. Available: www.ResearchSLCE.org

ABOUT THE AUTHORS

John Annette is a professor of citizenship and lifelong learning, dean of the Faculty of Continuing Education and pro vice master for Widening Participation and Community Partnerships at Birkbeck, University of London. He is on the executive of the Universities Association for Lifelong Learning (UALL) and chair of the Higher Education Community Partnership national network.

Richard Battistoni is a professor of political science and public service at Providence College. From 1994-2000, he served as the founding Director of the Feinstein Institute for Public Service at Providence College.

Matthew Bernacki is a doctoral student at Temple University pursuing a degree in the psychological study of education and is a research coordinator at the Faith-Justice Institute at Saint Joseph's University.

Frank Bernt is an associate professor and director of the Faith-Justice Institute at Saint Joseph's University.

Richard Bradley is a consultant and trainer for Learn & Serve Ohio, The John Glenn Institute at The Ohio State University, and the Meharry State Farm Project.

Dean Elson, is the senior director of evaluation at Jumpstart.

Robin L. Ersing is an assistant professor in the School of Social Work, University of South Florida.

Janet Eyler is a professor of the practice of education and associate chair of the Department of Leadership, Policy and Organizations of Vanderbilt University.

Margo Fryer is the president of the Canadian Association for Community Service-Learning (CACSL) and the founding director of the University of British Columbia's Learning Exchange. She is an assistant professor in the School of Community and Regional Planning, and also the director of the UBC-Community Learning Initiative.

Sherril B. Gelmon, is professor of public health in the Mark O. Hatfield School of Government at Portland State University and founding chair of the International Association for Research on Service-Learning and Community Engagement.

Irwin Goldzweig is an assistant professor in the Department of Family & Community Medicine and program director of the Meharry–State Farm Alliance, Metropolitan Demonstration Project and the Teen Occupant Protection Project.

Susan C. Harris is an associate director and director of research and academic affairs for the USC Joint Educational Project (JEP).

Steven Hart is an assistant professor in literacy and early education at California State University—Fresno.

Angela Harwood is a faculty member in the Department of Secondary Education at Western Washington University.

Judi Jetson is director of the USF Collaborative, University of South Florida

Lauren Johns was the service-learning project manager at Jumpstart until May 2007.

Robin Jones is the coordinator of the community initiative in the Department of Geography at the University of South Florida.

Paul Juarez is a professor of family and community medicine and vice-chair, Department of Family and Community Medicine at Meharry Medical College.

Harold R. Keller is a professor of school psychology and associate dean for academic affairs, College of Education, University of South Florida.

Alisha Lund-Chaix is a doctoral student in the public administration and policy PhD program at Portland State University.

Martha Merrill is dean of academic programs for the International Partnership for Service-Learning and Leadership.

Lauren McClanahan is a faculty member in the Department of Secondary Education at Western Washington University.

Trula Nicholas is a faculty member in the Department of Human Services and Rehabilitation at Western Washington University.

Jessica Taisey Petrie is a research manager at Jumpstart.

Margaret D. Pusch is associate director of the Intercultural Communication Institute and chair of the board of trustees of the International Partnership for Service-Learning and Leadership. She is also executive director of the Society for Intercultural Education, Training and Research in the United States.

Margaret W. Sallee is a doctoral candidate and research assistant in the Center for Higher Education Policy Analysis at the University of Southern California.

Kalawathie (Bella) Sattar is the director of the Centre for Quality Promotion and Assurance at the Durban University of Technology (DUT) in Durban, South Africa.

David Schlundt is an associate professor in the Department of Psychology at Vanderbilt University and an adjunct associate professor in the Department of Family and Community Medicine at Meharry Medical College.

Deon Tolliver has a masters in public health from Meharry Medical College.

Margaret Vickers is a professor of education and associate dean of community engagement at the University of Western Sydney.

Robert Wallis is pro vice-chancellor (rural and regional) at Deakin University and is currently president of the Australian Universities Community Engagement Alliance.

Nicole Webster is assistant professor at the Department of Agricultural and Extension Education at The Pennsylvania State University.

Printed in the United States
R3506700002B/R35067PG89564LVX1B/1-48/A

9 781593 118457